"The world is urbanizing. And wherever I go, I hear Christians talking about urban mission. But few books on urban mission provide anything but an introduction to the issues. In *Sowing Seeds of Change*, Michael D. Crane addresses this need. Michael takes research on urban mission to the next level. He invites us to engage in serious research and theology and missiology and practice. Michael's aim is to 'construct a theological and missiological foundation for engaging the whole city in a gospel-centered approach.' And he does this admirably, as he draws from the image of a tree canopy ecosystem to address such issues as transforming urban spaces, creating healthy urban churches, and much more. This is one of the best books I've read on urban mission. It provides much needed theological and missiological foundations. It's essential reading for anyone engaged in urban mission today."

Graham Hill
Vice Principal of Morling Baptist Theological College, Sydney, Australia
Author, *GlobalChurch*

"Ministry in and to the city has become popular recently, but why? Many offer pragmatic reasons, but few ground their pragmatics in faithful, text-driven theology. In *Sowing Seeds of Change* my friend Dr. Michael Crane gives us a treatise on urban mission that is at the same time rich in theology and imminently practical. If you care about God, the gospel, mission and the city, you should read this book."

Micah Fries, Vice President of LifeWay Research
Co-author of *Exalting Jesus in Zephaniah, Haggai, Zechariah, and Malachi*

"*Sowing the Seeds of Change* is a deeply insightful charge to the Church as we seek the welfare of the city. Crane's 'Canopy Ecosystem Approach to Urban Transformation' provides a refreshingly innovative and comprehensive response to the greatest missiological challenge of our time."

Curt Alan
Pastor of church planting & missions
Summit Church, Durham NC

1

"Global urbanization is one of the critical issues facing missions in our day, and an increasing list of books calls for more conversation, more engagement, and more study. What's been missing is application—we get the call to the city, but what do we do when we get there? Michael Crane has a theologian's mind and a missionary's heart, and has helped us immensely with *Sowing Seeds of Change*. I'll be putting it in the hands of students and missionaries as often as I can."

Jeff K. Walters, Ph.D.
Assistant Professor of Christian Missions & Urban Ministry
The Southern Baptist Theological Seminary

"*Sowing Seeds of Change* is an outstanding book on city transformation that deserves a permanent place on the bookshelf or desk of any kingdom leader committed to city transformation. Michael's scholarship and use of historical documents blended with current thought-leaders and practitioners serve to put into our hands a roadmap for urban transformation."

Eric Swanson
Leadership Network
Author of *To Transform a City: Whole Church, Whole Gospel, Whole City*

Sowing Seeds of Change

Cultivating Transformation in the City

Michael D. Crane

Series Editor

Stephen Burris

Urban Loft Publishers | Portland, Oregon

Urban Loft Publishers
2034 NE 40th Avenue #414
Portland, OR 97212
www.urbanloftpublishers.com

ISBN-13: 978-0692509531

Made in the U.S.A

Interior graphics: Patty Chen
Editorial: M. Sutton Seng

Table of Contents

Series Preface

Urban Mission in the 21st Century is a series of monographs that addresses key issues facing those involved in urban ministry whether it be in the slums, squatter communities, *favelas*, or in immigrant neighborhoods. It is my goal to bring fresh ideas, a theological basis, and best practices in urban mission as we reflect on our changing urban world. The contributors to this series bring a wide-range of ideas, experiences, education, international perspectives, and insight into the study of the growing field of urban ministry. These contributions fall into four very general areas: 1—the biblical and theological basis for urban ministry; 2—best practices currently in use and anticipated in the future by urban scholar/activists who are living, working and studying in the context of cities; 3—personal experiences and observations based on urban ministry as it is currently being practiced; and 4—a forward view toward where we are headed in the decades ahead in the expanding and developing field of urban mission. This series is intended for educators, graduate students, theologians, pastors, and serious students of urban ministry.

More than anything, these contributions are creative attempts to help Christians strategically and creatively think about how we can better reach our world that is now more urban than rural. I do not see theology and practice as separate and distinct. Rather, I see sound practice growing out of a healthy vibrant theology that seeks to understand God's world as it truly is as we move further into the twenty-first century. Contributors interact with the best scholarly literature available at the time of writing while making application to specific contexts in which they live and work.

Each book in the series is intended to be a thought-provoking work that represents the author's experience and perspective on urban ministry in a particular context. I have chosen those who bring this rich diversity of perspectives to this series. It is my hope and prayer that each book in this series will challenge, enrich, provoke, and cause the reader to dig deeper into subjects that bring the reader to a deeper understanding of our urban world and the ministry the church is called to perform in that new world.

Stephen Burris,
Urban Mission in the 21st Century Series **General Editor**

Other books in the Urban Ministry for the 21st Century series include:

Crossroads of the Nations: Diaspora, Globalization, and Evangelism by
    Jared Looney
Mind the Gap: Reflections from Luke's Gospel on the Divided City by Colin
    Smith

Dedication

To Karen, who consistently demonstrates what it means to seek the welfare of the city.

List of Figures and Illustrations

Foreword

Pastors, missionaries, and committed laypeople are among the busiest people on the planet. We work hard but not always smart. We are like Pig-Pen, that wonderful character in the Charlie Brown cartoons by Charles Schultz, who travels in a personal storm of dust and shares soiled candy from his pocket. As a pastor, I often felt like Pig-Pen, so busy with the tyranny of urgencies and preparations but doubtful if some of my activity was any real substitute for productivity. I knew what I needed. I needed to stop and climb up a ladder out of the fog of hourly necessities to take a far look to see what was strategic and transformative. But what I really needed was a consultant.

Consultants, often, are the people we pay well to tell us what we already know. But consultants are really more than that. To be a credible consultant you, must have had boots on the ground and be smart enough to read the good books and to know which ones are the best books. Michael Crane, the author of *Sowing Seeds of Change*, is just the kind of urban missions consultant that I am talking about, and this book is his consultancy.

In ministry I need a consultation that is biblically sound and not just picking and choosing pet passages. I need a consultation that respects God as the same God yesterday, today, and tomorrow, Old Testament and New Testament. I need a consultation that knows Jesus is Lord and is full of joy and hope. I need a consultation that knows how to keep effective church planting, urban transformation, and disciple making as the key chords in applying the gospel. I need a consultation that recognizes what it means to call a city the New Jerusalem on one page and then to call the city the whore of Babylon on the next. It is not either-or, but both-and. There are pages in this book that brought me face-to-face with the horror and the hope that are the cities to which we are called.

I need a consultation that is down to earth enough to point out steps for leading a church to partner with other churches in the city to move towards urban transformation and not merely community development without evangelism. How else can we express our joy and gratitude to the Lord for the salvation that has come to us? I need a consultant who is not afraid to give me a grid to test if I really have taken any steps toward city transformation, how many steps, and what the next step is toward God's presence and work. I need a consultant to remind me that all of this effort really is participating in what the Father, Son, and Spirit is up to in your city and mine. We don't really do things for God—not the things that last—we do things with God.

The consultant that I require will acquaint me with wider and deeper perspectives of the organic life in the city and the church. He or she must enable me to grasp the urban ecosystems that affect each other and what is necessary to see transformation start and gain momentum in the urban environ. I would expect my consultant to be an expert on the significant other experts in the field and to steer me away from those whose approach is lacking deep theology and wise missiology. The bibliography alone in *Sowing Seeds of Change* is worth the price of the book. I will be using this book, its diagrams, and its bibliography for years to come.

Rodrick Durst
Professor of Historical Theology
Director of the Bay Area Campus of Golden Gate Seminary

Preface

The mass migration of the world's population to cities demands a response by the Church. This unprecedented rate of urbanization has meant more than just a change of address; it has meant significant cultural change all over the world. The Church has been slow in responding to these tectonic cultural shifts. During this time of urbanization it is critical for the Church to engage our growing cities in a manner consistent with the gospel.

Although I was not always aware of it, I have come to realize that I have always loved cities. I was raised in the booming metropolises of Southeast Asia (Singapore, Manila, and Kuala Lumpur). As I grew older, my love for cities never faded, but I also began to see that cities growing at a scale never before witnessed in human history are facing overwhelming challenges. There has been a growing realization that the Church can be part of the answer to helping cities flourish. The people of God have always had the mandate to be a vessel of blessing to every family on earth. In our growing cities we have an opportunity to respond to this mandate.

Through the process of working on my Ph.D. in urban missiology, I began to see that most of what was written on this topic was at the introductory level. The writings were at a nascent level because the early advocates for urban missions were attempting to alert the church to the needs and opportunities of urbanization. We are now at the point—standing on the shoulders of these prescient proponents of urban missions—to take our research and practice to the next level. Now that cities are on the Church's radar, a lot of effort and money is being thrown at programs, some of which do little long-term good. We need more comprehensive thinking about the city both from a theological perspective as well as a missiological one. This book comes in response to that need. In this book I present a theological and missiological foundation for engaging the whole city in a gospel-centered approach. I draw from the image of a tree canopy ecosystem to illustrate a model for the Church of a city to work together to "seek the welfare of the city" (Jer. 29:7).

An effort like this is not created in a vacuum. I can only mention a few of the influencers, but there are many others who have played a role in the development of these ideas. From an early age, my parents showed me how to engage the world as a Christian and how to think critically. In my academic journey I have been blessed to have mentors and supervisors, like Rick Durst and Thom Wolf at Golden Gate Seminary, Mark Terry and Troy Bush at Southern Seminary, who taught me, prodded me, and patiently worked with me as these ideas were being formulated. This book would never have been published if it were not for the long hours of editing work by M. Sutton Seng. And, my wife, Karen, has been my life-long sounding board and ministry partner as we continually strive to be good neighbors and good citizens wherever God has taken us.

Although this book would not be possible without those mentioned here and many more, I take full responsibility for what is written here. It is my prayer that the ideas presented in this book will lead many to "glorify God on the day of visitation" (1 Pet. 2:12).

Chapter 1

Introduction

In truth, these two cities are entangled together in this world,
and intermixed until the last judgment effect their separation.
                                    --St. Augustine (1950, p. 38)

We are subjects of the city and involved in its condemnation,
and yet we are the possible artisans of her adoption by God.
                                    --Jacques Ellul (1970, p. 71)

Surging Cities, Flailing Response

We are in the midst of an urban revolution (Brugman, 2009). This revolution can be summarized by two simple facts with complex implications. First, the world's population is moving to the cities. With the urbanization rate exceeding the general population growth rate, the United Nations (2008) predicts the world will be seventy percent urban by 2050. Urbanization changes not only where we live, but also the ways we interact, do business, and even think. Second, this unprecedented mass migration to the world's cities is overwhelming their infrastructure and economies, leading to increased urban blight, poverty, and crime (Ali & Rieker, 2008; Gottdiener & Hutchison, 2006). When a city like Mumbai goes from a population of 1.5 million in 1941 to more than 15 million at the end of the century, infrastructure development struggles to keep pace (Kotkin, 2005). Cities can't build housing fast enough to accommodate the rising urban population, for example. The realities of urbanization and overwhelmed cities now confront the Church and her mission. Should the Church be concerned with these developments? If so, how should she respond to these trends?

Urban transformation has become a hot topic in both secular circles and the Church.[1] This might be due, in part, to the irrefutable trend toward urbanization (United Nations, 2008) and the resulting burden on urban infrastructure. It may also result from the rising influence of global cities in the media, market, and globalized cultures (Magnaghi, 2005). The sheer volume of humanity moving to cities and their longing for transformation should increase our interest in the subject. Many in the church have shifted from a dualistic approach (focusing on the soul as opposed to the body) to a holistic approach, ministering to both physical and spiritual needs, thus developing a deeper concern for urban transformation. A recent proliferation of books and websites draws attention to the impulse toward urban transformation. Examples are *To Transform the City* by Sam Williams and Eric Swanson (2010) and *For the City* by Matt Carter and Darrin Patrick (2010), both published in 2010, and James Davison Hunter's *To Change the World* (2011), one of *Christianity Today's* selections of "Best Books in 2011" (2011) To this we can add another pile of works calling for a change in our cultural or public engagement (Carson, 1996; Crouch, 2008; Hunsberger, 1996; Newbigin, 1986).

Many of the popular books written for Christians interested in making a difference in their cities are theologically anemic. The advice often given can be summed up by saying "do nice things in your city" and is supported only by one inspirational story after another. In the academic sphere, there are a broad variety of voices calling for change,

---

[1] Two major periodicals, one Christian and one secular, have begun segments featuring different cities and the issues faced in urban life. ("The Atlantic Cities," and "This Is Our City | ChristianityToday.com")

but the diverse theologies and models promoted by these voices can be dizzying for those called to be change agents in their cities. The sheer size of cities can feel overwhelming to those who want to bring changes, a feeling worsened in the face of so many models, theories, and ideas on how to transform our cities. Further complicating the situation is the fact that each city is so different and most models are developed around what worked in a particular urban context. Practitioners are often bewildered by the abundance of issues, opinions, and approaches set forth in the literature.

Graham Hill calls for an end to the detrimental bifurcation between sound theological reflection and missionary practice (Hill, 2012). This book seeks to answer that call by helping cut through the fog of the myriad solutions and ideas with analysis driven by biblical theology and missiology. I will propose a model of urban transformation that is theologically and missiologically sound and is also adaptable to a variety of contexts.

Globalized People in a World of Cities

The United Arab Emirates (UAE) has become a major player in the global financial services market and gained a reputation for being an attractive place for investment and entertainment. Over the last few decades, small sand-swept towns have emerged as global cities, with the country now boasting an 85% urban population. The story of UAE isn't only about urbanization, but also immigration and globalization; over 80% of the population does not carry an Emirati passport ("The World Factbook," 2014). The city of Dubai is a city bustling with people from every continent involved at every level of the economy. This globalized, urbanized world is the new reality for our time. The Church must learn how to engage this new world effectively through the cities or it risks limiting its voice to the margins of society.

The future of the world is urban. Isaiah 14:21 says the ambitious would cover the earth with their cities, a prescient observation which humanity is rapidly fulfilling. Harvey Cox famously predicted: "Future historians will record the twentieth century as the century in which the whole world became one immense city" (Cox, 1966, p. 273), and the trend of urbanization continues into this century. Every day, about two hundred thousand people move to cities around the world (Neuwirth, 2006). This growth of cities around the world led Viv Grigg (2009) to dub this millennium the "urban millennium." But these statistics are significant beyond just a tipping of the urban/rural scale, as Jeb Brugmann (2009) observed, "...we are overlooking the main event: half the world *has become a* City." An increasingly urban world means increased global interconnection, concentrating particularly among cities. In the past, a journey of significant distance involved horse carriage, train, or bus routes with stops at cities and towns along the way. Long distance travel today is often air travel, meaning people bypass all the small towns along the way and go straight from one city to another. The increase in the centrality of cities is cause for the Church to take more interest in impacting the cities of the world.

Cities are strategically influential for missions because they have a disproportionate amount of influence and power. Money and power drive a city (Hiebert & Meneses, 1995). Government seats and other significant decision makers are urban-based. Economically also, cities are also highly influential (J. Jacobs, 1985; Saches, 2005). Missionary statesman Roland Allen noted that all of the cities on Paul's missionary itinerary were centers of administrative power or cultural influence (R. Allen, 1962).

New ideas start from the cities. Cities accumulate creative talent and, thus, foster new innovations and ideas.[2] Cities foster an openness to new ideas as well; therefore, these ideas disseminate quickly. Missiologists and pastors are constantly searching for ways the good news of Jesus can be spread quickly and efficiently. Cities are the perfect context for spearheading the spread of the gospel. Wayne Meeks notes

---

[2] Most research and development happens in cities. Eighty-one percent of patents are filed by urban dwellers in OECD (Organization for Economic Cooperation and Development) countries. (United Nations Population Division, 2008, p. 3)

the impact of urbanization on the spread of Christianity: "I have suggested...that the rapid spread of Christianity through the lands of the Mediterranean basin was facilitated in manifold ways by the urbanization that had begun there before Alexander and accelerated during the Hellenistic and Roman imperial times" (Meeks, 1982, p. 25) Others have noted the way in which cities were particularly fertile ground for new religious ideas like Christianity (Bosch, 1991; Stark, 2006). The density of cities opens the way for Christianity to spread quickly. Tim Keller succinctly writes, "As the city goes, so goes the culture" (Keller, 2006, p. 37)

Cities are the gathering points of the nations, attracting and influencing people of diverse backgrounds (McMahan, 2012). As the church endeavors to obey the Great Commission (Matt. 28:18-20), cities are strategic places to engage the peoples of the world. Paul was prepared to go to Rome in the first century (Acts 19:21) because all of the peoples from conquered nations were now in Rome. Now, he could reach the nations in one city (Recker, 2002).

All of these reasons and more compel us to make cities a priority. But this is no simple task. Cities have grown exponentially larger since the days of Paul. Many of characteristics of Paul's entrée into cities were unique to the cities of the Roman Empire in the first century.[3] Rome was unparalleled in size and influence in the first century, but today at least three hundred of our world's cities are larger than ancient Rome.

Defining Terms

Any study of this type needs a clarification of the terms being used. I will define transformation at greater length in the next chapter, but will define other terms briefly here to avoid the ambiguity to which they are sometimes subject.

---

[3] Paul was able to take advantage of several characteristics common to most, if not all, of the cities he entered: common Greek language and culture, Roman citizenship gave him legal entry everywhere he went, and the presence of a synagogue or praying community with whom he could make first contact.

City. Defining a city is virtually impossible. Experts from diverse urban disciplines struggle to give cities a specific definition. Basing definitions on sheer numbers is problematic due to the lack of a consistent population across all nations and studies. One urbanologist might only consider a population of 200,000 as qualifying for a city. Norway, on the other hand considers an agglomeration of 200 or more as urban (G. Smith, 2004). In some cases, cities with smaller populations can seem more urban than other locations with large populations. Population density does not serve as a good measure either, because population densities vary so much around the globe. Other definitions have focused almost entirely on the physical environment of the city; permanence of the site, durability of the shelter, and facilities conducive to economic life (Beall & Fox, 2009). Macionis (2004) takes a stab at a definition: "a city is a relatively large, dense settlement that has a complex social structure that greatly reflects, intensifies, and re-creates cultural values and forms" (p. 253). This definition is not quantifiable, but it does capture the defining characteristics of a city. Other definitions capture different elements of the city such as the concentration of power[4] or the theological perspective of the city.[5] I will use Macionis' definition as the basic definition of the city in this book.

Global City. Global cities are a fairly recent development (Conn & Ortiz, 2001). The global city has a popular definition and a more academic definition. A city may be described as a "global city" in popular media simply because of its international recognition due to the media spotlight or because it is a crossroads for international travel. However, the notion of the global city has been studied more rigorously.

---

[4] Lewis Mumford defines a city as a "point of maximum concentration for the power and culture of a community." (Kostof, 1991, p. 37)

[5] For example, Conn's definition of the city as "a relatively large, dense and socially heterogeneous center of integrative social power, capable of preserving, changing and interpreting human culture both for and against God's divine purpose." (Conn & Ortiz, 2001, p. 233)

Sociologist Saskia Sassen coined the term "global cities" (Garner, 2004). Sassen's *The Global City: New York, London, Tokyo* (2001) is, to date, probably the most definitive work on global cities. She begins her book with a series of interconnected hypotheses related to the exigent role of global cities in globalization, economics, politics, and even social spatiality. She defines global cities primarily in economic terms as "cities where the dominant economic sectors are oriented to the global market and have been the object of considerable foreign investment and acquisition" (p. 87-88).[6] This definition definitely captures the economic element of global cities but might place too much focus on this aspect (Orum & Chen, 2003). As scholars continue to analyze and define global cities, other influences and dynamics are found to impact the fabric of global cities (W. I. Robinson, 2009). For instance, politics also influence the global nature of a city. In Kuala Lumpur, Malaysia, much of the labor force is made up of workers from other Asian nations like Indonesia and Bangladesh. The influx of in-migration labor is negotiated between the governments (ex. "President urges Malaysia to recruit more manpower from Bangladesh," 2012; Sijabat, 2010). Mark Abrahamson (2004) analyzes global cities more in terms of international influence. The presence of global media companies, multi-national corporations, and foreign-born citizenry combine to establish whether a city is worthy of "global city" status. Every two years Foreign Policy takes a similar approach by listing the cities considered most global based on the criteria of global influence ("The 2008 Global

---

[6] Sassen (2001, pp. 87–88) describes the functional importance of these cities: "Beyond their long history as centers for international trade and banking, these cities now function in four new ways: first, as highly concentrated command points in the organization of the world economy; second, as key locations for finance and for specialized service firms, which have replaced manufacturing as the leading economic sectors; third, as sites of production, including the production of innovations, in these leading industries; and fourth, as markets for the products and innovations produced. These changes in the functioning of cities have had a massive impact upon both international economic activity and urban form: cities concentrate control over the vast resources, while finance and specialized service industries have restructured the urban social and economic order. Thus a new type of city has appeared. It is the global city. Leading examples now are New York, London, Tokyo, Frankfurt, and Paris" (pp. 3-4).

Cities Index," 2008, "The Global Cities Index: 2010 Rankings," 2010). All of these characteristics combine to increase the global footprint of a city. Global cities are urban areas that impact the world far beyond its city limits through a combination of economic services and trade, political influence, and cultural dissemination.

Urbanization. According to Harvey Cox (1966), there is no agreed upon definition of urbanization. But it is agreed that urbanization is not measured quantitatively. Population size or density does not indicate the extent of urbanization. There are two ways to consider urbanization. First, urbanization refers to the physical growth of cities both in terms of population growth and geographical growth. China offers examples of each type of physical growth. In terms of population growth it is estimated that thirty million people move from rural regions of China to the cities every year.[7] China now boasts over ninety cities with populations exceeding a million (D. W. Smith, 2001). The geographical expansion of cities is also noteworthy.[8] In China, some municipalities, like Chongqing, are expanding their borders (Larson, 2010). In other parts of China, like the Pearl River Delta project, groups of cities are connecting their infrastructures to become urban

---

[7] The masses are moving to these because they dream of economic prosperity. The cities of China are positioning themselves to lead the global economy. (Groll, 2012)

[8] A World Bank report reveals the growing expanse of urban land use: "In total, urban built-up areas in the world consumed some 400,000 square kilometers in 2000, or 0.3% of the total land area of countries, estimated at some 130 million square kilometers. The land taken up by cities amounted to some 3% of arable land, estimated at 14 million square kilometers in 2000. Cities are now expected to grow 2.5 times in area by 2030, consuming some 1 million square kilometers, or 1.1% of the total land area of countries. They may possibly consume as much as 5–7% of total arable land, depending on the future rate of expansion of arable land, which is currently 2% per annum." (Schlomo, Sheppard, & Civco, 2005, pp. 1–2)

agglomerations of proportions never before seen in history.[9] Secondly, urbanization refers to the growth of urban influence even to rural populations. Influence spreads through urban-based media outlets and telecommunications technology.[10] This is defined by "diffusion of the system of values, attitudes and behavior called 'urban culture'" (Castells, 2002, p. 21). David W. Smith emphasizes the reach of this kind of urbanization: "For better or for worse, such urban settlements spread their influence over vast areas beyond their walls, and this suggests that the unprecedented physical expansion of cities at the present time will leave very few parts of the world unaffected by 'urbanization'..." (D. W. Smith, 2001, p. 18). The process and impact of ongoing urbanization demands innovative solutions that are flexible or organic rather than static. In other words, solutions cannot be confined to municipal boundaries but must extend through the paths of urbanization beyond city limits (Solecki, Seto, & Marcotullio, 2013). The vast reach of urbanization demands missiological awareness and adaptation in order to maximize effectiveness.

Projection of This Book

This book aims to blend theory and praxis. Theory without praxis results in empty rhetoric and ideas that remain detached from the complications of the messy reality we live in. Praxis without theory can lead to superficial results or, worse yet, unintended and unwanted results. Although theory and praxis are woven together in this book, the theoretical portion is concentrated in the first part and the latter three

---

[9] This ambitious effort is bringing several cities together through economic, transportation, and communications infrastructure to create an economic powerhouse. The cities brought together in this plan include Hong Kong, Macau, Guangzhou, Shenzhen, Dongguan, Foshan, Zhongshan, Zhuhai, Jiangmen, Huizhou, and Zhaoqing. This urban agglomeration will be home to more than 55 million people and boasts an economy that would rank 12th in the world if it were its own nation. (Ali & Rieker, 2008, p. 9; Enright, Scott, & Petty, 2010)

[10] "The Internet is an urban infrastructure, wedded to the markets and social realities of individual cities." (Brugmann, 2009, p. 9)

parts move towards praxis. Part 1 begins with a theological justification for urban transformation in Chapter 2. Chapter 3 surveys the wider range of Christian approaches or models of urban transformation, and Chapters 4 and 5 look more closely at what makes a city good. Chapter 4 answers this question from a secular urban studies perspective and Chapter 5 answers this question from a theological perspective.

In Part 2 of the book I introduce my model of urban transformation using the metaphorical image of a canopy ecosystem. Chapter 6 offers a broad overview of the model. In Chapter 7, I describe the importance of a root system grounded in sound theology and missiology. Chapter 8 highlights the need for an incarnational presence in the soil of the community. In Chapter 9, I assert that just as a tree canopy cannot exist without trees, gospel-centered urban transformation requires the presence of healthy churches. These are the bigger pieces of my model for urban transformation.

Part 3 goes into greater detail on important aspects of urban transformation that should emerge in a thriving ecosystem. Chapter 10 builds on the presence of churches by adding ministries and parachurch organizations that contribute important elements of ministry to the city. Given that more than half of the world's urban population is among the urban poor, Chapter 11 addresses healthy responses to urban poverty. Chapter 12 highlights the role of the church in advocating for justice in the city. Chapter 13 provides a short treatment of the need to reimagine the role of the church in the public square. Chapter 14 seeks to recover a theology of the importance place, not just in terms of church buildings, but valuing place as an essential aspect of life. Chapter 15 asserts that vocation is vitally important to city life, which means it is an important area in which to infuse transformation.

Part 4 provides next steps and concluding thoughts. Chapter 16 aims to illustrate how bringing healthy churches and ministries together into networks can function like an ecosystem to provide a vital spiritual environment. Chapter 17 explains key elements necessary for perpetuation of transformative movements to facilitate long-lasting impact. Chapter 18 provides a conclusion. Although the book is designed to be read from beginning to end, it can also serve readers as a topical resource.

Questions for reflection and discussion:

1. How are globalization and urbanization changing our world?
2. Is your city a global city as the author describes them? How have you seen evidence of globalization and urbanization in your city?
3. How has your church been affected by globalization and/or urbanization?

Part 1
Developing a Clear Understanding of the City,
Transformation, and the Role of the Church

Chapter 2
The Case for Urban Transformation

What renewal in the city there would be if Christians by the tens of thousands, with ministers of the gospel in the lead, would fan out across the neighborhoods and barrios, towering apartments and seething slums, distributing God's Word, explaining its contents, translating its message into the languages and cultures of urban people, and making themselves instruments of God for the salvation of souls and the transformation of urban life.

--Roger Greenway (1978, p. 55)

If you want to know what your suburb, small town, or rural area will look like in 20 years, look at the nearest major city to you ... It is fair to say that the urbanization of the city urbanizes the communities around it.

--Ray Bakke and Jon Sharpe (2006)

Almost everyone wishes for the city they live in to be a secure, thriving, wonderful city. If you know anything about your own city, you most likely grieve that it is not flourishing in the ways you would like. But what does it take to transform a city from the subject of negative headlines to a place of flourishing and justice? What role, if any, does the church play in working towards such transformation? In this section we will define urban transformation and establish it as a viable mission of the church. In doing so, a theological understanding of the city and the role of the church in it will begin to take shape.

"Transformation" is one of the latest buzzwords in Christian circles, but this concept has lacked definition, theological undergirding, and comprehensive strategic thinking. Transformation sounds nice as our stated goal, but its implementation is undermined by simplistic or single-pronged approaches to changing our cities for the better. A linear approach is insufficient for making an impact on the complex web of the city.[1] Social change works better through an organic web-based approach or a "systems" approach. Social, spiritual, and cultural changes each affect the other in important ways. In other words, if we want to see transformation in our cities, we will need an approach that encourages interpenetrating impact on multiple spheres of society.

Defining Urban Transformation

The word "transformation" is ambiguous because it is used in so many different ways, yet it is a valuable word because it is nearly always used positively, often with hope and anticipation of a brighter future. The English language so loosely defines the notion of transformation that it can describe any change in a person or thing. It can refer to a relatively minor adjustment (i.e., a radio station's format being transformed from classic rock to modern rock) or can indicate a radical restructuring to the point that the object in question is like new (i.e., a caterpillar transforming into a butterfly).

Evangelical missiologists are not in agreement regarding the notion of transformation. Some would limit the purview of transformation to the individual only. Theologically, personal transformation is a vital part of the Christian life as taught by the New Testament (2 Cor. 3:18; Rom. 12:2). As a result, many advocate a primarily evangelistic missiological task for the church. David Hesselgrave (2005), an advocate for this evangelistic priority, says the news of eternal salvation

---

[1] It is not as simple as using a 12 step process for urban transformation.

should always be primary. This argument says society can begin to change only through the change of individual lives. Hesselgrave speaks in opposition to a growing body of literature advocating for a holistic missiology—one that seeks to address the whole person, including temporal needs (Heldt, 2004; J. E. L. Newbigin, 1982; Russell, 2008; Stearns, 2009) as described in Scripture (Jer. 29:4-7; Is. 58; Matt. 5:14-16; Acts 5:12-16; 1 Pet. 2:12-15).[2]

The 1974 Lausanne Conference on World Evangelization brought transformation back to the forefront of mission strategy (Carrasco, 2007: p. 393).[3] As a result, transformation has been a significant conversational theme in missiology over the course of the last four decades.[4] From the 1983 Consultation on the Church in Response to Human Need, a document emerged, "Transformation: The Church in Response to Human Need," that provided a foundational rationale and a working definition for the church engaging in transformation. Many Christian relief and development agencies used this document to provide a theological foundation for their work (V. K. Samuel & Sugden, 1999), making it a "landmark" in formulating a

---

[2] These verses only offer a small sampling of passages advocating for a more holistic approach to engaging society. I will return to these specific passages throughout the book.

[3] Here is an excerpt from the Lausanne Covenant's section on Social Responsibility: "We affirm that God is both the Creator and the Judge of all people. We therefore should share his concern for justice and reconciliation throughout human society and for the liberation of men and women from every kind of oppression.... The salvation we claim should be transforming us in the totality of our personal and social responsibilities." "The Lausanne Covenant," *The Lausanne Movement*, 1974, http://www.lausanne.org/en/documents/lausanne-covenant.html (accessed November 23, 2012).

[4] It could be argued that transformation has always been part of the conversation in missiology, but the term "transformation" has increasingly been the chosen term starting with the document produced by the World Evangelical Federation Consultation on the Church in Response to Human Need in 1983. (V. K. Samuel & Sugden, 1983)

transformational missiology.[5]   Since the 1983 Consultation on the Church in Response to Human Need, "transformation" language has featured prominently in important publications: David Bosch's magnum opus *Transforming Mission*,[6]   Paul Hiebert's *Transforming Worldviews* (2008), and an academic journal, *Transformation: An International Journal of Holistic Mission Studies*. Vinay Samuel and Chris Sugden (1999) wrote a seminal missiological treatment of transformation in *Mission as Transformation*, yet even here the concept of transformation suffers from a lack of definition (Grams, 2007).

Transformation is difficult to define fully because it is more of a process than a finished product. Jack Dennison (1999) captures this idea in his definition: "[T]he process whereby individuals, peoples, and the city as a whole increasingly and dramatically become more like God's intention for them." Importantly, transformation is an ongoing process. Randy White (2006) likewise addresses the ongoing nature of transformation:

> To say a community is 'transformed' does not mean all need is erased or all conflict overcome. It is not a state that a community arrives at. Every community is made of individuals whose personal sin has clear ripple effects in the lives of others. For that reason, it's best that we speak of community transformation as an ongoing process.

---

[5] Charles Van Engen (2005) also notes the increased emphasis on transformation in the 1980s. He speculates about the cause of this emphasis: "I believe an impetus for this may have been the fact that the predominantly North American-based sodality mission agencies, active for more than 50 years, now have second- and third-generation converts and maturing churches in Africa, Asia and Latin America.... These new generations of converts are now living in circumstances of oppression, persecution, disease, hunger, and abject poverty. And they are beginning to ask their brothers and sisters in the West what should be the impact of the Gospel upon the reality they are now experiencing." (V. Samuel & Sugden, 1987, p. xi; Van Engen, 2005, p. 7)

[6] Bosch's definitive work on a theology of mission, while thorough, does not offer a definition or rubric for understanding what he meant by "transforming". Al Tizon describes the limited nature of Bosch's definition: "So transformation in Bosch's thinking denotes a comprehensive, divinely inspired process that affects both the object and the subject of mission; all parties involved undergo transformation. Beyond that, he did not say much else about the term." (Bosch, 1991; Tizon, 2008, p. 7)

As Indian churchman Richard Howell noted, 'Transformation is not changing what is, but creating what isn't.' He is referring to things like job opportunities, new housing, new social relationships—new levels of shalom. This type of transformation is important because every community has institutions whose very systems and ways of operating have been founded on greed, expanded through exploitation or embedded with oppressive values. (p. 124)

As Evangelicals, we have a tendency to think of sin in terms of personal choices. The suggestion that the compounding impact of sin seeps into our formal and informal social structures makes us chafe. I believe this is partly due to the fact that many Evangelicals have been insulated from institutional forms of oppression. It seems like every day I read another story about women being trafficked as sex workers after being conned with an offer to work in a restaurant. I just read one article telling of 184 women from seven different countries "rescued" from forced prostitution in Malaysia ("136 Vietnamese…," 2015). I say "rescued" because then these women, as is the practice in such cases, were detained by the police and held in deplorable facilities. These women, seeking honest labor, were forced into sinful acts. Our sin is not neatly confined by our skin. It is entirely plausible at least one of these women is a Christian. What is the impact of this institutional sin on her personal faith? In other words, we cannot settle for a response that does not go beyond the individual. We are social beings who innately create social structures. Since we are innately sinful, we create innately sinful social structures.

Human trafficking, to many readers, may sound like a distant problem that we have little control over. However, even in the West, many restaurants and other businesses in the service industry are staffed by in-migrant workers trapped in their jobs by tyrannical bosses who withhold wages and confiscate passports. Every day we make choices-some knowingly, some not- that either perpetuate systemic sin or cut against it. I participated in a consultation on a "Theology of Work" as a part of a Lausanne Movement working group.[7] One pastor attending was appalled when he realized a church member, who was always pleasant on Sundays at church, was a ruthless employer on Mondays at work. We all have blind spots where our old selves betray the gospel we say we believe to the world around us. The gospel changes our sinful hearts, but it must move from our hearts into the broad boulevards of our lives as well as the dark alleys.

Just as sanctification is a lifelong process, so too humanity's sinful nature guarantees a continuous need for transformation of our cities until we reach the time when the kingdom of God is fully consummated. Awareness of our sinfulness also reminds us that urban transformation must be reliant on God as is personal transformation (Swanson & Williams, 2010; Tink, 1994).

Another defining aspect of transformation is the forward looking vision of a better city in accordance with God's intentions. The Lausanne committee's definition describes it this way: "A framework that points to the best of a human future for our city-regions can then be rooted in the reign of God" (G. Smith, 2004). An eschatological perspective imbues the present work of transformation with hope (Tizon, 2008).

Therefore, I will define urban transformation as *the ongoing process of participating with God, individually and collectively, in seeking the welfare of the city so that gospel-centered living becomes normative and all city-dwellers have an opportunity to live an abundant life, both now and forever.*

Core Components to a Theological Definition of Urban Transformation

Four key theological components are necessary for a theologically sound definition of urban transformation.

---

[7] For more about the Lausanne Movement see www.lausanne.org.

Transformation is the Work of God and is in Alignment with God's Purposes

Transformation in accordance with the purposes of God should reflect the kingdom of God. Romans 12:2 indicates a difference between the patterns of the world and the patterns transformed by God (Dayton, 1987). Wayne Bragg (1987) rightly states that transformation results from "God's continuing action in history," and it is a corrective response to individual and corporate sin. J. N. Manokaran (2008) says the fall of humanity had holistic consequences which were devastating for humanity. In Christ's death and resurrection, humanity has been holistically restored. In other words, the saving work of Christ brings holistic healing to all that went wrong in humanity's sinfulness (Col. 1:13-23). Just as personal holiness requires our ongoing obedience, holistic healing that reflects God's kingdom in our cities is only possible with the participation of Christians. We must work toward community transformation just as we work toward individual sanctification.

Transformation is Gospel-Centered

Transformation should be rooted in the gospel of Jesus Christ. The church must follow the model of Jesus, who emptied himself for the sake of the world (John 1:14; Phil. 2:5-11). Joel Edwards says, "Transformation is the inevitable result of incarnation" (Edwards, 2008, p. 97). Samuel and Sugden (1987) set forth a posture of cruciformity in our approach to transformation:

> As we engage in the struggle for justice, as we undergo suffering for God's sake, we are not constructing the kingdom of God here on earth by seeking to create perfect structures and model situations that can be proclaimed "foretastes of heaven." The sign of Christian development and social change is not the New Jerusalem but the cross. (p. 147)

Too many models of transformation skip right past the cross. If the Son of God chooses not to assert his reign through force and domination, then certainly the church should avoid these tendencies. Romans 12:1-2 captures this idea by describing the church as having a sacrificial posture in her worldly presence as part of her God-glorifying worship.[8] This sacrificial posture is infused with life as a result of Jesus' resurrection. Luke 24 offers a glimpse into the disciples' dejected comportment after the death of Jesus before they realize he has risen. With the news of the resurrection, everything changed for the disciples as they experienced a new reality of life, and it transformed their engagement with the very people who had called for Jesus' crucifixion (D. W. Smith, 2001).

One needs to be careful at this point; transformation is not the same thing as salvation. However, God's people, having experienced salvation, are able to introduce true transformation in the city. Transformation is a broader term that refers to a more general improvement of life and applies to a broad spectrum of society. To clarify, transformation is inclusive of God's "saving/redemptive grace" as well as "common grace." "Common grace" is a term used by John Calvin and is defined as the space at the intersection of God's purposes and the interests of society (Bavinck, 1909; Keller, 2010b). It captures God's goodness to everyone (Lk 6:35; Mt 5:45) (Rusaw & Swanson, 2004). "Saving grace" is the grace extended to all of those who believe and confess Jesus' atoning sacrifice on our behalf (Rom. 10:9). Harvie Conn (1992) elucidates the relationship between these two categories: "The very real mercies of common grace provide the field of operation for redemptive grace." (p. 42) When we talk about transforming cities, only individuals can benefit from saving grace, but there is a goodness that can be brought to bear on the whole city. When churches are an integral part of seeking the goodness for the whole city (common

---

[8] Richard Hays (1996) explains the corporate nature of the passage: "Paul's formulation in Romans 12:1-2 encapsulates the vision: 'Present your bodies [*somata*, plural] as a living sacrifice [*thysian*, singular], holy and well-pleasing to God...And do not be conformed to this age, but be transformed by the renewing of your mind' (p. 196).

grace), they create space for individuals to hear and embrace the gospel (saving grace). Good cities can provide economic opportunities, security, and community on a wider scale. As such, cities can be conduits of common grace while creating space for redemptive grace to enter the hearts of citizens in the city.

Transformation is Kingdom-Oriented

Transformation should always be oriented to the kingdom/reign of God.[9] The simple definition of the kingdom of God is God in his kingly rule (Flew, 1938; Ladd, 1993). The kingdom of God was central to Jesus' teachings and actions (Caragounis, 1992; Ladd, 1993). In Jesus, the kingdom of God was inaugurated, but reaches final fulfillment in the *eschaton* (the new era of Christ's return, renewal, and reign) (Goldsworthy, 2000). In practical terms, the inaugurated reality of the kingdom is the catalyst for the start of communities (churches) who are collectively submitted to God's reign. These communities must then interface with a fallen world, seeking its transformation until God's kingdom is fully implemented. The Church is not the author of transformation, rather it becomes a vessel of God's work of transformation in the city.

The process of transforming implies an end vision. That which is transforming is moving toward being transformed. Jesus taught that our basic orientation should be toward the kingdom of God (Matt. 6:33). This reality of God's reign was introduced by Jesus (Matt. 4:17) and therefore becomes an active reality for the church to follow. At the same time, Jesus taught a prayer that looks forward to God's reign on earth being completed, like it is in heaven (Matt. 6:9-15). Like Graham Cray (1999) says, "It is an 'upside-down Kingdom' which presents a direct

---

[9] Some scholars have chosen to use alternate terms for "kingdom of God," attempting to avoid the potential mental pitfall of imagining a kingdom with borders as we have with geopolitical nation states. A substitute term often used is 'reign of God'; this better communicates a borderless domain of authority. Jesus, along with John the Baptist, announced that 'the kingdom of God is near' (4:17). (Guder et al., 1998, p. 90; Jeremias, 1971, p. 96) I will use "kingdom of God" and "reign of God" interchangeably.

challenge to and reversal of accepted social religious values." (p. 29) Jesus' description of the kingdom of God provides us with a vision of what life could be like, characterized by justice, peace and joy (Rom. 14:17) (Hunsberger, 1998).

The church that has a beautiful vision of society perfected by God's kingdom must also acknowledge limitations in the current age. The Church remains imperfect and thus is an imperfect force for transformation,[10] and the notion of the kingdom does not give license for the implementation of a theocracy (Saucy, 1988). Yet this does not remove the Church's responsibility to enact the ideals of the kingdom in obedience to the King (Ladd, 1974). The Church points to the kingdom of God as a signpost and a foretaste. The Church's posture should be one of influence and sacrifice rather than of power and coercion (Cray, 1999; Saucy, 1988).

Transformation is Holistic

True transformation is holistic in scope. Holistic mission combines evangelism and social responsibility together as essential to the missions task (McConnell, 2000; Russell, 2008). The Bible consistently challenges readers to be concerned about people physically and spiritually (cf. Is. 58).[11] Correctly understood, John Perkins says the whole person needs a holistic gospel (Perkins, 1982). "Bluntly," says Christopher Wright (2006), "we need a holistic gospel because the world is in a holistic mess." (p. 315) Holistic transformation extends to cities as well; "…the urban environment cannot be transformed without a significant cultural transformation" (Jardine, 2004, p. 261). This holistic approach to mission pertains not only to the reuniting of the physical and spiritual, but also includes holistic theology. The Church

---

[10] Berkhof imagines the potential impact of a church that is not in a fallen state: "if all those who are now citizens of the Kingdom would actually obey its laws in every domain of life, the world would be so different that it would hardly be recognized." (Berkhof, 1941, p. 408)

[11] When the church overemphasizes one over the other it distorts the biblical message.

needs a theology that touches every aspect of life, including urban life.[12] Grams (2007) notes the impact of a holistic perspective on many theological ideas:

> ... an already/not yet eschatology; sin/redemption; personal/social sin; personal/social transformation and salvation; physical/spiritual; evangelism/social involvement; Church/world; culture is both good and bad, needing transformation; the need for both mercy and justice; love for both the Church and the larger community; partnership in missions; and parity between the purpose and means of raising funds. (p. 194)

This commitment to holistic theology impacts missional practice, affecting the way a person or church approaches city transformation. Advocates of transformational missiology consider this holistic tension of theological commitments to be more faithful to the Bible as a whole than those who maintain a more dualistic theological framework (Grams, 2007).

Core Components to a Theological Definition of Urban Transformation
• Transformation is the work of God and is in alignment with God's purposes.   • Transformation is Gospel-centered.   • Transformation is Kingdom-oriented.   • Transformation is holistic.

Figure 2.1 Core Components to a Theological Definition of Urban Transformation

---

[12] Christopher Wright (2010) observes God's holistic purposes: "Amos probably surprised his listeners by insisting that God was actually more interested in what happened 'in the gate' than in the sanctuary (Amos 5:12-15)." (p. 224)

Urban Transformation as a Biblical Priority

Cities are Gifts from God

There is a long history of debate about whether God holds cities in a positive or negative light. The issue cannot be settled with a simplistic either/or answer. Scripture mentions 119 different cities and refers to cities at least 1,227 times; therefore, space does not permit a full survey of the biblical view of cities (Rubingh, 1987). The French sociologist Jacques Ellul (1970) argues that cities were created in rebellion against God and that they are to be judged by God. Ellul builds his case on the first recorded city in the Bible in Genesis 4:17.[13] Even after God promises his protection over Cain, Cain builds a city, presumably for security. The combination of the human pride and lack of faith displayed by Cain persuades Ellul to see the building of cities as mired in rebellion and ultimately accursed by God. According to Ellul, all cities of humankind fall into this category and are symbolized by Babylon. The only hope for humanity is the new city that is "solely the work of God" (p. 188). This view taken at face value might cause the church to abandon the city and its well-being completely, but Ellul's anti-urban interpretation goes beyond the text in Genesis (Stockwell, 1992).

The biblical record related to cities is exceedingly more complex than the view averred by Ellul. The Promised Land delivered to the Israelites is full of cities that were to be restored after being delivered to God's people. "The city is an integral feature of the theological topography of the promised land, no less than God's gift to Israel" (Brown & Carroll, 2000, p. 7). And new cities were built: "Steps were soon taken to restore the shattered cities or to found them afresh, e.g., Nu. 32:16, 24, 34, 38, 42; Ju. 1:26. Even Jericho rose again, 1 Kg. 16:34. Once settled in the land, Israel could not do without the

---

[13] DuBose (1978) rightly observes that Cain's city in Genesis 4 is paradigmatic for Ellul. (p. 103)

protection of cities and placed its confidence in them, Dt. 28:52" (Strathmann, 1964, p. 523). Cities were an essential feature of the land provided by God. Furthermore, some cities were even established as cities of refuge, symbols of God's desire for justice in a broken world (Deut. 4; 21; Josh. 20). Put differently, "The cities of refuge were to be symbols of life, not death, of divine protection rather than self-protection" (Conn & Ortiz, 2001, p. 89).

Cities are not innately bad; they are gifts from God that we are to be stewards of and through which we can reflect God's glory. The Promised Land given to the Israelites was not an empty tract of land. In Deuteronomy 6:10-12, God reminds his people that there are already "good" and "great" cities provided from them. They, in turn, are to take care of these cities in manner that brings honor and glory to God's name.

Personal Transformation Should Have Social Implications

Transformation cannot stop at the individual; real transformation should impact the individual's social network (V. Engen, 1996). When speaking of Christian transformation, it is most common to think and speak in terms of the individual being transformed, but this tendency is formed by and feeds back into a culture increasingly fixated on individual consumerism. However, individual transformation can never be complete without impacting other people and even social structures (Matt. 7:15-20). Paul Hiebert (2008) connects individual transformation to the transformation of the church community: "Spiritual transformation is the work of God in the life of a sinner, making him or her a child of God and a citizen of the kingdom of God. It is also the work of God in the church, the community of those who follow Christ. Because it is the work of God, we cannot fully comprehend it" (p. 307). The Christian is transformed and, as a part of the church, brings transformation to the church community. Randy White (2006) avers: "Our own transformation makes us avenues of transformation in the city" (p. 121). Swanson and Williams (2010) consider individual transformation as partnered to community transformation rather than as a substitute. The church community, and the individuals that comprise it, should be threaded into the surrounding community and should be an agent of transformation in that community.

The Apostle Paul, in the New Testament, recognizes the social implications of personal transformation when a runaway slave, Onesimus, becomes a Christian. Paul pleads with Onesimus' owner, Philemon, who also is a Christian, to receive him graciously as a brother in Christ. Both men, undergoing personal transformation, are immediately facing an issue that challenges traditional social structures in Roman society.

Cities Serve a Redemptive Role in God's Purposes

God has consistently used cities as means of common grace as well as gathering places where his name is exalted. Psalm 107:4-7 describes people who were wandering and hungry until God led them to a city to dwell in. Cities are used by God to provide community, sustenance, and security. This is a manifestation of God's grace that everyone can benefit from. But cities are not always places of such pleasant accommodation for new arrivals. It is incumbent on the people of God in the cities to ensure that cities are places of justice, refuge, and opportunity.

God also uses cities to make his saving grace known to the nations. God intended the nations to know him through the Israelite cities. Jerusalem becomes a city that praises God through inviting the nations to join in the praise (Is. 62). When the people of God failed to be a light to the nations, God made himself known by sending people to the pagan cities of the nations. For example, the prophet Jonah was sent to the city of Ninevah, which had a well-earned reputation for being fearsome and terrible (Nah. 3:1). The message was to call this people who seemed too far from God to hear the message of repentance. God loved this city of 120,000 inhabitants so much that he sent a messenger with a life-altering message (Jon. 4:11).

Ultimately, the lasting city is the final destination of Christians, because Jesus died outside the city in order to create for himself a new city (Heb. 13:12-14). The promise of the new city accompanies our entry into even the most difficult urban communities. Conn and Ortiz (2001) explains: "Now, in the fulfillment time of the new Jerusalem, God's new benefactor people move through other city gates with the same mandate and a victorious Messiah to make it happen" (p. 154). This promise offers confidence for those ministering in the midst of risk.

Whole City Impact is the Best Way to Care for the Poor and Marginalized

When the poor and marginalized are mistreated in the Bible, the whole city is held accountable (cf. Isaiah 1; Ezek. 16). More than half of the world's urban dwellers are counted among the poor. The causes of poverty are too complex to cover here, but suffice it to say the whole city contributes to the well-being of its citizens. Cities are liable for acts of injustice, both at a personal level as well as at a structural level (Gen. 18:16-33; Ezek. 16:49-50; Jer. 23:13-14) (D. W. Smith, 2001). In fact, acts of injustice repulse God. Isaiah 1:15 indicates our prayers are void unless we repent of our participation with oppression.

If the whole city is culpable for oppression, then the whole city must be involved in restoration. If the poor are trapped in systems and structures that keep them poor, then no amount of personal transformation is enough to help them come out of poverty. The Bible clearly indicates that the people of God should go out of their way to help the poor among us (Deut. 15).[14] The people of God must work in

---

[14] This is not a contradiction of Jesus' statement that the poor will always be among us (Matt. 26:11). In fact, Deut. 15 describes cycles of restoration every seven years which acknowledges the reality that the brokenness of human nature inevitably results in a return to poverty for some. The admonition to have no poor among us still calls for compassion and generosity from the people of God.

cities in a way that moves the whole city towards a state of equity and justice.

Our Calling is to Seek the Welfare of our Cities

Our calling is to seek the welfare of our cities, which includes all aspects of city life. Jacques Ellul (1998) has objected: "There is one thing which is not asked of us, and that is to *build* the city. We are to live in the city already existing. But we are asked neither to materially found a new city, nor to participate in spiritual building projects, that is, to share in that which forms the very being of the city" (p. 97). On the contrary, Scripture has many examples of God's people being commanded to contribute to the building and restoration of cities. I have already referenced Numbers 32 where the Israelites are commanded to build new cities for the people of God, but there are other examples of God instructing his people to actively engage and develop the city, including its built environment.

In the exile, King Nebuchadnezzar forcibly removed many of God's people and took them to Babylon. God's people were tempted to remain on the edge of the oppressive, pagan city until God rescued them (Jer. 28). This temptation is understandable given the descriptions of Babylon at that time. The city was imposing in every way. It was quite possibly the greatest city in the world at that time.[15] Aristotle remarks that when Babylon fell, it had been taken for three days before some parts of the city realized it (Mumford, 1961). For the Jews taken as captives to Babylon, it would have been physically, emotionally, and spiritually overwhelming.[16] The city featured a grand avenue used as a

---

[15] Among other great achievements, Babylon was possibly the first city to have a grid system of streets, over a thousand years before it became the urban norm. They were *avant-garde* in their incorporation of organic greenery in the Hanging Gardens and the terraces of the ziggurat. (Kostof, 1991, pp. 104, 226)

[16] Andrew Davey (2002) speaks of the incomprehensibility of the city for the Jews: "Babylon and Nineveh are cities of the imagination, of a size and an order of which exiles and prophets had no previous experience or comprehension." (p. 63)

royal processional way passing by the great public buildings along the river front right up to the Ishtar Gate (Kostoff, 1991). Walter Brueggemann (2010) sums up the unrivaled importance of Babylon during that period: "There is no doubt, however, that Babylon was the defining, generative power in international affairs, and so constituted an immediate threat to Israel" (p. 2). In spite of all this, God instructs them to approach the city of Babylon not with fear or resentment, but rather with integration, to a degree, building houses and planting gardens in that hostile city (Jer. 29:4-6). This unusual command from God forces the people of God to engage the people of the city through their physical engagement of the city. Ultimately, they are called to "seek the shalom of Babylon" through living fully in the city (Jer. 29:7). As Christopher Wright (2004) notes: "The shalom of the people of God was bound up with the shalom of the pagan nation among whom they now resided" (p. 240). It is clear from this passage that God expected his people to actively seek the good of the city, which included a concern for the physical elements of city life. It is not only an Old Testament priority; but the New Testament continues this emphasis of seeking the good of the broader community (Matthew 5:16; 1 Peter 2:12, 15) (Gornik, 2002; Winter, 1994). First Peter is written in the midst of persecution, yet the command is to do good works that are observable and recognized as good in the pagan society. Bruce Winter links the passages together: "A paradigm for the role of the Christian in society in 1 Peter can be found in Jeremiah 29:7. This appears to have been foremost in the thinking of the writer of this letter, for the self-definition of Christians is expressed in terms of the 'Diaspora' (1 Peter 1:1)" (Winter, 1994, p. 15). Acts portrays the early church consistently engaging in public good works, even in the midst of opposition (i.e. Acts 3, 5, 6).

The Well-Being of Urban Dwellers is Directly Related to the Well-Being of the City

The characteristics of a city impact the people of the city holistically. The inhabited environment can affect the way someone conceives of her/himself, relates to others, treats the oppressed, and even worships God. Cities are not fully comprehensible in isolated pieces. Nicholas Wolterstorff (1983) describes the human tendency to miss the forest for the trees when we look at cities. It is better, he says, to see the city as an integrated whole rather than viewing it atomistically. Wolterstorff uses the example of aesthetic contributions of the built environment to make his point. In interesting and unpredictable ways, beauty in a city's buildings can positively affect the quality of life in the city.[17] Cities are so tightly woven together that one element has a ripple effect on the rest of the city. Perhaps this explains why the prophets addressed cities as a whole for systemic injustice (cf. Jer. 6:6) (Cleaerbaut, 1983). Economic systems invariably favor one segment of the citizenry over another segment, and this is true of all of the systems operating in a city, whether it is politics, education, or public transportation.[18]

It is naïve to assume that an approach that ignores the systems of the city will be effective in moving toward transformation.

---

[17] Historic downtown George Town, Malaysia was looking its age with many buildings falling into disrepair when Lithuanian artist Ernest Zacharevic began painting unique murals on blank walls along side streets. This, then, sparked other works of street art in the area and spurred local businesses to spruce up their businesses. The street art and revitalized aesthetic of the businesses now gives tourists and locals a reason to wander and explore the unique small side streets of this post-colonial city. Once-abandoned shop lots have new shops, and the city buzzes with vigor.

[18] For some readers this statement might be difficult to digest. I am not advocating a type of socialism here, but observing the societal consequences of individual sin. One example is the practice of redlining a neighborhood (now illegal, but still practiced under the table). Redlining a neighborhood means refusing bank loans, building permits, or supermarkets in poor neighborhoods. Sometimes this is done so that real estate prices will bottom-out and developers can enter with projects lucrative for them. The poor in the community are eventually displaced and have little control over it. The topic will be taken up again in Chapter 13.

Anthropologist and missiologist Sherwood Lingenfelter (1992) encourages serious consideration of the importance of systems and structures in society: "While the spiritual battle relating to conflicting ideologies is crucial for the propagating of the gospel, the truth is that oftentimes the ministry of making disciples and planting churches is thwarted by conflicts that reside primarily in the spheres of economic and power relationships" (p. 203). One's spiritual status cannot easily be separated from his/her social and economic realities.

A well-known example of urban restoration from the Old Testament is found in Nehemiah. Nehemiah was called to aid in the reconstruction of Jerusalem after the exile. He was distraught at the situation in Jerusalem as he surveyed a city in ruins and a people lacking in social or spiritual vitality. Nehemiah began his ministry with organizing a collective effort at rebuilding the wall of Jerusalem. Clearly, the people of Jerusalem desperately needed spiritual help as well, but Nehemiah saw the value of building the city wall, which dramatically impacted the welfare of the city. After a long exile, citizens of Jerusalem, having rebuilt the wall, were then able to hear the Scriptures read to them after such a long void and return to living by the law of God (Neh. 8). Speaking about Nehemiah, Tollefson (1987) suggests:

> The Nehemiah model of cultural revitalization suggests that Christian missionaries have a unique mission and message that can significantly influence the economic and moral development of human societies. In fact, it may just be the most dynamic and viable option available. According to the Nehemiah model, Christian mission becomes an endeavor in 'community development' to assist and encourage local communities to solve their own problems and to care for other people. (p. 31)

Again, the example of Nehemiah illustrates that urban transformation is a vital part of mission. Much more needs to be said about the nature of transformational engagement of the city, but it is clear that there is ample biblical precedent for a theology of urban transformation. Jack Dennison (1999) states it in unequivocal terms: "The bottom-line goal for any city-reaching effort must be transformation" (p. 104).

Cities are the Best Context to Welcome the Stranger and Love Our Neighbors

Eric Jacobsen (2003) offers a strikingly simple way to differentiate between a city and a village: "A city is a place where it is acceptable to be a stranger" (p. 139). All over the world, cities are attracting *strangers* from the surrounding countryside and faraway lands. Cities are becoming so globalized that it is becoming normal to be foreign (Crane, 2014). God's Word repeatedly implores his people to welcome the foreigner in our midst (Ex. 23:9; Lev. 19:34; Deut. 10:19). There is no better place to do this than in our cities. Jesus broadens the command by calling us to love all of our neighbors, no matter who they are (Lk. 10:27). Looking forward, we even see foreigners contributing to the New Jerusalem (Is. 60:6-14).

What kind of welcome does a visitor experience at your church? Quite often we treat the visitor to a plastic smile and a noncommittal handshake. That is not the biblical idea of welcoming! We are called to the kind of hospitality we might extend to a family member. We are to love the stranger like we'd love ourselves (Deut. 10:19). This love for our neighbors includes offering physical help when needed as well as welcoming them into our spiritual family (Deut. 29:10-13). In order for the Church to obey this command well, the Church needs to be established in the cities and seeking out ways to welcome the foreigner and love our neighbors. Engaging community members with hospitality and love cannot help but have a ripple effect on the city as a whole.

We Should Live in a Vision of a Transformed City

When the Bible describes the future completion of the new creation, it is described as a city. Isaiah, Ezekiel, and Revelation all describe a "new city" in the *eschaton*. Sean Benesh (2011a) puts it this way: "Cities are not inherently evil; otherwise it would seem silly that God would incorporate them into eternity" (p. 31). If the city was innately cursed and evil, it would not be featured so prominently in eschatological texts. The importance of present cities, then, cannot be discounted: "This urban eschatology is important for urban mission. It is a powerful incentive not to abandon the city. Our work and testimony in the city are not insignificant" (Murray, 1990, p. 57). By reflecting on the biblical narrative that leads to the new city, we should be impassioned to engage cities today with this eschatological hope (Van Engen, 1996). .

The ways we live, speak, and call others to live should reflect the future hope of life made complete (Phil. 1:6). There is a biblical notion that we will somehow contribute to this glorious city. Passages describing the future city indicate human labor and cultural offerings will be incorporated by God into the city (Is. 61:4; Rev. 21:26). We have been created to be involved in God's New Creation. The prophetic call for a more just, more equitable, and more merciful city anticipates a future holy city where creation is restored and reflects the God who brings this marvelous event to fruition.

Questions and Objections

Why use the term transformation?

The Wheaton Consultation used the term "transformation" intentionally instead of other terms like "development." Development often implies only economic rehabilitation of those who need it, whereas transformation entails the holistic needs of a person or community (Samuel & Sugden, 2003). Another reason is given in the Wheaton Consultation document: "Western nations, for example, who have generally assumed that development does not apply to them, are, nevertheless, in need of transformation." (Samuel & Sugden, 1983, p. 3). Many can benefit from development or economic assistance, but everyone needs transformation. Other terms imply a humanistic animus powering the transformation, but transformation is more easily considered in theological or spiritual terms (Dayton, 1987; Swanson & Williams, 2010). In accepting the development approach, churches are uncritically accepting the basic assumptions behind it (Paredes, 1987). Thinking only in terms of economic prosperity or development can lead to the false conclusion that the "good life" has been achieved when, in fact, transformation exclusive of spiritual rebirth falls short of being holistic (Bragg, 1987; Elliston, 1989). It is through the power of God, the Creator and Sustainer of the universe, that transformation takes place.

Does transformation distract the church from the priority of evangelism?

Not everyone agrees that church should be involved in urban transformation. Darrin Patrick's *Church Planter: The Man, the Message, the Mission* (2010) argues theologically for the transformation of the city in its last chapter. Mark Dever's endorsement of the book contained this one objection: "I disagree with some things, like Darrin's correlation between the resurrection of Christ and the transformation of cities, but this book has been exciting and helpful and I appreciate [it] a great deal" (see further Dever, 2013). Dever is not the only one who is skeptical about urban transformation being part of the role of the church (Hodges, 1978). These objections deserve an answer.

In essence, Dever and others claim that the church's job is primarily to evangelize and disciple individuals through the local church. Efforts at addressing systemic evils in the city or broad-based urban transformation initiatives are derailing the church from the primary task of evangelism and discipleship. First, it should be said their criticism is not without merit. There are many churches that have become distracted by programs and projects that do not result in Christian disciples growing deeper. However, Dever's (and others') approach goes to the opposite extreme and fails to acknowledge the complexity of God's commands to love those around us more completely. Although more could be said on the subject, I want to respond to such objections with just two points.

First, we must remember the potential of our collective impact as much as our individual impact. Just as an example, imagine Joe becomes a Christian in his city and is discipled in a local church. The church teaches Joe to care for God's creation and one simple way to do so is to recycle. Joe decides to recycle but quickly realizes that his neighborhood has no recycling service. This means many others are also not recycling. An individual might quickly give up on the issue and start throwing cans away like everyone else. However, if the church saw itself as an agent of transformation in the city, it could play a larger role in calling for a recycling service and possibly offering its property as a location for collection. In doing so, the church, by being stewards of God's creation, points to the Creator God. It is through small actions like this one the church becomes an active and concerned member of the community. When the church becomes involved in the issues of the city, it is more capable of being a prophetic voice to not only call for changes but draw people to God.

Second, the individualistic view of transformation is naïve about the compounding impact of systemic and structural oppression. There are urban communities in every city that have developed systemic patterns and sub-cultures that, left unaddressed, make it very difficult to grow as a new Christian. Perhaps a young woman is being forced into prostitution or a young man's mom is threatened unless he sells drugs. The church has a responsibility to help address these systemic issues so that young disciples of Jesus can grow and bear fruit. Quite often those promoting an exclusively individual evangelism approach live in communities where systemic issues pose no obvious threat.

If our cities are temporary, isn't urban transformation a wasted effort?

Some argue that the cities we live in are temporary and therefore we should not expend great efforts at transforming them; instead we should be getting people saved out of them. Of course, opinions vary widely on the eschatological views of continuation or discontinuation from this world to the next. Without having to appeal to one particular view of the end times, there is a biblical precedent for investing deeply in our cities even if it is only for a time. We return to the passage in Jeremiah 29 referenced earlier in this chapter, where God's people are taken into exile to Babylon and called to seek the welfare of that city (v. 7). After the citizens of Jerusalem have been forcibly dragged to the city at the center of the brutal conquering empire they are called on to actively pursue the good of the whole city, capital of the enemy empire. It is an astounding command because in the same passage God clearly states this will be a temporary arrangement, lasting only seventy years (v. 10). Furthermore, God speaks through Jeremiah declaring the judgment and destruction of Babylon (Jer. 50). In fact, Babylon is used symbolically in the Bible to describe the city in the hands of evil humanity. Yet, God calls his people to love and invest in that city, however temporary it may be, so that God may be known even in the most hostile of cities.

Questions for reflection and discussion:

1. According to the author, what are the four defining characteristics of a theological understanding of transformation? Do you agree?
2. Before reading this chapter, what was your view of cities? Has this reading affected your understanding of God's view of cities?
3. In terms of both geography and engagement, where is your church in relation to the city?

Chapter 3
The Spectrum of Christian Models of Urban Transformation

There are nearly as many theories of right, biblical, and sane methodologies and goals as there are evangelical urbanologists.
--Sydney Rooy (1992, p. 223)

...it should be clear at this point that good intentions are not enough to engage the world well. The potential for stupidity, irrationality, cruelty, and harm is just as high today as it has ever been in the past. God save us from Christians who are well-intentioned, but not wise!
--James Davison Hunter (2010, p. 273)

Jun Vencer (1989), former international director of the World Evangelical Alliance, offers a poignant question for the urban church: "If the mission of the urban church is to establish the Kingdom of God in the city by incarnating and proclaiming the gospel of Jesus, what would be the activities of that mission?" (p. 131) In other words, idle church presence is not enough. Churches will need to make choices to establish a transformational engagement with the city. In a sea of models of urban transformation, the "right model is needed" (Duncan, 1996, p. 119).

There are dozens of resources available that promote urban transformation or at least an aspect of urban transformation. At first blush, these resources can all appear beneficial for the mission of the urban church. However, deeper analysis reveals that one cannot put two of these approaches in practice without them being in conflict with one another.

The approach one chooses will most likely be a reflection of his or her stance toward the city. Responses of Christians to the city vary from a largely negative view of the city with a more confrontational style of engagement to the other extreme in which the city and its systems are viewed as good and the church's role is simply to support these good elements. As tends to be the case with many matters of theology and missiology, the evangelical response to urban transformation occupies a nuanced middle area on the spectrum between hostility and positive affirmation. Even within the evangelical response, there exist a number of models that approach urban transformation in different ways. In this chapter, I will provide an overview of different Christian approaches to urban transformation. In some cases, these approaches are intentional models for urban transformation; in other cases, they are more or less default approaches towards urban transformation.[1] For example, those who seek to change society through one soul at a time may train their focus on individuals without contemplating the city.

Churches and individual Christians employ a wide variety of models in approaching the city and its transformation. A model, as I'm using the term, is not necessarily an intentional set of practices, but may

---

[1] Those who have written on urban transformation have used different terms. Here I differentiate between "approach" and "model." Approach is a broader term referring to one's theological perspective of the city. Model, on the other hand, is a more specific strategy for bringing change to the city. Carter, Patrick, and Maggay prefer the term "approach," while Conn and Hunter use "model." (Carter & Patrick, 2011; Conn, 1997; Hunter, 2010; Maggay, 2004)

be the default mode of interaction with the city due to one's posture toward it.[2]

Introduction to the Broad Spectrum of Christian Responses to the City

The range of Christian models of urban transformation is vast, and models differ partly because views of the city differ (see Stockwell, 1992). Different views of social transformation also contribute to variations among the models. Some scholars have attempted to categorize the different models, and in this section I will summarize a few of these categorizations.

Sociologist Melba Maggay (2004) is an Evangelical as well as a social activist. She has observed four common approaches for transforming society. First is, "The City on a Hill" in which proponents demonstrate potential societal transformation in alternative communities. The second is "The Idea of Christendom," where transformation is introduced through Christian influence in the prevailing power structures. The third, "The Gospel of Liberation," seeks to bring transformation to current power structures that disadvantage the poor and oppressed. And fourth is "The Practice of Compassion," in which acts of kindness and mercy are offered to those in need. Maggay provides the biblical support for each model followed by a critical assessment of each one. Her taxonomy is helpful, and her assessments are incisive, but the categories are broad and unnuanced. Ultimately, she does not favor any of the four approaches, but proposes a model that, while loosely patterned after the incarnation of Jesus, lacks cohesion.

James Davison Hunter (2010) introduced his own categories of social transformation in *To Change the World: The Irony, Tragedy, and Possibility of Christianity in the Late Modern World*. His three categories

---

[2] Conn cautions his readers about the risks in using "models." By this, he refers to a defined blueprint for building or doing a task. Here "model" will be used more generally to describe an approach with many possible variations according to urban ministry practitioners. (Conn, 1997, p. 196)

are: Evangelism, Political Actions, and Social Reform. To summarize Hunter's view, he contends "that the dominant ways of thinking about culture and cultural change are flawed, for they are based on both specious social science and problematic theology" (p. 5). Like Melba Maggay, Hunter captures a broad spectrum but over-generalizes. Using his expertise in sociology, Hunter helpfully exposes the problematic tendency of some Christian writers to proof-text sociological ideas, following the logical trajectory of their arguments to reveal inherent flaws or difficulties.

Borrowing from Niebuhr's *Christ and Culture* (1975), Harvie Conn developed a helpful typology delineating different models of the church's cultural engagement with the city. In Conn's understanding, typical Christian postures are: 1) Christ against the city; 2) Christ and the city in paradox; 3) Christ transforming the city. Conn suggests the third one as the most biblical response, and he sees a link between creation and redemption. In Conn's estimation, Evangelicals have underemphasized creation in order to highlight the importance of redemption.

I find that two of Conn's categories—"Christ against the city" and "Christ and the city in paradox"—are too similar to be easily distinguished, so I have adapted Conn's typology by changing one of his three categories.[3] I have chosen to group various approaches to the city into three broad categories: 1) the church against the city, 2) the church for the city and, 3) the church transforms the city. These approaches to the city are influenced by differing theological understandings of the city, different convictions regarding the relationship between Christ and culture, and different theological understandings of the mission of the church. As with any attempt to categorize models, my framework is susceptible to generalizations and exaggerations in order to delineate the differences between the models. I have attempted to note where this

---

[3] Conn uses his terms differently than I do here. For him, "model" denotes a general attitude to the city, which then informs the approach one takes toward urban transformation. (Conn, 1997, pp. 196–202)

might be the case. The focus here is on approaches to urban transformation rather than approaches to Christ and culture, although the two topics are very much related. Cities are, after all, "places where 'Christ' and 'culture' meet" (Graham & Love, 2009).

It should be noted that all of these models hope to introduce transformation to the city. Some have critiqued Niebuhr's category "Christ against Culture" as misrepresenting the desired posture of advocates of that position (Grams, 2007). Many from the Anabaptist tradition who represent that model have noted that they do still wish to engage culture with transformation in view (Stassen, Yeager, & Yoder, 1995). I do not intend to imply that transformation is not in view. I acknowledge that each approach is aimed at transformation but think it is important to note that each model within the approaches is born of certain theological commitments that establish different postures toward the city.

A Typology of Approaches and Models of Urban Transformation

In the chart below are three broader approaches to the city with a selection of models that fall into each category.[4] Brief descriptions of those urban transformation models follow the chart.

---

[4] "Approach" here refers to broader theological perspectives of cities, missions, and culture. "Model" is more specific as it prescribes solutions or practices that will lead to urban transformation. I have used "posture" more loosely to refer to both approaches and models.

Approach to the City	Models of Urban Transformation Corresponding to the Approach
The Church Against the City	• Transformation through One Soul at a Time • Transformation through Strategic Organized Prayer • Transformation through Influence in Key Areas • Transformation through Escape to an Alternative City
The Church for the City	• Transformation through Solidarity with Other Institutions • Transformation through Solidarity with the Poor and Marginalized
The Church Transforms the City	• Transformation as Part of the City • Transformation through Incarnational Presence and Holistic Revival • Transformation as a City within the City

Figure 3.1. Macro-Perspective of Models of Urban Transformation

The Church Against the City

As the title would suggest, advocates of this approach generally understand the city as negative. Similar to the perspective espoused by Jacques Ellul, advocates of this approach often describe the city as cursed or under the control of the evil one. This anti-urban posture has been very common, particularly within the church.[5] Harvie Conn (1994) observes the embeddedness of anti-urbanism in America: "By the middle decades of the nineteenth century, this image of the 'wicked city' had become a stereotype already deep in the national consciousness" (p. 38)

While many Christians with this view would like to see cities change for the better, expectations of urban impact are very low and evangelism is expected to be very difficult (Keller, 2002). Within this approach are a variety of models. Advocates of the models under this approach tend to come from the most conservative wing of the church, mostly fundamentalist churches or charismatic churches.[6]

Transformation through One Soul at a Time

Many Christians, particularly from fundamentalist traditions, believe the city is beyond hope except for the salvation of individuals. This view of urban transformation considers the only real solution to be the evangelism of individuals. In other words, personal evangelism is the key to urban transformation. Matthew Recker (2002), a Baptist with fundamentalist connections, describes transformation primarily as saving one soul at a time. With this attention on the individual, it is rare to find a developed approach to urban transformation from churches with this perspective. Quite often, the city is only considered a place of temptation and violence vying against the church for the soul of each individual. Matthew Recker's approach, while placing the

---

[5] In the introductory essay to *Gods of the City*, Robert Orsi deals extensively with the development of anti-urbanism in America, especially among the religious. Among the influencers of this stance are novels that teemed with dramatic images of the "dark" city. Interestingly, he also notes that the writings of those who sacrificed much for the sake of the city (i.e. David Wilkerson, Jane Addams, Billy Sunday) also painted the city in sinister colors. Orsi goes so far as to call such descriptions pornographic because it is intended to be titillating. (Orsi, 1999, pp. 6–12)

[6] I am using "Fundamentalists" as differentiated from Evangelicals in their desire to be separated from mainstream culture and high value for agreement in all areas of doctrine. (McIntire, 1984; Smidt, 1988, pp. 601–602)

priority on evangelizing individuals, does acknowledge the value of holistic concern for the individual. Recker gives an extended example in his book about someone with addiction issues. He states that it helps for the individual to have a way to get out of the vicious cycle in which he or she is trapped. But, even more importantly, they must have a genuine salvation experience, or the rest is useless. "Let us never forget that to preach the gospel is to give man what he really needs" (p. 113). The logic explicates that, the more individuals saved, the more the community shows signs of transformation. Hunter (2010) captures the underlying assumption of this approach, "if a culture is good, it is because the good values embraced by individuals lead to good choices" (p. 7). Ultimately, however, advocates of this approach believe only the city of God can undergo transformation. The city of God is regarded as completely separate from the city of man and consists only of those in the church. The societal separation envisioned by this approach is where the "against the city" posture is evidenced.[7] Everything about the earthly city will pass away.

Seeking to change the city by focusing on individual souls has its strengths. The transforming nature of the gospel is a priority, so God is acknowledged as the source of real change. Another strength is the formation of communities that seek to be different by their commitment to biblical values. This difference can demonstrate, in a microcosm, what a society submitted to God can look like. Also, the focused commitment to evangelism is a strength.

This approach also has several weaknesses. A focus only on individual evangelism, when carried to its logical end, winds up with a focus only on the eternal destiny of individuals and neglects the biblical admonitions to love our neighbor, even our enemy (Mt. 5:44; 19:19). In other words, discipleship in this approach would primarily focus on how to evangelize and would limit disciples' understanding of living as

---

[7] Mohler exemplifies this kind of separation in his stance on public schools in America as a lost cause. He calls for Christian families to choose other educational options that are more separate from mainstream society (Mohler, 2011, p. 157).

transformed children of God to selected issues of individual morality. The theology of the city as negative impacts churches' approach significantly at this point. When someone believes the city is evil and little can be done to change one's individual plight, "then avertive religion in one or another of its forms or some inwardness version of formative religion will prove irresistibly attractive, and the social activism inherent in world-formative religion will seem profoundly irrelevant" (Wolterstorff, 1983, p. 11). Put differently, if our outlook on society is hopeless, we will not seek to make change in society.

Another weakness is the lack of awareness of the strength and influence of social systems in our lives. A boy forced into a violent gang as a child might be open to the evangelistic message of the gospel, but never understand how to reconcile his faith with his lifestyle. Those with an exclusive emphasis on "one soul at a time" hold a critical assumption about Christianity as a social order. Grams (2007) notes that the individual evangelism approach often overlaps with a perspective of Christianity as a social order: "...the more one identifies Christianity with a social order, the more one will understand evangelism and conversion in terms of belief as opposed to action" (p. 198) The presumption is the social order will (eventually) take care of the non-spiritual needs of individuals. In other words, social order is thought to be an automatic consequence of the accumulation of individuals experiencing conversion, so a positive change in social order can be achieved only through conversion efforts, rendering pointless the church's involvement in social systems.

Transformation through Strategic Organized Prayer

For some, corporate prayer is the key to transforming cities. Of course, all of the Christian approaches to transformation would see prayer as vitally important, but in this instance prayer is the central strategy. Advocates of this model, like George Otis Jr. (1999a; 1999b), believe unseen powers are at work in cities. These powers can be detected through a process called "spiritual mapping" which "enables us to 'see' things that were previously undetectable with our natural eyes" (1999a, p. 81). These things include angels, demonic strongholds, and spiritual pacts that obstruct the advance of the gospel. A strategy is then developed to combat these strongholds.[8] These strategies often include concerts of prayer, praying in strategic locations, and marching around the city in prayer.[9] This more supernatural-reliant model is a particularly popular approach among Pentecostal churches.

The strength in this view is that the spiritual realm is acknowledged and addressed. The Bible clearly reveals a spiritual realm that impacts the physical realm (Eph. 6:12).[10] In combating evil, whether in spiritual form or physical form, the Church must rely on the power of God. The Church needs to unite in prayer and make a clear stand against evil influences in our communities.

I find three major problems with this model. First, the scriptural support for this approach is thin. C. Peter Wagner has admitted this weakness and humbly receives correction when his use of the Bible has exceeded the exegetical intent of the passage.[11] Nevertheless, their methodology draws from obscure references in the Old Testament (e. g.

---

[8] "Those who pray to deliver people from demonic oppression have long since learned that, generally speaking, results are much greater when the evil spirits are identified and specifically commanded to leave in the name of Jesus rather than ministering with a vague prayer such as, 'Lord, if there are any spirits here we command them all to leave in Your name.' We suspect that the same may be true of praying deliverance over neighborhoods, cities or nations. Spiritual mapping is simply a tool to allow us to be more specific, and hopefully more powerful, in praying for our community." (Wagner, 1993, p. 18)

[9] "Marching in silence around a wall for days on end made no sense militarily, but the people were gaining spiritual authority by the exercise of faith, obedience and self-control. That they had to march in silence is probably a clue to the nature of the unseen realm over Jericho." (Dawson, 2001, p. 4)

[10] Missionaries from the West, with their rationalist worldview, underestimated the unseen realm. Since Hiebert's seminal article, the unseen realm has become an important topic in missiology. (P.G. Hiebert, 1982)

[11] For example, Wagner used Revelation 12:7 in his argument for strategic-level spiritual warfare. After receiving criticism for relying on such a literal view of Revelation in his theology, Wagner has minimized his use of this apocalyptic book. (Wagner, 1996, p. 226; Wagner, 1993, p. 19)

Ezek. 4:1-3 for spiritual mapping), and is applied literally in the contemporary context. The descriptions we have of Jesus' and Paul's ministries do not look similar to these prayer strategies. Second, some of the language they use almost has a ring of occultic or animistic formulae.[12] The ideas of discovering secret pacts made with demonic forces and discovering the names of spirits ruling over specific territories receives much attention (e.g., Bailey, 2010; Moreau, 2010). Neither Jesus nor Paul employed this approach, and it does not integrate easily with scriptural mandates for mission. Third, this approach assumes a hostile posture to the city using military terminology and a presumption that the city is occupied by the enemy. This posture creates an "us against them" attitude that devolves into increased polarization between Christians and the rest of society.

Transformation through Influence in Key Areas

This model says the way to change the world is through the penetration and influence of key areas of society. The goal is to establish Christians and Christian ideas in these spheres of society. Within this model are many variations. Ed Silvoso (2007) seeks influence through marketplace penetration and influence with his International Transformation Network. The subtitle of one of Silvoso's books communicates his approach: "Change the marketplace and you change the world." He uses the term "marketplace" quite broadly to include all of mainstream society including government. This approach shares many points of overlap with the previous approach of strategic organized prayer. The goal in this model is to harness Christian influence to impact the highest levels of society. Silvoso persuades his readers "to reclaim the marketplace...for the kingdom of God" (p. 31) and this will, in turn, transform society at large. Vishal Mangalwadi (2009) shares a similar emphasis, contesting for worldview change in

---

[12] Priest, Campbell and Mullen argue persuasively that many of the practices of these strategic level intercessors are more rooted in animistic ideology than in Christian theology. (Priest, Campbell, & Mullen, 1995)

every sphere of society. Silvoso tells many stories of Christians appealing to top government leaders in order to influence change in the nation, so that the nation may be saved.[13]

Bob Roberts also advocates a model similar to this through his T-Model ("Glocalnet: Connecting for Glocal Transformation"; Roberts, 2010). Roberts seeks to use influence in every sector of society at a local level and at a global level. Through naturally occurring networks via work and community development, Roberts emphasizes the role of lay Christians as ministers of transformation.

The leaders of the Seven Mountains Movement or 7M Mandate place a heavier emphasis on prophecy and politics in their articulation of the model (C. Jacobs, 2010, p. 168). The Seven Mountains Movement advocates exerting Christian influence over the seven key spheres or mountains of any society. These spheres are religion, business, government, education, media, arts and entertainment, and family ("Reclaiming the 7 Mountains," n.d.). The basic idea was originally developed by Loren Cunningham, Bill Bright, and Francis Schaeffer,[14] but has now morphed and is being promoted by others (Enlow, 2008; Hillman, 2011; Wallnau, 2009). The biblical characters Daniel and Joseph become key role models for Christians today (Enlow, 2009). Similar to Silvoso's strategy, the Seven Mountains Movement transforms through the influence of the dominant sectors of society.

This approach has some positive characteristics. Advocates value every aspect of life as sacred and connected to the spiritual world. Prayer is given high value. Practitioners of this approach are entering these seven spheres of society with the intent to proclaim the good news of Jesus. Most of the models of transformation listed in this chapter do not offer such a thorough plan of societal penetration.

---

[13] He builds his case on his interpretation of Matt. 28:18-20 and Rev. 21:24-27. (Silvoso, 2007, pp. 40–42)

[14] The "Reclaiming the 7 Mountains" website indicates that Francis Schaeffer developed this approach separately from Bright and Cunningham.

The primary trouble with this approach is that it is essentially a dominionist approach. That is, the goal is not only to wield influence in these areas, but dominate them for the sake of the kingdom. One of C. Peter Wagner's latest books is titled *Dominion!: How Kingdom Action Can Change the World* (2008). Silvoso (2007) avers preaching the gospel of the kingdom of God "means stating and also *enforcing* the will of the King" (p. 59, emphasis added). It is no wonder that this model is perceived by the media as an attempt at theocratic society (Meacham, 2011; B. Wilson, 2009). When the church seeks to influence through worldly power, it ends up becoming a slave to power structures that are antithetical to kingdom power structures. The life and teachings of Jesus consistently demonstrate a radically different approach to worldly power, summed up by the phrase "the last will be first" (Matt. 20:16, ESV). Jacobsen (2003) critiques this dominionist tendency to "claim" a city for Christ by referring to Paul, who was "aware that Christ won a decisive victory on the cross, and nowhere seems to imply that we need to improve the effectiveness of his victory by claiming things" (p. 48).

Transformation through Escape to an Alternative City

Many Christians become so frustrated by the difficulties of ministering effectively in cities that they established their own communities/cities built on a better foundation. This is one way of understanding the Puritan mindset as they established cities in New England. The Church's flight to the suburbs away from the evils of the city is one manifestation of this approach. Christian schools provide children with a completely separate education that establishes the building blocks for a different society. That approach is sometimes more of a reaction to perceived urban evils than an intentional plan for transformation, but other groups have developed this approach with more intentionality. Christian communes and monasteries are also types of the alternative city approach.

This approach draws on the utopian visions of new garden cities that arose out of the industrial era. One of the most extreme examples is found in Jakarta, Indonesia. During our family's stay in Jakarta in 2008, I learned about a city within Jakarta called Lippo Karawaci that was designed to be a fully functioning city complete with its own residences, schools, hospitals, and even a megamall. Stable sources of water and electricity are built into the design. It seems that everything has been thought of, and it provides a solution to all of the problems faced when living in Jakarta. Lippo Karawaci was designed for up to a million residents and is one of two such cities built by the Lippo Group. It is a utopian city within a dystopian city. What makes this even more interesting for us is the fact that this city was the dream of a Christian, James Riady. The Christian school was intentionally established to integrate discipleship into the children's education (Hogan & Houston, 2002).

One can definitely see the benefits of living in this environment; it is clean and safe and provides all of the modern utilities. Citizens in these communities no longer have to rely on inefficient or dysfunctional institutions for basic infrastructure and they have more control over the foundational ethos for their children's education.[15]

The separate city within a city strategy developed by Riady might sound extreme, but it actually represents a trend of living, working and being entertained in private spaces or "fortified enclaves" (Caldeira, 2005, p. 83). This approach to urban transformation is weakened by the fact that it is primarily about self-preservation and self-interest. Andrew Davey (2002) observes the tendency of suburban congregations to develop programs that meet only their own interests and "will often use the rhetoric of transformation and change but will ignore or fail to promote critical reflection on wider issues of lifestyle, social responsibility or power." (p. 93). One common example is the church

---

[15] This model might have stronger appeal in majority world nations that have high levels of corruption and underdeveloped infrastructure. In Indonesia it was common to hear people refer to the government as mired in KKN (*korupsi, kolusi, nepotisme*, the Indonesian words for corruption, collusion, and nepotism). Corruption is so deeply woven into government procedures that many of the educated elites, like the Riady family, find it easier to circumvent the government by developing their own infrastructure.

that builds a "community" center that is only available to the congregation and not truly available to the community. Returning to the example of Lippo Karawaci, the city of Jakarta has no water supply or sewage system. The issue is solved privately or within a small group of buildings with a well and septic tank. This solution leaves the remaining millions of Jakarta residents unable to afford those utilities facing water and sewage problems (Hogan & Houston, 2002). Garner (2004) critiques this approach:

> A theology which posits the city as a cursed and condemned place and rejects in principle any active attempt to work for its redemption is flawed.... First, it is contrary to the Christian doctrines of creation and incarnation and, second, it fails to recognize that Christians are ineluctably wedded to the secular world— they work in it, buy its goods, are susceptible to the lures and demands of the global market. Retreating into privatized communities achieves nothing in terms of healing or salvation and simply leaves the city to rot. (p. 69)

In other words, when Christians separate themselves from the problems of the city, they no longer share in the problems. In addition, there is a tendency of those who adopt this model to be among the wealthy, with the unintended consequence of reaching and blessing only other wealthy people to the exclusion of the poor. As a result, they offer little in the way of engagement or transformation of the whole city.

The Church for the City

The church that is for the city expends its resources for the sake of the city. This approach is generally more optimistic about the will of the city aligning with the mission of the church. Whereas the previous category considered the city in its current state as being at odds with God's intentions, this category considers the city to have tremendous potential. A few well-designed initiatives can put the city on the path to being a good city. Advocates of this approach tend to hold a hold a theological perspective, according to Timothy Keller (2002), "that views all historical movements that work to emancipate the oppressed as the Kingdom of God (whether Christian, non-Christian, or even atheistic)" (p. 1). Concern for the city is very much focused on the present needs of the city dwellers and is less concerned about their spiritual state. Advocates of these models tend to come from mainline Protestant churches but include a few evangelicals as well.

Transformation through Solidarity with Other Institutions

This approach seeks the good of the city as defined by the people in the city. Peter Robinson (2010) considers solidarity to be "the key value which sustains human society so that it is worthy of human beings" (p. 61). In contrast to other models presented in this chapter, the church does not engage the city prophetically but rather joins ongoing efforts at improving the city. Elaine Graham and Stephen Lowe (2009) state the task of the church is "to be transformative, embodying vision and signaling justice" (p. xi). In their case "vision" means trying to satisfy the "demand for happiness" from those in the city. In essence, advocates of this model suggest the church find the appropriate niche in which to contribute to the good of the city. Dieter Georgi (2005, p. 353-364) suggests the church can play a role in humanizing the urban experience for city dwellers by offering rites of passage, welcoming other faith communities to become established, and being the city's conscience in regard to matters of human dignity and ecological concern.

The source of transformation is described with theological vocabulary. For example: "If the act of preaching in the urban environment can be seen as a tactical act of resistance to all that prevents human flourishing, then that is a key part of allowing hope and even transformation to emerge" (P. Robinson, 2010, p. 55). While frequently employing terms like "evangelism" and "gospel," proponents of this model seem to be advocating humanism with a spiritual gloss rather than the expansion of the kingdom of God. Robinson concludes his two chapters on evangelism by saying, "It wasn't so much the words that were proclaimed but the proclamation itself within the act of solidarity" (p. 62). Jesus' work on the cross is relegated to moral example inspiring a type of self-actualization. And he is to be found in marginalized communities (Davey, 2010), thus reducing the incarnation of Christ to an ideal rather than an historical event.

This approach does have three key strengths. Proponents of this model have studied urban trends by keeping up with the many disciplines that inform urbanology. Cities are more globally connected than ever before, and Andrew Davey (2002) and others have reflected on the church's role in the city as this occurs. Many of the advocates of this model have personal insight into the day to day realities facing urban dwellers in the old industrial cities. Whereas evangelical churches have the liberty to move to a bright new suburb, the parish church system maintains a presence in the urban core, even when it is in decline. The commitment of urban parish ministers to more challenging parts of the city gives them a presence among the urban poor and marginalized.

Proponents of this model advocate for the distinctive contribution of the church and even for theological engagement in the public square (Garner, 2004, p. 90; Georgi, 2005, pp. 348–355; Graham & Lowe, 2009, pp. 23–48). These authors rightfully lament the loss of the Christian voice in the public square. Public theology is valuable if it engages the public in a distinctive, transformative manner. Unfortunately, this is where the solidarity with institutions model fails. Advocates of this model rarely represent the distinctives of orthodox Christian theology; rather, their message is moralistic and universalistic. Georgi (2005) even counters the need for Christian uniqueness by calling it "Christian colonialism." There is, I think, a problem of diagnosis. The problems of a city do not stem only from sinful structural powers, but from the fact that every city dweller is innately sinful and in need of individual redemption from the bondage of that sinfulness. Scripture is clear that it is only through Jesus that we can secure such redemption (Acts 4:12). This is not colonialism; rather, it is the trumpet sound of freedom!

Transformation through Solidarity with the Poor and Marginalized

A number of urban ministers and missiologists suggest the church's primary role in urban transformation is through solidarity with the poor and marginalized. Cities throughout history have been centers of social segmentation, particularly along the lines of economic power. Davey (2002) calls the church to,

> ...stand with urban communities in the midst of the shakings of globalization; this will involve living alongside the anger, the pain, and the misunderstanding of those areas, and the churches may need to be prepared to take the brunt of it.... In the global context, it is on such fault lines that the church needs to locate itself. (p. 118)

Here the Church is called to be a voice for the voiceless and draw from a global network to address structural and systemic ills in our cities. Advocates of this model draw heavily from liberation theologians.[16] While intent on fomenting a balance in the welfare of all urban dwellers, they do not, however, espouse a violent revolutionary mindset as some of the liberation theologians have done in the past.[17]

This model has aspects that are commendable. The Church is clearly called to care for the poor and marginalized, and even to stand for them against their oppressors. The Church's call is to follow the example of Jesus who "inverted the typical understanding of cultural values in his teachings through his perpetual lifting as important people

---

[16] For succinct introduction to moderate liberation theology for the urban context see (Davey, 1998)

[17] Maggay refers to those on the more violent edge of this movement as "extreme liberationists", but she goes on to say that most contemporary advocates place more emphasis on grassroots political empowerment. (Maggay, 2004, p. 81)

or situations that society, in most instances, viewed as having lesser value" (Peters, 2007, p. 65). Parallel to this inversion of cultural values is the valid and necessary recognition that there are structures in place that give advantage to some and disadvantage others. Christians should be aware of these types of injustices and seek to address them.

However, an exclusive focus on the well-being of the urban poor and socially marginalized neglects the damaging effects of sin at every other level of society. Beyond ignoring those who are not classified as poor or marginalized, this approach perpetuates the unhealthy divisiveness that already plagues the city. Wolterstorff (1983) concludes:

> In short, the liberation theologians' analysis of the misery of their people leads them to the conclusion that those people are being wronged—they are being exploitatively dominated by the core areas of the world-system and by the small but powerful oligarchies in the periphery. Their analysis leads the liberation theologians to take sides with those whose cries they hear, to stand against those who oppress them (p. 44).

The danger in this approach is that the wealthy and powerful are viewed as enemies of the Church rather than people in need of the gospel. The physical concerns of the urban poor are certainly an important concern for the church, but the resources to address these deep-seated issues are found only in new life in Christ, of which both poor and rich are in need. The soteriological element is completely missing from many of the advocates in this approach.

The Church Transforms the City

In between the two polarities of a negative view of the city and an optimistic expectation of the city, is the messy middle perspective inhabited by many Evangelicals. This posture portrays a theological perspective of the city that feels the gravity of the fallen state of the city and yet envisions a participatory role for the Church in urban transformation. Augustine (1950) espoused this perspective in his magisterial contrast between the city of God and the city of humankind: "In truth, these two cities are entangled together in this world, and intermixed until the last judgment effect their separation" (p. 38). Harvie Conn (1997) links these two cities through the biblical themes of creation and redemption:

> Redemption means putting on 'the new man' (Eph. 4:24; Col. 3:10). And that means putting on 'the new Adam,' and a new start for a new creation (Gal. 6:15; Eph. 2:10). This is the attitude of a property owner, of earth's inheritors (Matt. 5:5). The church has begun to exercise creation rights of urban ownership before the closing papers of the final eschaton are signed. All things are now ours, because we are Christ's and all things belong to him (1 Cor. 3:21-23) (p. 201).

The three models featured in this approach each offer valuable components to urban transformation and will remain a part of the dialogue in the rest of the book.

Transformation as Part of the City

The city is transformed through the transformation of communities within the city. Advocates of this model encourage long-term engagement of urban community needs. There are many advocates of this model and many variations within it. This model can be further divided into two categories: 1) the Christian community development model and 2) the socially-engaged church model.

John Perkins (1982) founded the Christian Community Development Association (CCDA) after investing many years of engaging in evangelical community development in Mississippi and California. He developed the "Three R's" of Christian community development, which has become the core philosophy for many practitioners: relocation, reconciliation, and redistribution.[18] This model starts in specific communities of the underprivileged: "Whether it is one building, one block, or a larger neighborhood, effective rebuilding depends upon having a well-defined concrete geography or focus area" (Gornik, 2002, p. 150). The starting place is community development done by Christians with the hope that a church or churches might be among the fruit of this community development.

Robert Linthicum (1991a, 1991b, 2003) advocates a similar approach as a way to address oppressive systems and structures in a city and offer practical guidance for community organization. Linthicum's model seeks to organize disenfranchised urban communities to the point of leveraging their relational power in order to confront systemic injustices in the city. This process empowers the local community to initiate their own problem-solving process as well as address systemic powers of the city. His model is unique in the degree to which government is engaged in the process of seeking the good of the city.

This model shares similarities with the "Transformation through solidarity with the poor and marginalized" model, as they both direct their efforts and resources toward the poor and marginalized. Also, they both also recognize the power of systems and structures that contribute to an unjust imbalance of resources. The uniqueness of Christian community development, explains Perkins, is maintaining that the key to social change is spiritual. For Perkins, evangelism is central to any real attempt at community transformation: "To be Christian, by definition, is to live and speak in such a way that our lives continually point to the wonderful person of Jesus Christ."[19] Many variations of this model exist, but the implementation has been primarily in North America.

---

[18] Perkins has written about these concepts in a number of works (1982; 1993; 1995). Other urban ministry practitioners have incorporated the three R's into their models, including Mark R. Gornik (2002), Wayne L. Gordon (1999), and John Fuder and Noel Castellanos (2009).

[19] As quoted in (Reed, 1995, p. 41)

The socially engaged church model takes a "just do something" approach to the city. In a way, this approach came as a reaction to churches that focused all of their resources internally on programs, buildings, and member privileges. Movements of missional churches[20] and externally focused churches (Rusaw & Swanson, 2004) are now emphasizing the outward mission of the church. The goal with both of these groups is to see missional engagement of the community threaded into the DNA of the church. They urge the church to spend more time, energy, and even dollars outside the walls of the church. The externally focused church approach does not advocate that churches develop their own ministries as much as partner with government and non-government initiatives already going on. When churches set up their own ministries, they limit their contact with others endeavoring to do the same work and even create a competitive spirit. The idea is for the whole church to have maximum transformational engagement with the world: "Our understanding of the church is shifting from seeing it as a place where the many send the few ('Lord, thank you for raising up that dear, sacrificial family to faithfully work in Guatemala') to seeing it as a place where the few equip and send the many (Eph. 4:11-12)" (Swanson & Williams, 2010, p. 21).

This model recognizes that cities left on their own are deeply troubled both spiritually and physically. In contrast to the "church against the city" posture, this model sees the potential formation of partnerships in the city as a way to engage the city and introduce holistic transformation. With partnering as a priority, citywide consultations are a significant step toward transformation. "A consultation is a time when the churches in the city get together to discover each other's gifts and the signs of grace God is already doing in

---

[20] The inspiration for the missional church movement came from the late missionary statesman, Lesslie Newbigin, who called the church back into a missionary posture with the surrounding culture in the West. His writings provided the initial theological impetus for what has become an avalanche of books about missional churches. One of the most influential works, *The Missional Church*, came from a collaborative effort sponsored by the Gospel and Our Culture Network. (Guder et al., 1998)

their cities" (Bakke & Sharpe, 2006, p. 136). In contrast to evangelistic crusades or charity programs, the consultation brings local Christian leaders together to impact the city.

Transformation through Orders of Incarnational Presence and Holistic Revival

This particular model uniquely emphasizes both the importance of incarnational presence in community and of a holistic revival. The emphasis on both elements is distinctive to Viv Grigg (2009). In Grigg's model, transformational revival movements are the key to initiating change. The Holy Spirit is the source of change which should include intentional efforts at a holistic outworking in all of the sectors of a city. Grigg also emphasizes the importance of incarnational work among the urban poor as part of the broader model of urban transformation. His model is a hybrid combining elements of different approaches and adding the holistic emphasis in revivals.

Orders of incarnational presence are becoming more prevalent throughout the world.[21] Practitioners of this model share a conviction that the best way to reach the urban poor is through living among them at their standard of living.[22] Advocates of this approach, like Shane Claiborne (2006), model their practice on a literal application of Jesus' life and teachings. Scott Bessenecker describes organizations promoting this approach as the "new friars" and notes that they share a few common characteristics.[23] First, the new friars take a vow of poverty of some kind and sometimes a vow of abstinence from entertainment

---

[21] Orders originated out of the early Roman Catholic monastic tradition and have been adapted by different Protestant traditions. Not everyone is comfortable with the term "order." It is not used as an institutional term, but to signify a deep level of commitment to the poor. (Bessenecker, 2005; 2006; House, 2005; Wilson-Hartgrove, 2008)

[22] For more on incarnational missiology, see: Barker (2012); Langmead (2004).

[23] Among these organizations are InnerCHANGE, Servant Partners, Servants to Asia's Urban Poor, Urban Neighbours of Hope, and Word Made Flesh. (S. A. Bessenecker, 2006, p. 24)

media (i.e. television or internet). Second, these organizations also prefer to work communally for the sake of accountability and spiritual growth.[24] Third, each of these organizations strives to be missional, sharing the good news of Jesus with the urban poor.[25]

The passion of the new friars is admirable. Many of them are reacting to the excesses of churches spending on themselves. The urban poor currently make up fifty-five percent of the world's urban dwellers and this percentage is projected to increase.[26] Given that over half the world is urban, this means that more than one in four people in the world lives in urban poverty. A segment of the global population this large certainly deserves missionary attention, yet the tendency is for missionaries in urban areas to focus on the upwardly mobile classes instead of the poor (Bonk, 2000). These new orders are not simply community development organizations, but see church planting as central to their work ("8 Signs…" 2012). The incarnational approach taken by the new friars is a healthy model for discipleship because the disciples hear the gospel and see Jesus' life modeled (Neely, 2000, p. 475).

Transformation as a City within the City

The church is the starting point for authentic transformation according to this model. Planting churches in the city is considered essential to reaching the city. This model is more consciously patterned

---

[24] Grigg notes that Protestant missionaries have preferred business structures for missions, but he "realized that we must first establish caring communities, not work teams, for the human costs are high." (Grigg, 2012, p. 20)

[25] There are two movements that are similar, the new monastics and the new friars. Scott Bessenecker makes a distinction between these two movements by noting that the new monastics are "cloistered" communities entering dying neighborhoods in order to draw the poor to their community. The new friars, on the other hand, intentionally go places where the gospel is not known. Both are missional in that they incorporate intentional gospel proclamation in their work. (S. A. Bessenecker, 2006, p. 21)

[26] By 2025, it is projected that sixty-six percent of urban dwellers will be poor. (Johnson & Crossing, 2013)

after the apostle Paul's methods: "The churches Paul planted were the leaven of society. They were models of righteousness" (McClung, 1991, p. 149). Advocates of this model attempt to strike the balance between being in the city but not of the city, in other words, striving to become a city within the city (but not in the exclusionary sense of escape described in one of the previous models). Vencer (1989) describes the urban church as "the sacred city in a secular city that needs to experience the *shalom* of God in all areas of life. It should not abandon or isolate itself from the life of the city but neither should it be absorbed into it" (p. 115). The primacy of the church for the work of urban transformation is central to this model (Roberts, 2010). The church is to become the city of God with the purpose of weaving itself into the cities of the world in order to be witnesses of the gospel and live out transformation (Murray, 1990, p. 47).

One of the most visible advocates of this approach today is Tim Keller, the planter and pastor of Redeemer Presbyterian Church in New York City. Keller's model advocates for a movement of gospel-centered churches that seek the welfare of the city as a city within the city (2009; Keller & Thomson, 2002). Keller sees the church as essential to urban transformation. Therefore, Keller's model prioritizes establishing healthy, gospel-centered churches that can implement change for the good of the whole city.

Many other approaches resort to power or influence for the sake of transformation. Advocates of this approach consciously limit their use of power, and they can even be critical of the times when the Church did use power exploitatively. When the Church reaches for power, it actually begins to withdraw from the power of God working through it (Murray, 1990). Instead, the Church should seek transformation by establishing a city within the city, one that is established on the gospel of Jesus Christ. Unlike the previous approach in which transformation is sought through escape to an alternative city, this city within the city is not separated by physical barriers or geographical distance. Rather, it is a city of God intertwined with the city of man as Augustine described. Yet the church is a distinct community that should: "Resist the evil one; endure suffering; persist through conflict; trust him whose city this is" (Seitz, 1997, p. 27). As a city fully integrated into the city, yet not assimilated, the church serves as a foretaste of the future new city to come through service and a lived-out alternative worldview.

Assessment of Urban Transformation Typology

I will offer a few general observations on the range of approaches outlined above. These nine models represent the broad spectrum of Christian approaches to urban transformation (see Figure 2.1). Although these descriptions are oversimplified in the interest of brevity, they demonstrate the essential relationship between theological assumptions and the model chosen for urban transformation. I will lift out a few of these theological assumptions because they will be pivotal for a detailed theology of urban transformation.

It is clear that the approaches under the "Church Against the City" paradigm remain more aloof from the city as a whole, while many of the other approaches involve an incarnational ministry element. Even within the incarnational methods there are significant differences in approach.[27] Some theologians contest the imitability of Jesus' incarnation as a missiological principle (Schnabel, 2004, p. 1575; Starke, 2011). Others build their missiology on the incarnation, making incarnational ministry the foundation of the missiological task.

The doctrine of sin also emerges as an important issue in transformation. In essence, developing a right doctrine of sin in order to foster transformation is akin to diagnosing an ailment. The approaches to transformation are solutions to a problem, but the problem needs to be defined before it is fixed. Is sin appropriately understood in

---

[27] Billings draws a distinction between those who define incarnational as "with" the people only and those who broaden the definition to include "with" and "for". In Billings' view, incarnational ministry patterned after Christ must include the more proactive "for" along with the "with". Otherwise, he argues, the missionary merely engages in passive solidarity with their people and no change occurs (Billings, 2004).

individual terms? Or has sin had corporate or even systemic repercussions? Can the unjust systems of a city be transformed by the transformation of individuals? Or do we need a solution that addresses corporate sin as well as individuals?

What are the powers that rule a city? Are these powers essentially evil (i.e. demonic spirits)? Or are they essentially good? This issue is related to the diagnostic questions surrounding the doctrine of sin and profoundly important for developing a sound theological approach to urban transformation.

A theology of transformation is partly determined by an understanding of the purpose of the Church as it relates to the future. In other words, one's eschatology will determine one's approach to seeking the good of the city. If one believes only individuals are salvaged from the city, then the approach will reflect this conviction. Others view the welfare of the city as related to spiritual growth, and therefore, they use a more city-positive approach.

Views of the kingdom of God and ecclesiology are at the core of the theological foundation for the Church's approach to seeking the good of the city. If the kingdom of God is viewed only in individualistic and spiritual terms, then missional engagement with the city will focus primarily on individuals. If, on the other hand, the kingdom of God is a reality whenever something good happens, then the Church's purpose is radically changed to a supporting institution for good works. One's understanding of the kingdom will dictate his or her view on the purpose of the Church and ultimately governs the approach to missional engagement with the city.

Approach to City	Model of Urban Transformation	Description of Each Model	Weaknesses of Each Model
The Church Against the City	Transformation through One Soul at a Time	Personal evangelism is the key to urban transformation. Transformed individuals make the city better.	• Evangelism becomes only priority. With little attention to holistic discipleship. Relies on healthy government social order. • Negative view of the city averts focus only to eternity. • Ignores influence of systems/ structures in the city.
	Transformation through Strategic Organized Prayer	Strategic prayer is central to city transformation. Hindrances to transformation are unseen spiritual forces. This approach sometimes includes "spiritual mapping" and discerning territorial strongholds.	• Very little scriptural support for territorial spirits. • Language sometimes similar to occultic practices. • Creates hostile interaction with the city. • We are not called only to prayer.
	Transformation through Influence in Key Areas	The way to change the world is through the penetration and influence of key areas of society. The goal is to establish Christians and Christian ideas in these spheres of society. Within this model are many variations.	• Dominionist strategy that seeks to take control of each sphere of society. • Can be humanistic. • Creates hostility and leads to power-lust. Church becomes slave to power structures. • Sometimes (e.g. 7 Mountain Mandate) draws on occultist practices.
	Transformation through Escape to an Alternative City	Christians establish their own communities/cities built on a better foundation. This approach is sometimes an unintentional escape, but maybe more intentional as with communes, monasteries, or all-inclusive communities.	• It communicates that the church is more concerned with self-preservation and self-interest. • Requires resources, primarily serves middle & upper class • Does not seek the welfare of the city.

The Church for the City	Transformation through Solidarity with Other Institutions	The church seeks the good of the city as defined by the city itself. In contrast to other models, the church does not engage the city prophetically but rather joins ongoing efforts at improving the city.	• Loses Christian distinctiveness. Christ is not the solution, solidarity and service are. Seeks to find common moral or ethical stances, diluting the prophetic voice of the church. • Sin only understood as structural and not individual.
	Transformation through Solidarity with the Poor and Marginalized	The church is called to be a voice for the voiceless and draw from a global network to address structural and systemic ills in our cities. Advocates of this model draw heavily from liberation theologians.	• Isolates poverty as the priority issue of transformation and neglects other areas of sin and brokenness. • Perpetuates division, wealthy are blamed for societal ills. • Ignores eternal implications for humanity.
The Church Transforms the City	Transformation as Part of the City	The city is transformed through the transformation of communities within the city. Advocates encourage long-term engagement of urban community needs. Sub-models: 1) Christian community development; 2) socially-engaged church.	• Scatter-shot, "just do something" approach can be inefficient and lacking in strategy. • Assumes a vibrant Christian presence from the outset. • When done without reflection, defaults to addressing popularly perceived needs rather than deep issues.
	Transformation through Incarnational Presence and Holistic Revival	This model uniquely emphasizes both the importance of incarnational presence in community and the necessity of holistic revival. (Another group primarily focuses on incarnational presence with less emphasis on gospel proclamation.)	• Grigg's model is complicated. • Model prioritizes poor communities over rich. • The incarnational approach can be slow in development.

	Transformation as a City within the City	Planting urban churches is the starting point for authentic transformation. The church becomes the city of God in order to weave itself into the cities of the world as a witness to gospel transformation.	• Model is best suited to reaching educated urban professionals. Less so with the poor and working class. • Model relies on extensive resourcing and cities with the freedom of public gatherings. • Does not actively engage systemic sin.

Figure 3.2 Distinctives of Models of Urban Transformation

Questions for reflection and discussion:

1. What are the three broad approaches to the city that Christians and churches tend to take?
2. Which model of urban transformation do you currently align with most? Do you agree with the author's assessment of its strengths and weaknesses?
3. Which approach and model of urban transformation does your church take? Do you feel it has been an effective way to engage your city?

Chapter 4

An Urban Studies Perspective on What Makes a Good City

A city without a vision is a city in trouble.
--Robert Lupton (2005, p. 151)

The earthly city, which does not live by faith, seeks an earthly peace, and the end it proposes, in the well-ordered concord of civic obedience and rule, is the combination of men's wills to attain the things which are helpful to this life. The heavenly city, or rather the part of it which sojourns on earth and lives by faith, makes use of this peace only because it must, until this mortal condition which necessitates it shall pass away.
--Augustine

If transformation of a city is to be effective, then we must have a clear idea of what makes a good city. Agreement on this issue is not so easy to come by, as Eric Jacobsen (2003) discovered when he embarked on a conversation with his Sunday school class at his church about what a redeemed city would look like. He asked a series of questions that brought back interesting responses. Among the questions were these: Would there be less work for police officers? Would there be fewer food banks? Would houses be closer together or farther apart? Jacobsen describes the response, "It was fascinating to observe how unanimous the response was to certain questions and how divided we became over others. A few left us in absolute confusion" (p. 49). Any discussion of transformation necessitates a clear idea of what a transformed city might look like, but what is a Christian vision of a good city?

Not a Utopian City

One must be careful not to confuse God's vision of a good city with a humanistic utopian vision. The good city that we seek is the result of the City of God (God's Kingdom) overlapping with and blessing the City of Man. The good city will never be perfect, never be totally free of the problems cities face. As we seek to create good cities, we must not place our trust in a utopian vision as so many throughout history have done.

The early Greek philosophers, Plato and Aristotle, devoted much thought to designing a utopian society but never succeeded in achieving it.[1] The dream of a utopian city has been revisited throughout history. Many types of cities have been built with utopian ambitions, some grand and some not so grand. The Garden City, developed by Ebenezer Howard, sought to create new, smaller-scale cities that would be more open and less dependent on capitalism.[2] This experiment was somewhat socialist in design, but was never carried out according to plan (D. W. Smith, 2001). The City Beautiful Movement grew out of the displayed "White City" at the World's Fair in Chicago in 1893. Daniel Burnham gathered the nation's architects to design a magnificent series of structures that became the inspiration for grand public buildings all over the United States. This movement contributed to the beautification

---

[1] Plato and Aristotle dreamed of communities where virtue remained intact, but as the ancient Greek cities took shape, the lust for control and power derailed their utopian vision. (Mumford, 1961, pp. 200–3)

[2] The Garden City was created as a solution to the problems facing an overcrowded London at the end of the nineteenth century. Howard wanted to design smaller communities that would maintain a balance of habitat, employment, and recreation. (P. Hall, 2006, pp. 704–705)

of America's cities, but it did not address the problems of housing shortages and urban poverty. It also placed too much faith in the potential of good governance (Palen, 2008, pp. 271–3; Sine, 1999, pp. 82–83).

Prior to World War II, urban historian Lewis Mumford was optimistic about the potential of cities to continually improve, envisioning an eventual urban utopia. The war destroyed his optimism, and when he returned to the notion of an urban utopia in the 1960s, he ended up viewing cities as the downfall of civilization (Kornbluh, 2003, p. 483).

The utopian city has been a failure. We cannot simply build a set of glorious buildings and infrastructure and expect perfection. History teaches that the best cities have been built over centuries, which should keep our attempts at city transformation humble and our focus on the immediate community and the people in it. We err when we begin to think of the city as an abstraction and lose sight of real people and real life (Jacobsen, 2003, p. 15). Even the "godfather" of the City Beautiful movement, Charles Mulford Robinson, recognized this when he said that cities are intended to be lived in, rather than only observed (Rybczynski, 2010, p. 17). Roger Greenway (1989) puts it in eschatological perspective: "All utopian schemes for the creation of a perfect city on earth are immediately discarded once the postfall city is understood in biblical perspective" (p. 8). As admirable as the utopian city sounds, it is a project doomed to fail because it does not take into account the fallenness of humankind and the ripple effect of that fallenness in our societal structures and systems.

The urban planning movement attempted transformation by offering solutions to perceived urban problems within established cities (Ali & Rieker, 2008). But urban planning has not lived up to those idealistic hopes. In *The Death and Life of Great American Cities*, Jane Jacobs has led the charge in critiquing these grand plans on the grounds that they fail to account for the ways in which people actually live in the city.[3]

A more recent effort at planning the good city has come to be known as "New Urbanism." Proponents of this movement describe it this way:

> New Urbanism promotes the creation and restoration of diverse, walkable, compact, vibrant, mixed-use communities composed of the same components as conventional development, but assembled in a more integrated fashion, in the form of complete communities. These contain housing, work places, shops, entertainment, schools, parks, and civic facilities essential to the daily lives of the residents, all within easy walking distance of each other. New Urbanism promotes the increased use of trains and light rail, instead of more highways and roads. Urban living is rapidly becoming the new hip and modern way to live for people of all ages ("New Urbanism").

In essence, this new movement values dense, walkable, mixed-use neighborhoods that are interconnected through public transportation. It

---

[3] Two paragraphs from the opening pages of this classic work are worth quoting in full:

> There is a wistful myth that if only we had enough money to spend—the figure is usually put at a hundred billion dollars—we could wipe out all our slums in ten years, reverse decay in the great, dull, gray belts that were yesterday's and day-before-yesterday's suburbs, anchor the wandering middle class and its wandering tax money, and perhaps even solve the traffic problem.
>
> But look what we have built with the first several billions: Low-income projects that become worse centers of delinquency, vandalism and general social hopelessness than the slums they were supposed to replace. Middle-income housing projects which are truly marvels of dullness and regimentation, sealed against any buoyancy or vitality of city life. Luxury housing projects that mitigate their inanity, or try to, with a vapid vulgarity. Cultural centers that are unable to support a good bookstore. Civic centers that are avoided by everyone but bums, who have fewer choices of loitering place than others. Commercial centers that are lackluster imitations of standardized suburban chain-store shopping. Promenades that go from no place to nowhere and have no promenaders. Expressways that eviscerate great cities. This is not the rebuilding of cities. This is the sacking of cities. (J. Jacobs, 1993)

is a reaction against urban sprawl and some of the tendencies of suburban developments, such as cul-de-sacs and curvilinear streets (Palen, 2008, p. 287). Eric Jacobsen (2003) makes the case for New Urbanism from a Christian perspective in his work, *Sidewalks in the Kingdom: New Urbanism and the Christian Faith*. This movement embraces several principles that contribute positively to the good of the city. However, as the other well-intended movements for urban improvement, the New Urbanism movement relies on the impractical ideal that urban dwellers will adjust their lifestyle to the prescribed principles (Palen, 2008). For example, New Urbanism emphasizes walkable communities, but many urban dwellers are now conditioned to drive everywhere. The movement's success would require not only city design that creates walkable, mixed-use communities, but also people that become pedestrians.

Planned cities have not been the panacea often imagined by urban designers. Cities evolve over the centuries on layers of built environment as well as intellectual and cultural development (Rybczynski, 2010). In other words, cities are not built on a blank slate. A city always develops in the midst of a particular context. Neither is technology the salve for the ailments of urban breakdown. Advances in technology create new challenges as quickly as they do solutions to previous problems. In some cases they even lead to the utter destabilization of a city.[4] Full transformation of the city is rendered impossible by the sinfulness of humanity (Eph. 2:1-3; Rom. 3:23). Biblically, transformation of cities is not based on hope in humanity. Rather, transformation must be rooted in the work of Christ and a forward-looking hope of the completely good city to be established in the eschaton (Heb. 13:14; Rev. 21:9-27) (Gallagher & Hawthorne, 2009, p. 40; Gornik, 2002, p. 27).

The dreams of great utopian cities have been deflated, but the church still has a responsibility to seek the good of the city. What

---

[4] The authors site examples from Siberia and Nigeria to make their case for the dangers of relying too heavily on technology. (Ali & Rieker, 2008, pp. 4–5)

constitutes a good and vibrant city? In some ways we need what
Manuel Castells calls "utopian vision" because it helps urban
institutions avoid short-sited planning and stagnation and urges people
to dream and design cities with the greater good in mind (Davey,
2002). Although we are not capable of creating the utopian city, we are
called to imagine the best cities possible. Urban transformation requires
that we have a vision of the good city in order to "think the
unthinkable" and operate outside status quo urbanism. From a
Christian perspective, David Smith says: "To be bereft of any vision at
the point at which cities were about to expand as never before would
open up the terrible prospect that the emergent urban world would take
forms dictated by the purely pragmatic interests of those who hold
power within the market system" (D. W. Smith, 2001, p. 69). To
summarize his point, if the church is concerned about the well-being of
the increasing number of people who dwell in cities, then the church
needs to understand the characteristics essential to a good city.

What is the Good City?

Cities are becoming increasingly complex, making the already
difficult task of identifying a set of variables that make for a good city
even more challenging (Hern, 2010).[5] When we add that each city has
unique issues, our analysis is further complicated (Evers & Korff, 2000,
p. 6). The quest to discover criteria for the good city is mired in debate
but can be simplified by examining what urban experts contend makes a
good city, which we will do here. In the next chapter we will evaluate
what the good city ought to be from a Christian perspective. After
these perspectives are each described, the ideas will be brought together
for the sake of a simplified rubric for evaluating the good city. We need

---

[5] Michael Batty (2007) describes the complex nature of extended urban areas far beyond
the CBD (Central Business District): "In short, our traditional image of the city no
longer holds. Cities appear much more complex than we generally assume" (p. 17–18).

to have an idea of what makes cities flourish, so that we are able to love, serve, and bless our cities well.

The study of cities is extraordinarily interdisciplinary. The most loved books on cities are written by architects, journalists, anthropologists, sociologists, economists, and philosophers. Each author naturally tends to see solutions as coming from his or her own field of study, making consensus on good city criteria hard to reach. However, such diversity of perspectives makes the criteria that do reoccur that much more compelling, and a list of interdependent elements of the good city emerges (Graham & Lowe, 2009, p. 39). Those elements are density, vibrancy, diversity, security, economic opportunity, and organic growth.

Characteristics of a Good City: The Urban Studies Perspective

- Density
- Vibrancy
- Diversity
- Security
- Economic Opportunity
- Organic Growth

Figure 4.1 Urban Perspective on Characteristics of a Good City

Density

"The density of cities," says Brugmann (2009), "is their most basic advantage over any other kind of settlement.... Density increases the sheer *efficiency* by which we can pursue an economic opportunity" (p. 27). Scripture affirms this as a positive quality of cities. Psalm 122:3 describes Jerusalem as "built as a city should be, closely compact..." (translation L. C. Allen, 2002). In this Psalm extolling the virtues of Jerusalem, urban density is one of its prized attributes. It is urban density that opens the way for commerce, competition, and social interaction (Toh, 2012).

Intrinsically related to urban density is the value of walkability. Density directly contributes to the ability to access work, shops, restaurants, and neighbors on foot. A walkable neighborhood can reduce automobile use and thereby can reduce energy consumption, traffic congestion, and parking problems (Graham & Lowe, 2009, p. 57; Kunstler, 1994, pp. 260–262). Walkability requires a level of intentionality beyond mere density. It takes coordinated design on the part of urban planners. Successful walkable neighborhoods require mixed use communities within a relatively small geographical area (Kelbaugh, 2002, pp. 354–355), taking full advantage of the city's density. Walkable communities have proven to be healthier (Benesh, 2011, p. 158; Owen et al., 2007) and to foster community.[6] Well-planned density with built-in pedestrian enclaves can improve the well-being of city dwellers.

Urban density becomes the seedbed of innovation, creativity, and even culture itself (Brugmann, 2009, p. 29; McMahan, 2012, p. 3). Density forces diverse people, skills, and professions into close proximity. The combination of proximity and diversity fosters the exchange of ideas and the freedom to innovate (Badger, 2013). Jacobs posits that urban density is indispensable to cities: "The district must have a sufficiently dense concentration of people, for whatever purpose they may be there" (J. Jacobs, 1993, p. 277). Cities become cities when there is enough density for thriving businesses, municipal services, and social energy. Density creates the possibility for critical mass when issues need to be addressed (Brugmann, 2009, pp. 78–9), which leads us to the second characteristic of a good city: vibrancy.

---

[6] When members of a community walk, they interact incidentally. This incidental contact, Jacobsen argues, is crucial for the development of deeper levels of community. (du Toit, Cerin, Leslie, & Owen, 2007; Jacobsen, 2003, pp. 89–91)

Vibrancy: Active Citizenry

The best cities in the world—the ones people love to visit—have a vibrancy to them. This vibrancy stems from human activity. The sidewalks are busy with activity, and the public spaces are being used in diverse ways. This happens when the citizens demonstrate involvement in the city and the everyday matters of the city. Cities depend on engaged citizens (Hern, 2010). Joel Kotkin (2005) describes the way citizens contribute to a vibrant city:

> A busy city must be more than a construct of diversions for essentially nomadic populations; it requires an engaged and committed citizenry with a long-term financial and familial stake in the metropolis. A successful city must be home not only to edgy clubs, museums, and restaurants, but also to specialized industries, small businesses, schools, and neighborhoods capable of regenerating themselves for the next generation (p. 154).

In other words, there is a practicality in the ways good cities allow the citizenry to interact, network, and function. The downfall of the utopian urban designs was that they removed vibrant life from the streets, which reduced involvement in city life (Tink, 1994, p. 25). High civic involvement often includes municipal governing that creates avenues for citizens to provide input into urban affairs.[7] When civic involvement ebbs, municipal governance more often falls prey to self-interest groups and local citizens lose their opportunities for providing input.

Vibrancy also engenders pride in the city. This happens in a variety of ways, but a common way is through public built space. MIT urban geographer, Kevin Lynch (1960), says even "awkward 'beautification' of

---

[7] These avenues for citizens to respond can be either official or unofficial. But if the municipal government is democratically elected, then citizens have a chance to make their voices heard. This kind of local community activism spurs invested interest in the common good of the community or neighborhood. (Gottdiener & Hutchison, 2006, pp. 241, 243)

a city may in itself be an intensifier of civic energy and cohesion" (p. 117). In any city, the citizens begin to refer to landmarks in the city. Only sometimes are these landmarks intentionally built as landmarks; more often they are a busy intersection, a unique business, or a public space where people can naturally gather. These are the spaces that generate a sense of hometown pride and thus contribute to the vibrancy of the city.

Diversity

Aristotle said "a city is composed of different kinds of men; similar people cannot bring a city into existence" (Sennett, 1994, p. 56). Commerce, education, and culture benefit from the diversity of nationalities, talents, and perspectives in a good city. The very act of being around people different from us challenges stagnant ways of thinking, promoting innovation and development. Continued contact with diverse people is actually a good thing for people (Conn, 1987, pp. 44–45). In addition, urban diversity gives a city a competitive edge in this globalized economy (Batty, 2007, p. 376). Diversity in the city "becomes a part of the stimulus and spice of urban life" (Hiebert & Meneses, 1995, p. 315).

Jacobsen (2003) suggests that this kind of diversity actually defines the city: "A city is a place where it is acceptable to be a stranger" (p. 139). Kotkin (2005) describes the process of learning how to interact and coexist with strangers from different backgrounds. He says of the experience of early urbanization, "This required them to develop new ways to codify behavior, to determine what was commonly acceptable in family life, commerce, and social discourse" (p. 158). The variety of people and talents became the seedbed of new ideas that created new markets that then became the engine of increased research and development. This diversity of people and cultures also generates a deepening of cultural and artistic expression (Graham & Lowe, 2009, p. 57; McDonogh, 2005, p. 372). Urban diversity contributes to both the economic well-being of a city and the aesthetic well-being of a city.

Security

One of the distinguishing marks of a city in ancient times was high, solid walls around the perimeter. People made sure they were within the walls by nightfall in order to avoid those who might do them harm. The collectivity of people in close proximity ensured greater safety in ancient times and still does today. More densely settled populations can pool their resources to set up informal and formal security systems. It is the collective density of cities that generated the resources for other security measures. In the seventeenth century, Paris was the largest city in Europe. Municipal taxes were used to create the first modern police force as well as a street-lighting project (Glaeser, 2011, p. 106).

Security has always been a significant value for humankind, and exaggerated perceptions of crime in cities keep many in fear of them. Despite perceptions, urban crime is significantly lower than it was in the nineteenth century (Blokland, 2003, p. 194; Fischer, 1984, p. 103), and big cities are no less safe than small ones. Although it is true that certain types of crime are more prevalent in the city than in rural areas, overall crime rates per capita are not significantly affected by city size (Macionis, 2004, p. 360; Palen, 2008, p. 179).

The most secure cities in the world are the ones that seek solutions on a citywide level. There has been a trend towards fortifying private compounds within bourgeoning cities (Palen, 2008, pp. 178–179). Mike Davis (2003) critiques this trend due to the fact that it contributes toward further insecurity of the city and disrupts municipal functionality. There are many variables involved, but studies show that increased attention to citywide security proves beneficial for the well-being of the city (Palen, 2008, pp. 178–179). Safety is a major consideration when people have choices about where to live, and companies are more likely to invest in a city deemed secure. However, we do more harm to the city as whole when we address security only for individual dwellings or neighborhoods.

It stands to reason that as the population of a city rises, crime will scale with the number of residents. But crime is not evenly distributed; it is reduced in communities where the citizenry is more socially integrated (Glaeser, 2011, p. 107). The concept of social capital comes into play here.[8] When people are familiar with each other, they are more prone to protect each other (Portes, 1998, pp. 9–10; Putnam, 2000, pp. 307–318). This principle is true for congregations as well. The more churches engage their community, the lower the crime rates (Desmond, Kikuchi, & Morgan, 2010). Social capital is more than security; it is the social "glue" that brings a community together (Garner, 2004, p. 127; Stockwell, 2002, pp. 165–166). Increased security is a byproduct of increased social capital in a community, the engagement of its people. Therefore, the safety of the city is intertwined with the vibrancy of the city.

Economic Opportunity

Economics and cities have been intertwined since the very beginning of cities. Psalm 107:4-7 tells of people who are economically disadvantaged and thus, hungry and thirsty. God meets their need by leading them to a city in which to settle. Likewise, the masses migrate to cities often because of the economic opportunities made possible by urban density (Bertinelli & Strobl, 2007). Max Weber proffered that cities were primarily places of commerce. Cities, by their very nature, are hubs of trade. A city grows where a marketplace emerges and becomes a gathering point for the region (Orum & Chen, 2003, p. 9). The global economy runs on urban economies (J. Jacobs, 1985, p. 31). Even the rural economy depends on vibrant commerce in the urban

---

[8] Social Capital is defined as "the resources embedded in social networks accessed and used by actors for actions." (Lin, 2001, p. 25)

centers.[9] The absence of a solid economy spells certain death to a city (Orum & Chen, 2003, p. 96). A good city must provide economic opportunity for the majority of urban dwellers.

Economic factors of a city are complicated by the fact that they lead to policies that so easily and so often become tools for oppression and unjust advantage. Susan Fainstein (2002) acknowledges that restructuring the economies of cities will positively benefit the global economy but is at the same time clear that focusing only on central business districts can actually hurt the urban economic ecosystem: "Efforts to spur central business district development and the 'realistic' dismissal of manufacturing as the future basis for growth have displaced residents and small firms and left blue-collar workers stranded" (p. 113). This can even play out in the built environment as large corporations have learned how to manipulate public policies and funds for their own purposes. As an example, in downtown Los Angeles, international investors built corporate megastructures like CitiCorp Plaza and then channeled public funding into the removal of pedestrian access from the older, minority communities to these new commercial spaces (Abrahamson, 2004, p. 33). In this way public funds and policies have been manipulated to give advantage to a few. In essence, this diminishes economic opportunities for many in the city. The difficulties with the economic-progress-equals-development mindset became apparent in the 1970s and 1980s. The problems meant to be solved by economic progress were much more complex and socially related than was assumed (Beall & Fox, 2009, p. 14). This is where urban theory becomes increasingly complex. Many theorists have reacted to the abuses of the rich and powerful in the cities by developing theories based on Marxist principles (Castells, 1985, 2002; Harvey, 2009; Mitchell, 2003). As I noted in Chapter 3, placing the blame on the rich and powerful does

---

[9] Jacobs provides a detailed scenario that not only makes the case for the dependency of agriculture on the urban economy, but also avers that the skills, methods, and tools for a thriving agrarian life stem from the urban centers. (J. Jacobs, 1970, pp. 3–31)

not lead to whole city transformation.[10] In other words, the good city should strive to provide economic opportunities for all of its citizens.[11]

The value of vibrancy and density comes to play in fostering economic opportunity for all (Toh, 2012). Cities are more than vessels for commercial activity: "It is possible to articulate and develop genuinely democratic and inclusive strategies that are not self-defeating, that don't reduce 'community' to a commodity" (Hern, 2010, p. 131). Beall and Fox (2009) describe it in terms of freedom. All people should have the freedom to pursue economic opportunities (Hern, 2010, p. 59).

Organic Growth

The best cities of the world have grown organically and sustain themselves organically. What is meant by this is that the most interesting and vibrant parts of cities are those that look and feel like the people of that community had a hand in creating them, where there are old buildings and new ones and where there are stores, cafes, and residences. Matt Hern (2010) says great cities are built bit by bit by a huge number of people, rather than by developers and urban planners. He goes on to say, "Great cities have to be inherently democratic projects built in ways that can never be planned or predicted, as products of a vibrant everyday life" (p. 55).

This notion of the organic city has grown in reaction to attempts at building fully planned cities. These all-encompassing plans resulted in even worse problems in the cities they were meant to improve. One

[10] One of the flaws of Marxist theory is that it assumes that once the rich and powerful are brought down society can move forward. In reality, it replaces the rich and powerful with others who become rich and powerful. It is more beneficial to look at acts and policies that lead to injustice and exploitation rather than rotate those in positions of power and privilege.

[11] Neo-Marxist theorists like Harvey and Castells have provided good analysis as it relates to the economic realities for the masses. Their error is in only looking at the city through economic lenses. A complex understanding of the city reveals that other components play an equally important role in the city. (Orum & Chen, 2003, p. 44)

example found in cities all over the world is the replacement of poor slum communities with high-rise public housing. The poor are given little choice but to move into these large, sterile buildings, losing the many advantages of their old slum community. In the old slum community, they had small businesses, restaurants, places to socialize, and even small plots of land for growing vegetables. New public housing lacks all of those things and is devoid of all that makes for vibrant community life. Piecemeal growth is a necessary condition to wholeness (Hern, 2010). This is in contrast with the many attempts at building the ideal city, which have seen mostly failure. The best cities are ones that grew organically over hundreds of years.[12] Today, there are a number of urbanologists who advocate an organic approach to city building, but the pioneers who began to speak of the city in such terms are Jane Jacobs (1993) and Christopher Alexander (Alexander, Ishikawa, & Silverstein, 1977). Alexander used the phase "living city" to refer to an organic, unfolding city. He understands cities as complex systems which require solutions that maintain all of the nuanced complexities of each aspect of city life (C. Alexander, 1964). In other words, the city that grows organically can have remarkable complexity and still requires intentionality. Organic growth ensures a measure of flexibility and adaptability in the city. With the redefinition of urban planning, the role of urban planners has become negotiation rather than dictation (Beall & Fox, 2009, p. 207). The irony, says Jacobsen, is that the "organically grown city will in almost every case be more beautiful and interesting than the solitary work of subdivision or megamall, no matter how talented the architect or builder may be" (Jacobsen, 2003, p. 72).

---

[12] This does not mean that urban planning is totally unnecessary. Under scrutiny here is the kind of urban planning that prescribes exactly where every component should be located, rather than allowing owners of smaller land plots to decide for themselves how and what to build. (Jacobsen, 2003, p. 76)

Conclusion

From the secular perspective, these six characteristics—density, vibrancy, diversity, security, economic opportunity, and organic growth —can make a city good. Of course such a list could go on ad infinitum, but I would reduce it down to these essential characteristics.

If a city commits to developing these six characteristics in design, planning, and governance, urban life can be vastly improved. But as much as the secular literature can teach us about the welfare of the city and its inhabitants, we cannot neglect the spiritual condition of the urban environment. As in every endeavor, Christians must think deeply about the biblical perspective and strive to integrate the best of human knowledge into the truth of God's Word.

Questions for reflection and discussion:

1. From an urban studies perspective, what makes a good city? Do you agree with this assessment?
2. What elements of the good city are present in your city? Which are missing?
3. How might your church participate in addressing those missing elements?

Chapter 5
A Biblical Perspective on What Makes a Good City

The goal of urban mission or community ministry is not to obtain power or influence, nor can it ever be to 'take over' the neighborhood. Rather, the church's goal is to be God's peace in the broken places and to bear witness to the kingdom of God.
--Mark Gornik (2002, p. 124)

Whereas the city had no place in Yhwh's earliest dealings with Israel's ancestors and with the people itself, some of the First Testament's most spectacular visions relate to the city. The story that starts in a garden ends in a city.
--John Goldingay (2006, p. 449)

The Bible has a lot to say about what cities should be like and how we as God's people are to live according to this vision of the city of God. Our understanding of the good city should be rooted in the fact that cities are God's creation (McClung, 1991, p. 64). The characteristics described in the previous chapter are not contradictory to Christian core values, but they do not capture all that marks a city undergoing transformation from a Christian perspective. Three general characteristics of a transformed city according to biblical values are God-centeredness, *Shalom* social vision, and proliferation of Kingdom communities.

Characteristics of a Good City: A Biblical Perspective
• God-Centeredness • *Shalom* Social Vision • Kingdom Communities

Figure 5.1 Biblical Perspective of Characteristics of a Good City

God-Centeredness

The Scriptures clearly indicate that humankind was created to live in a way honoring towards God and was entrusted with the stewardship of God's earthly creation. T. Desmond Alexander (2008) writes that the meta-story of the Bible reveals that God's ultimate aim in human history is to dwell with humanity. We see this fulfilled in Revelation 21-22, when God dwells with humanity in the eschatological holy city. As Alexander concludes in his study, the Bible clearly portrays the purpose of humanity as centered around a relationship with God, the culmination of which is depicted by the vision of God living among his people in the New City.

If honoring God is foundational to humanity's urban residence, then this commitment should impact urban life in tangible respects. Many of the Psalms reflect a powerful relationship between God and the city, and at times depict God "animating its institutions," as Bakke (1997, p. 69) puts it. Psalm 48 offers characteristics of a city inhabited by God. The city is praised as beautiful due to God's presence (v. 1-2). The security of the city is assured because of God (v. 8). The people of the city meditate on God's love (v. 9), operate under God's just judgment (v. 10-11), and become a conduit of praise for God to the ends of the earth (v. 10) and to each generation (v. 13). From a biblical standpoint, God-centered living is essential for the good city.

This kind of city living is developed from God's inherent character.[1] The prophet Isaiah contributes significantly to this notion. The prophecy of Isaiah 24-27 says that only God provides a suitable foundation for the good city. Chapter 26 portrays those who put their trust in God inhabiting a city differently than those who inhabit the city without acknowledging God. It is because of God's holiness that Jerusalem was established to be a holy city. Thus the people of Jerusalem were to walk in this same holiness (Kim, 2008, p. 218). Although Jerusalem holds a unique role in God's redemptive plan, we are called to live in the same manner, as tangible demonstrations of God's love, holiness, justice, and mercy.

This vision for God's people to live out the pattern set by God is an important theme in the Scriptures. In our sin, humanity turned away from our God-centeredness, breaking our relationship with him and with one another. As we seek to become more like God, we should also embody God's love for the people of cities (McClung, 1991, p. 74). This is precisely the point made in Jonah 4 when Jonah is chastised for caring more about a plant than the people of the great city of Nineveh. As we seek to orient our lives toward God and his purposes, we must again embrace a *shalom* social vision, a better pattern of living established by God.

Shalom Social Vision

God created us in his image (Gen. 1:26-27) in order to live out a social vision that embodies the same moral characteristics as God himself.[2] The biblical message is to love as God loves (1 John 4:11), forgive as God forgives (Matthew 6:12), and be holy as God is holy (1

---

[1] Zuidervaart interprets Augustine's *City of God* to mean that cities need a Trinitarian anchor for the ordering of a society. (Zuidervaart, 2005, p. 143)

[2] Bakke uses the phrase "social vision" to describe the prophetic guidance issued for God's people to live more justly. (Bakke, 1997, p. 81)

Peter 1:15-16). Scripture is clear and consistent regarding how people are supposed to live.

By the third chapter of Genesis, this plan was disrupted severely. From that very first act of rebellion by humankind against God, there followed an irrevocable bent towards sin directed at God and one another. In Cornelius Plantinga's penetrating study on sin, he defined it thus: "All sin has first and finally a Godward force. Let us say that a sin is any act—any thought, desire, emotion, word, or deed—or its particular absence, that displeases God and deserves blame" (Plantinga, 1995, p. 13). Plantiga speaks in individual terms, but sin has a cumulative effect when considered in the city context. Sin is present wherever there are people, and, since cities have dense concentrations of people, sin is more densely concentrated (Conn & Ortiz, 2001, p. 345). Jacques Ellul (1970) adds an emphasis on systemic or structural sin that becomes embedded in city life: "No one does evil, everyone wishes for the best, but evil is still committed" (p. 67). Like a train off its rails, humanity is now careening out of control and not operating as intended. This state of humanity is grievous to God (Gen. 6:5-6). This reality means that cities are the focal points of spiritual contestation (Murray, 1990, p. 23), not because cities make people more sinful but because there are more people at stake within them.

This grievous state of humanity was not God's intention. Plantinga directs us to the Old Testament prophetic vision of humanity's restoration as one in which injustice and oppression are made obsolete. Humanity is able to flourish in all of the ways God has intended. This vision even portrays all of creation experiencing reconciliation. At the center of this is a restored relationship with God. Plantinga refers to this webbing together of God, humanity and all of creation as *shalom*. This web of restored relationships is how God intended life. Plantinga (1995) adds:

> We call it peace, but it means far more than mere peace of mind or a cease-fire between enemies. In the Bible, *shalom* means *universal flourishing, wholeness, and delight—*

a rich state of affairs in which natural needs are satisfied and natural gifts fruitfully employed, a state of affairs that inspires joyful wonder as its Creator and Savior opens doors and welcomes the creatures in whom he delights. *Shalom*, in other words, is the way things ought to be (pp. 9-10).

This idea of *shalom* has tremendous depth. Anton Zoughbie (1994) notes the scope of the word includes "the life of the community, the welfare of the individual, and the condition for political security and economic prosperity" (p. 6). In English translations, *shalom* is most often rendered "peace," thus losing the deeper sense of the all-encompassing nature of *shalom*. The same is true in Greek, but the New Testament usage incorporates the broader meaning conveyed by Hebrew (Beck & Brown, 1986, p. 780; Geddert, 1992, p. 604; Winter, 1994, p. 15). Because the fullness of meaning is not conveyed in translation, readers of the Bible can easily overlook the many references to *shalom* in God's Word, and yet it is a dominant theme in Scripture.[3] Every aspect of Jesus' life and death is couched in *shalom* terminology, and it is ultimately the essence of the gospel (Villafane, Hall, Agosto, & Jackson, 1995, p. 3).

Shalom is a comprehensive vision for life as God intended it.[4] Wolterstorff describes *shalom* as touching three areas. First, it means humankind has a restored relationship with God, one in which people no longer flee his presence but serve happily at his pleasure. Second, *shalom* means restored harmonious relationships with the rest of humanity and experiencing true community. Community as envisioned by *shalom* means that every human is valued and treated with dignity. Third, *shalom* means a restored relationship with humankind's physical surroundings. People are created as physical beings intended to have a

---

[3] Greenway (1978: p. 34) counts over 350 references to shalom or its derivatives in the Old Testament. Graham Cole (2009) sees shalom as an organizing idea of Scripture.

[4] It is comprehensive in that it concerns the spiritual, physical, psychological, and social. (Moreau, Corwin, & McGee, 2004, p. 84)

flourishing relationship with all of their physical surroundings, which includes nature (N. Wolterstorff, 1983, p. 70). This threefold view of *shalom* encompasses all of life and reflects the biblical message.

As stated earlier, humankind has fallen away from God's *shalom* vision (Norman, 2007, p. 430). This fallenness has disrupted all three aspects of *shalom*. Two chapters of Genesis illustrate the disruption of humanity's relationship with God, among people, and to nature. The relationship with God was changed forever in Genesis 3, with Adam and Eve hiding from God in shame. In the very next chapter of Genesis, the fracturing of human community is so severe that Cain kills his own brother, Abel.[5] And the choice of Adam and Eve to sin even resulted in a broken relationship between humanity and the earth (Stagg, 1962; Norman, 2007). It was only after the Fall that working the earth became a painful toil. The comprehensive disruption of *shalom* necessitates a comprehensive solution. "The gospel of peace is a radical alternative for the city" says Mark Gornik (2002, p. 99). The response to the sinful state of humanity is a holistic approach that addresses the need for restored relationships with God, with humanity, and with their surroundings.

Jeremiah 29:4-7 serves as a call to a comprehensive response to the state of humanity, particularly in the city context. This passage, referenced in Chapter 2, suggests the people of God are called to proactively seek and implement *shalom* characteristics in the city of their residence. They are to live as a fully devoted community of God while establishing life in the midst of a city hostile to the most high God and his holy justice. The call is to an effort to turn the city into a good city, with one important proviso—the good city is defined by God's standards for a good city. It is God's standards that determine the agenda for the people of God. In the same way, the Church is to seek the *shalom* of the city (Claerbaut, 1983, p. 27; Conn & Ortiz, 2001, p.

---

[5] Bonhoeffer (1965) observes that individual sinfulness and societal sinfulness have reciprocal and perpetuating effect on each other (p. 81).

110; Greenway, 1978, p. 31; Murray, 1990, p. 82; Swanson & Williams, 2010, p. 60).

God's standards for his people in a city can be seen in the eschatological passages casting a vision of the new city. For example, Isaiah 65:17-25 describes a future where oppression and injustice are noticeably absent. The relationships will be such that God can delight in his people and conversation with God is natural and immediate. This restoration of a harmonious relationship affects not only the human community, but extends even to the rest of creation. "Isaiah 65:17-25 gathers all these themes together in its eschatological vision of the coming *shalom*, painted now in terms of the restoration of the urban paradise of the Messiah" (Conn, 1992, p. 17). Several passages of Scripture present a clear understanding of God's will for humanity in carrying out justice and mercy to all others.[6] It is also clear from the Bible that God's people are called to participate in living out his will: "The prayer 'Thy will be done' is in vain if it is not made visible in action for the doing of that will" (L. Newbigin, 1995, p. 91).

Tied in with the idea of *shalom* is the idea of God's kingdom (Geddert, 1992, p. 604; Gornik, 2002, p. 102; Moreau, Corwin, & McGee, 2004, p. 84; N. T. Wright, 1997, p. 595). God's reign or kingdom is located where God's will is carried out. Johannes Verkuyl describes this kingdom this way:

> The kingdom to which the Bible testifies involves a proclamation and a realization of a total salvation, on which covers the whole range of human needs and destroys every pocket of evil and grief affecting [hu]mankind. Kingdom in the New Testament has a breadth and a scope which is unsurpassed; it embraces heaven as well as earth, world history as well as the whole cosmos (as quoted in C. Van Engen, 2005, p. 10).

---

[6] Amos 5:18-27; Isaiah 58; 61; Revelation 21-22. There are too many passages that offer descriptions of God's vision for his people to include a comprehensive list; these are a mere sampling.

The news of the arrival of God's kingdom is called good news in the Gospels and is both described and demonstrated by Jesus. Those who enter God's kingdom experience *shalom*.

God's kingdom is marked by justice, love, and holiness. Jerusalem was called to be a testimony to the world's cities of the *shalom* possible under God's covenant (Ps. 122:6-9) (Conn, 1992, p. 27; Lim, 1989, p. 25). Isaiah 2 also describes God's intention for Jerusalem as a model city, where his *shalom* is normative. The city's excellence was measured by the care given to the weakest members (Bess, 2006, p. 108). Throughout the Bible, Jerusalem comes under God's judgment for failing to measure up to this noble calling (Ezekiel 5:5-8; Jeremiah 6:6; Isaiah 1:21-31), abandoning its purpose in favor of a "pagan culture of death." (D. W. Smith, 2001, p. 188). Tragically, Jerusalem falls short of fulfilling its destiny. Jerusalem, it turns out, was no different than the surrounding nations (Murray, 1990, p. 30). Jesus stopped outside of the city to weep over it, lamenting its people's inability to detect the source of peace (Luke 19:41-44). Jesus' arrival signaled God making his move and, ultimately, *shalom* is secured through the cross of Christ (Col. 1:19-23).

While Jerusalem did not succeed in living out the *shalom* vision described by the prophets, her purpose and calling have been passed on to the church. Jesus made peace through his blood sacrifice with a goal of reconciling all things to him. Based on the work of Christ, Paul casts a vision for the work of the church to embrace this *shalom* (Cole, 2009, pp. 20–21; Martin, 1993). The church "must incorporate a vision of *shalom*" into the church's vision (Conn & Ortiz, 2001, p. 347). The church is called to be present in the cities of humanity, all the while demonstrating kingdom values.

Proliferation of Kingdom Communities

Jerusalem did not fulfill her intended role, so the responsibility shifted to a new group of people raised up as the new people of God (2

Cor. 6:16; 1 Pet. 2:9-10), the "true Israel."[7] The new people of God, made up of those who consciously choose to follow Jesus, is the church. In following Jesus as a community, the church chooses to accept and embody kingdom values.[8] The church serves as a community within the cities of the world: "In this way the church will be the holy city within the city until Christ comes again to redeem the faithful and the heavenly Jerusalem comes down to claim its eternal citizens" (Seitz, 1997, p. 27). The church, then, can fulfill the important role that Jerusalem was once tasked for, to be the city on a hill (Matthew 5:14).

The church is not just a rendezvous point to catch the train to heaven; it is the community set apart to live out God's kingdom ethos.[9] The church is the place where God is acknowledged as king, and his kingdom ethos is observed (Chester, 2000, p. 29). We have already established the importance of the previous two points: God-centeredness and *shalom* social vision. The church ideally brings these two together. A church that is truly focused on God should also be devoted to doing God's will. A church submitted to God "means that when we plant a church that throbs with biblical vitality, we introduce into urban life a force for good, for justice, and reconciliation.   It

---

[7] Not all scholars are in agreement that the New Testament church is the new Israel (cf. Dever, 770), but the evidence strongly favors this interpretation. Jesus used symbolically powerful imagery referring to a flock (Lk. 12:32) and the twelve disciples (Mt. 19:28). In Acts, Israel's history is brought forward to the church. Paul writes of two Israels (Rom. 9:6) and in his letter to the Galatians calls them the "Israel of God" (Gal. 6:16). Ladd concludes: "Jesus sees his disciples taking the place of Israel as the true people of God" (108). Even those who disagree with this view see continuity between the church and Israel. (Dever, 2007, p. 770; Flew, 1938, pp. 52, 64; Guthrie, 1990, p. 707; Ladd, 1993, pp. 106–8, 583; Seccombe, 1998, p. 371; Twelftree, 2009, p. 55)

[8] In the past, the church was often equated with the kingdom of God (i.e. Augustine). Most scholars today differentiate between the two while acknowledging a symbiotic relationship. Even though the church is not God's kingdom, it is entirely dependent on the reality and hope of God's kingdom. And God's kingdom relies on the church for propagation and embodiment of the Messiah. (France, 1984, p. 31; Ladd, 1993, pp. 103–117; Volf, 1998, p. x)

[9] The way one understands the Great Commission determines the mission of the church. William Taylor says that if mission is only understood in terms of proclamation, then the mission of the church is reduced to "spiritual anemia." (Taylor, 2000, p. 4)

happens when churches pursue the agenda of the kingdom of God, as Jesus did" (Greenway, 1997, p. 22). It is for the church, as the body of Christ, to continue the kingdom mission initiated by Jesus (Lk. 22:29).

To demonstrate the values of the kingdom, a community is essential. Christians who have embraced the release from the bondage of sin through Christ can begin to live freely as intended by their Creator. Gathered as the church, these Christians have the potential to embody this inward transformation in outward ways (Todd, 1976, p. 257). Lamin Sanneh (1989) describes how the early church lived life in a way that constantly acknowledged the kingdom of God:

> This vision of the kingdom infused a powerful sense of ethical seriousness into earthly conduct. How people treated each other, how they acquired and disposed of their wealth, how they behaved in the world, what motives existed for their actions, and how they practiced restraint, forgiveness, and charity toward others were all governed by the certainty that the kingdom of God (1 Thess. 4:16-18; 5:1-28) would appear in the foreseeable future. No one took the world as seriously as those who were called to make war upon it. God as Judge and Savior not only ensured the rule of justice and faith in redemptive steadfastness, but also called forth a strong sense of righteousness and trust in the salvific promise. Thus earthly existence had cast upon it this inexorable pressure to rise to the highest standards of ethical conduct (p. 12).

The church, in other words, made an impact much more broadly than just upon the members of their community.

Christians seeking to do the will of God will naturally hope to diffuse the practices they consider beneficial for the city.[10] Diffusion theory suggests that the earliest adopters try the new innovation, and, as others see its value, they will also adopt it. Once the adopters reach a "critical mass" (10-16%), it will diffuse naturally to the rest of the

---

[10] Diffusion theory attempts to explain how new ideas and innovations spread. (Rogers, 1995)

society (Stone, 2004, p. 72). The church ought to be among the early adopters of practices that lead toward the good city, providing a support community for those adopting and implementing kingdom values. The church as a whole can be a transforming presence, its members heralds of the King and early adopters of the *shalom* social vision.

The gospel is made manifest in the world by the church believing, proclaiming, and living it out (Newbigin, 1989, p. 223). The church's role in manifesting the gospel does not mean that salvation is only through the church; rather, the church is called to proclaim salvation through Christ to the world.[11] The church is crucial to the process of developing Christians into those who seek first God's kingdom. This process is most often called discipleship. There have been attempts by missiologists and Christian ministry practitioners to foment a form of Christianity without the church (see the following books for examples of churchless Christianity: Hoefer, 2001; Jamieson, 2002; Ward, 2002). Greenway (1992) repudiated this trend: "From my point of view, 'churchless Christianity' is in most cases something spurious, unbiblical, and empty" (p. 45). I have seen the churchless mission strategy first hand in my ministry experience in San Francisco, where amorphous Christian networking dissipated due to a lack of structure. The exigency of church is true everywhere, and even more so in the urban context. Institutions are essential to urban life, therefore the Church will need to be formally organized in order to engage the city in mission (P. Hiebert & Meneses, 1995, p. 283). The Church benefits from some level of formal organization in order to generate true disciples.

Since the Church intends to diffuse kingdom values that lead to a better city, she must also prioritize reproducing herself with the starting of new churches. Church reproduction is the "best way for a church to

---

[11] It is interesting to note that idea that salvation was found only in the Church can be traced back to Augustine's writings, but it should also be noted that this was not Augustine's intention. Instead, he was urging the Church to live in the manner of salvation for the sake of the world, working for a better society. The Roman Catholic Church had long declared there was no salvation outside of the Church (*extra Ecclesiam nulla salus*) but modified this position at the Vatican II Council. (Bevans & Schroeder, 2004, p. 132; Karkkainen, 2002, p. 29)

grow in an urban situation" (Wagner, 1972, p. 188). Tom Malluga (1999) captures the importance of church reproduction for the sake of transformation here:

> Imagine cities with a harvest of people being connected with the Good Shepherd through the starting of new churches. Watch as blighted neighborhoods become transformation zones. Smiles light up faces once shadowed by fear and despair. Hope replaces aimlessness, relationships are healed, and the actual appearance of buildings begins to change. A dynamic of transformation flows out of churches, progressively eliminating pockets of darkness in the community. People whose lives once seemed irreversibly broken are now the excited leaders of teams of change agents sent to start transformation zones in other city neighborhoods (pp. 172-173).

In this way, the proliferating churches are an important ingredient to urban transformation. Just as the gospel transforms individuals, those transformed by the gospel come together as a community agent of change.

What is needed for urban transformation is a network of God-worshipping, *shalom*-seeking, city-improving church members. Indian urban missiologist, J.N. Manokaran (2008) concludes: "Planting churches is the only hope for humanity" (p. 244). The church, as the people of God, is uniquely commissioned to bring transformation to the city. It is not merely a ministry option for the church, but is built into its DNA (Snyder & Runyon, 2002, pp. 51, 194). Elaine Graham and Stephen Lowe (2009) describe the Church of England as having 16,500 local outlets, 10,000 full-time employees, billions of dollars of assets, and the largest volunteer force in the country. The church is strategically positioned to be a transformative presence in cities around the world. Graham and Lowe go on to say: "This is much more than service provision. It is about hope, transfiguration and the Kingdom. It is not just a 'mission statement', but is proclaimed in word and deed and is fuelled by values" (p. xi). The Church is a core avenue of introducing needed change for the welfare of cities.

Conclusion: Bringing the Characteristics of a Good City Together

Urban centers are expanding every day all over the world. An understanding of the characteristics that contribute to the wellbeing of urban centers is essential for any hope of transformation. The characteristics described in this chapter are derived from two perspectives: urbanology and Christianity (see Figure 5.2 below).

Urbanology Perspective	Christian Perspective
Density Vibrancy Diversity Security Economic Opportunity Organic Growth	God-centeredness *Shalom* social vision Kingdom communities

Figure 5.2 Summary of Characteristics of a Good City

None of the characteristics stands alone. Each characteristic impacts the others interdependently. For example, vibrancy benefits from density. When people live in closer proximity, they share more community concerns, infrastructure, and economic opportunities, which then leads to community involvement (vibrancy). A vibrant community will grow organically and be more secure. In the same way, a lack of security can breed distrust in the community, becoming an obstacle to vibrancy and more oppressive forms of economic exploitation arise. Even though the characteristics blend into one another in this manner, they also need to be considered separately in order to intentionally seek the betterment of the city.

The perspectives of urbanology and Christianity are not mutually exclusive, but rather complement and inform one another. It is not as simple as following the urbanology set of characteristics to create a good secular city. Nor are the three characteristics from a Christian perspective all that is needed for a good, godly city.[12] As demonstrated above, Scripture supports several of the good city characteristics put forth by urbanology. Similarly, the urbanology characteristics benefit from the addition of Christian perspective (Graham & Lowe, 2009, p. 105). Economic opportunity for all citizens is difficult to achieve without any moral vision for social justice. Without such a vision, employers might refuse to pay the salaries of their employees, thus exploiting the poor, for example.[13] The Christian characteristics keep the other characteristics in check or in perspective. Security is an important characteristic of good cities and a basic human need. But the Bible makes it clear that humanity cannot be assured of their security outside of God. Security in God should be foundational to any other security provisions. It is the *shalom* social vision that spurs further security measures that seek to protect those disadvantaged in their communities.

The inclusion of the biblical characteristics of a good city helps restore a realistic view of the city and aids in our understanding of the root problems. The innate sinfulness of humanity renders utopian urban planning schemes futile, but neither are we forced to accept a dystopian future, because we live with the hope of restoration.

---

[12] It could be argued that the biblical characteristics are sufficient for the transformation of the city, but this would presume a *shalom* social vision that is fully informed by all of the factors that ensure the people of the city experience things like economic opportunities and security. Implicit in this statement is the idea that the church can benefit from the wisdom of others (cf. Acts 7:22).

[13] This is more difficult to imagine in the West where laws are in place offering ways for the employees to take legal action. It is a different scenario in many other countries. For example, in Kuala Lumpur, Malaysia, migrant workers and refugees number in the hundreds of thousands. Many employers (owners of factories, restaurants, etc.) exploit them for their labor but then do not pay their salary or "dock" their pay for reasons outside of workers' control. The legal system in Malaysia provides very few options for such workers to receive just treatment.

Variables taken from urbanology and Christian theology combine to contribute to the well-being of a city. However, each city will have a unique blend of these characteristics. Some of the characteristics listed above can be measured and compared more readily, such as density or economic opportunity. Vibrancy and organic growth, on the other hand, cannot be measured or compared so easily. A good city is marked by these characteristics, but will always continue to strike balances between them. Even though a precise formula does not emerge, these characteristics can serve as a rubric for evaluating the different models of transformation, including my own.

Questions for reflection and discussion:

1. What three elements does the author say encompass a biblical vision for a good city? Do you agree with this assessment?
2. How does your city reflect or not reflect a *shalom* social vision?
3. Does your church teach and act towards creating these biblical elements of a good city? How can your start or further the discussion of *shalom* and the good city in your church?

Part 2

A Canopy Ecosystem Approach to Urban Transformation

CANOPY ECOSYSTEM APPROACH
TO URBAN TRANSFORMATION

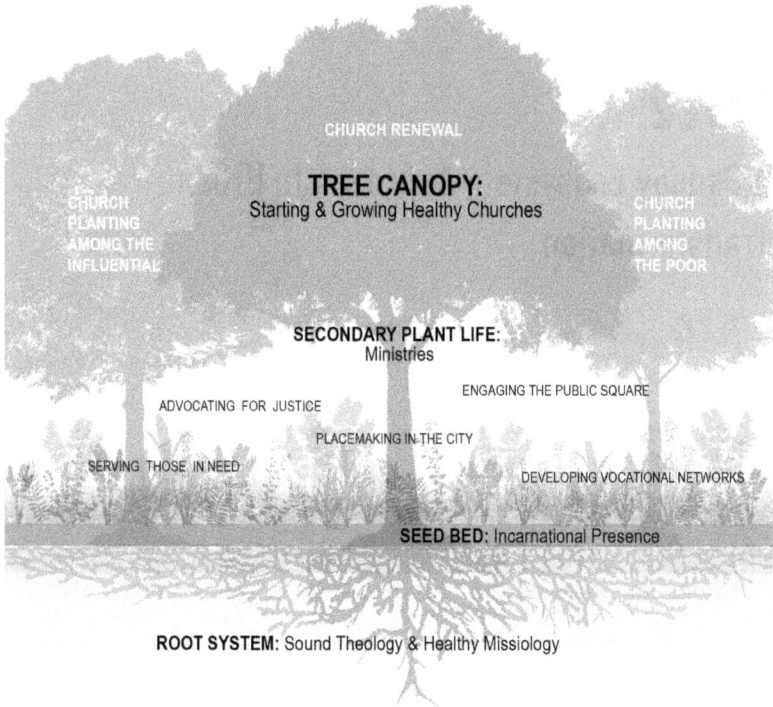

CHURCH RENEWAL

TREE CANOPY:
Starting & Growing Healthy Churches

CHURCH
PLANTING
AMONG THE
INFLUENTIAL

CHURCH
PLANTING
AMONG
THE POOR

SECONDARY PLANT LIFE:
Ministries

ENGAGING THE PUBLIC SQUARE

ADVOCATING FOR JUSTICE

PLACEMAKING IN THE CITY

SERVING THOSE IN NEED

DEVELOPING VOCATIONAL NETWORKS

SEED BED: Incarnational Presence

ROOT SYSTEM: Sound Theology & Healthy Missiology

ROOT SYSTEM ➡ SEED BED ➡ TREE CANOPY ➡ SECONDARY ➡ THRIVING CANOPY
PLANT LIFE   ECOSYSTEM

Chapter 6
Canopy Ecosystems and Urban Transformation

We can best grasp the challenges of urban mission, in fact, if we view it ecologically.

--Howard Snyder (2013, p. 48)

Just as a biological ecosystem is made of interdependent organisms, systems, and natural forces, a gospel ecosystem is made of interdependent organizations, individuals, ideas, and spiritual and human forces.

--Timothy Keller (2012, p. 371)

During the height of the modern era we looked at cities in very precise and static ways. It was common to view issues as problems to be solved with simple solutions. If more housing was needed, big high-rise apartment blocks were erected. If rush hour traffic was badly congested, wider elevated highways were built. It soon became obvious, however, that these supposedly simple solutions actually created a host of other problems. Wide, elevated highways did wonders for pumping cars in from the suburbs, but it was disastrous for street life below the highways. In reaction to the quick fix approach to urban planning, a number of urban thinkers began to describe cities using terms that conveyed the organic nature and complexity of the city and to propose appropriately nuanced solutions to its issues. Likewise, the Church can no longer rely on simplistic approaches to city transformation.

In the previous section we covered a lot of theoretical ground. We have begun to develop a theology of the city as well as a deeper understanding of what makes a city better. We also surveyed the wide range of Christian models of urban transformation. Each model was strong in some areas and weak in others. Now we will seek to build on what we have learned with the goal of developing a model that guides the Church in responsible and God-honoring urban transformation.

A Natural Metaphor for Urban Transformation

We need a model that is nuanced enough to pervade every corner of the complex city and adaptable enough to be applicable in cities around the world. The aim is to facilitate transformation for the whole city, not just the poor or certain other specific communities. Using only a linear approach to social change is not sufficient for making an impact on cities. As I mentioned in Chapter 4, cities are best understood as complex webs. Paul Hiebert suggests that social change works better through a web-based approach or a "systems" approach. Social, spiritual, and cultural changes each affect the other in important ways (Hiebert, 2009, pp. 132–134). In other words, change happens through an interpenetrating impact on different spheres of society. This eliminates overly simplistic models from consideration (D. Hall, Hall, Daman, & Bass, 213AD, p. Location 2670). The one size fits all approach is not sufficient for the diversity of cities and is not missiologically healthy.

Ecological images are well-suited for constructing models that address the complexities of the city. Cities are composed of human social ecosystems that are webbed together (Harden, 2013, p. Location 1960). Tim Keller uses the image of an ecosystem to capture the need for an all-encompassing and interrelated approach to impacting cities with the gospel (Keller, 2012, p. 375). Ecosystems have infrastructure that creates the right environment for vibrant life, and as such cannot be instantly implemented. Building this infrastructure requires a linear progression, particularly in the initial phases, so that the ecosystem can flourish. Howard Snyder (2013) relates the ecosystem imagery to cities: "There is such a thing as an urban ecosystem. Like all ecosystems, it involves inputs, throughputs, outputs, with complex interrelationships, and feedback loops" (p. 48). The development of this ecosystem is crucial. Here, I use the image of a *canopy ecosystem* to capture the complexity and comprehensiveness of the model needed, as well as to highlight the linear progression of the foundational infrastructure necessary for transformation to take place.

The image of the canopy ecosystem is useful for a number of reasons:

- *Flourishing organic and functional diversity.* Tree canopies establish a habitat for a rich diversity of plant life and other organisms that perform a variety of functions for the ecosystem (Asner et al., 2014). The canopy is not merely a few tall trees and some squirrels and birds' nests; we see mosses and fungi, ferns and flowers, insects and animals of all types. Biologists tell us that there is as much biodiversity in the tree canopies as there is on the ground (E. O. Wilson, 1986). Cities can also benefit from a symbiotic ecosystem of organizations committed to a better city.
- *Unique organisms.* Tree canopies not only host diverse organisms, but also organisms that are not found anywhere else. The coalescing of those compelled by the vision of city transformation can foster unique and innovative solutions not found anywhere else.
- *Long-term process.* Ecosystems do not pop up overnight. They require a long process of gradual growth. In the same way, cities will not be changed by a quick-fix mentality. Rather, a long-term perspective is crucial for a sound approach to urban transformation.

In the following chapters, we will use the canopy ecosystem as a metaphor for constructing a model of urban transformation. A canopy ecosystem begins under the ground with a deep root system. A Christian approach to urban transformation must be deeply rooted in solid, orthodox theology and sound missiology. The seed bed represents the importance of incarnational presence in the city. A canopy ecosystem does not exist unless there is a grove of trees in close enough proximity to each other to support the development of other species in the canopy. Launching healthy, gospel-centered churches plants the trees that create the canopy. The rest of the ecosystem is supported by the growth of vital churches through on-going gospel renewal. For these churches to thrive they must rely on a root system that ensures their continual growth. In and among the trees is secondary plant-life that both feeds off of and supplies nutrients for the trees. Specialized ministries serve the same function as the secondary plant-life by assisting the church in providing ministry to subcultures and other specialized groups of people in the city. As churches and ministries grow in close proximity, they can converge to form the beginnings of an ecosystem. This ecosystem network(s) should be forged by prayer and a shared vision for the city and unified around the gospel. From this prayerful, unified, shared vision, networks emerge and grow to collaborate for the sake of city transformation.

In these ways the canopy ecosystem functions well as a helpful metaphorical model for urban transformation. Of course, we must remember that this, and every, metaphor has its limitations. In the following chapters I will explain each element in more detail, but first, I will introduce a few concepts necessary to developing a spiritual canopy ecosystem in the city. Much like a thriving canopy ecosystem cannot develop without the right environmental conditions, certain "environmental conditions" are necessary for the development of a successful model for urban transformation: vision, prayer, and unity.

Vision

I love Ultimate Frisbee. Wherever I have lived, I have sought out a group to play Ultimate with on Sunday afternoons. When we are playing informally we sometimes don't keep score. While it is more relaxing to play this way, the level of play is sloppy and lackadaisical. If we suddenly decide to keep score and play a short game to five, everyone immediately steps up their speed, intensity, and quality of play. What has changed is that we're playing with a clear goal in mind, and this determines the quality of play even on the first point. The vision of victory drives us toward excellence.

Similarly, it is the victorious vision of the city of God that drives our desire for city transformation. We do not work halfheartedly like novices in a scrimmage, but as serious athletes competing for the life-altering win. The Bible repeatedly offers a vision of the new city of God. One place we see this vision is Isaiah 65:19-23:

> I will rejoice in Jerusalem
> and be glad in my people;
> no more shall be heard in it the sound of weeping
> and the cry of distress.
> No more shall there be in it
> an infant who lives but a few days,
> or an old man who does not fill out his days,
> for the young man shall die a hundred years old,
> and the sinner a hundred years old shall be accursed.
> They shall build houses and inhabit them;
> they shall plant vineyards and eat their fruit.
> They shall not build and another inhabit;
> they shall not plant and another eat;
> for like the days of a tree shall the days of my people be,
> and my chosen shall long enjoy the work of their hands.
> They shall not labor in vain
> or bear children for calamity,
> for they shall be the offspring of the blessed of the Lord,
> and their descendants with them. (ESV, 2008)

This beautiful vision of a just city should drive our visions for the cities we live in today. This passage indicates that we are, in some way, participants in the building of the new city. Of course God is the master architect, benefactor, and the primary labor force, but we are included in the building of the city of God! This does not mean that we will be able to turn the cities of our time into New Jerusalems, but it does set before us a standard and vision for what a city can be. Ray Bakke links this vision of the future with our current reality: "In fact, the biblical picture of God who integrates the redemptive threads of the universe into a transformed eternal city should give us more than adequate permission to try and get our heads and hearts around the urbanization of the world" (Bakke, 1997, p. 80). Then we as God's people begin to live according to this vision and dream about ways in which our cities can reflect this future reality.

We read about this magnificent vision for the city in the Bible and we return to our context and imagine what could happen in our cities. David Smith calls for "urban imagineers" who are unbounded and unrestricted in their dreams for what cities can become (D. W. Smith, 2001, p. 239). This is not a call for a revival of the power of the human spirit. In fact, Smith argues that reliance on humanistic thinking can bog down the vision of what God might want to do in a city: "the new vision of the city we so urgently need cannot come to birth as long as thought and action remain confined within a secular, materialist worldview" (D. W. Smith, 2001, p. 239). A God-centered vision for our cities should be birthed in our reading of the Scriptures. For a city to reflect God's new city, albeit imperfectly, it should carry the DNA of the city of God. When we, as God's people, inhabit our cities, we should reflect godly purposes within our cities.

The powerful impact of a compelling vision for the city is in the way it speaks to the present conditions of the city. Verse 22 of the passage from Isaiah 65 (quoted above) speaks of house builders who are building their own homes, not just homes for the wealthy. This verse at once anticipates the new city and speaks to the housing conditions of construction labor during the time of Isaiah's ministry. Our biblically informed vision of the City of God ought to inform how we seek the best for our cities today. As we look to the vision of what we want the city to become we must also see the city as it is in its current state. "Our vision of the city powerfully determines how we will engage with it" (Hillis, 2014, p. 5).

David Hillis (2014) tells the inspiring story of Sam Shoemaker. Shoemaker had already made an impact, one that continues until now, as a cofounder of Alcoholics Anonymous. And he extended his impact through writing books and pastoring in New York City. In 1952, Shoemaker went to Pittsburg with a vision to see the city transformed. He said simply: "I have a vision that Pittsburgh will one day be as famous for God as it is for steel" (p. 5). He would routinely take Christian leaders up to the top of a mountain that overlooks Pittsburg to pray for the city. As he did this, Christian leaders began to develop a vision for their city. Out of this vision formation came a network of Christian leaders who made it their goal to make Pittsburg "famous for God" (Hillis, 2014, pp. 9–21).

Too often our visions are too small. Our visions are sometimes limited to growing our own church or ministry. As a result, churches and ministries become either competitive with or isolated from like-minded organizations. When this happens, Christians become distracted by in-house politicking and tribalism. Church members can become prideful about their own church's growth despite the fact that the citywide Christian community is fractured and dysfunctional. Churches and ministries with such limited visions can be a hindrance to what God wants to do in the whole city.

Being limited by a small vision is not a new phenomenon. The people of God in the Old Testament struggled similarly with inwardness and small mindedness. The people of God were always intended to be a blessing to all of the nations (Gen. 12:1-4). In their persistent disobedience and lack of faith toward God, they were sent into exile for seventy years. When the people of God were allowed to return to the land God had given them, they were intent on building their nation back. God reminds them (Isaiah 49:6) that hoping only to restore their own nation is too narrow a vision; rather the God-sized vision was for this small nation of people to be a light for all of the nations to know God and experience his work of salvation.

The beautiful thing about large visions—and whole city transformation is definitely a large vision—is that it is impossible to carry out alone. When we consider whole city impact we are forced to draw on a whole network of churches and ministries to accomplish the task. Tim Keller planted Redeemer Presbyterian Church in New York City with this kind of thinking. It emerges from his understanding of the kingdom of God. He believes the Church should care more about the kingdom than it does a specific church or a particular denomination. A church should be willing to give ten people to start a new church for the sake of the eighty they might reach. In the big picture, the kingdom has gained, and that should give us cause to rejoice (Keller, 2008a, p. 4).

The individuals who make up a church intersect with the larger city culture on many levels. As churches internalize the kingdom vision for the city, its members become more engaged in the real affairs of the city, and when each member sees the ways their gifts and skills relate to the collective vision, they realize their calling. The Church has a responsibility to help its members process important social and ideological issues biblically:

> In the main, the social revolutions of our day are city-based. In the city, as nowhere else, the church must articulate biblical answers to the burning social questions being raised by students and proletarians alike. If we fail in the urban arena, we shall have failed indeed. The theological basis for a just and righteous society must be proclaimed and lived in the circle of the Christian community which is the church. The role of the local church cannot be overestimated as far as its influence on societal structures is concerned (Greenway, 1976, p. 18).

To return to our athletic metaphor, a shared purpose benefits both players and team. A shared vision for the city can spur on the depth of discipleship in individuals as well as a posture of engagement for the whole church, creating a mutually beneficial relationship among church, members, and the city.

Unity and Prayer

There is but one body of Christ. In this age of extreme individualism and autonomy, we have dishonored the biblical instruction for unity (John 17, Eph. 2, 4). The fractured state of the Church in our cities harms our witness, prevents our role in transformations, and misrepresents Christ's work of reconciliation. Wilbur Stone (2003), Global Studies director at Bethel Seminary, says, "The cities of our world will remain largely unreached until and unless the numerous components making up the collective Body of Christ begin to work together" (p. 86). Among those who teach and work in urban missions there is near unanimity on the issue of unity among the churches in the city. Churches' proximity and overlap of parish (whether recognized or not) necessitates unity and collaboration.

Quite often when I speak to church leaders about this topic, the reply I hear is: "Well we are unified in spirit, which is what really counts. We're too busy to do things together." But that is rubbish; most churches are unified with one another in neither action nor spirit. I constantly hear about the terrible things other churches do. But when I ask where the information came from, the source is clearly interchurch gossip, often the result of viewing other churches as competitors rather than teammates. Even if we are too blind to see it, non-Christians in the city see the division and disunity quite clearly. We need to prioritize unity by finding ways to be physically present together. We need times of prayer among leaders and/or to "...hold citywide or regional celebrations occasionally to endorse and reaffirm the Church's diversity and its unity in diversity" (A. G. Smith, 2009, p. 39). Although these events might not feel like time well-spent and the results cannot be measured numerically, there are intangible benefits to gospel impact on the whole city.

The Praying Body. Unity seems critical for the growth and health of the church in cities. One important way for the whole Church to come together is through organized prayer. A unified prayer emphasis is one effective way to promote unity. Mac Pier (2008) has been a leader of the prayer emphasis in New York and attests to the exigency of a united prayer effort. Pier made it his life's work to organize prayer around the city. Since they started 25 years ago, 1000 churches in the city have joined in praying for their city, and they have seen tangible changes:

- The churches used to be openly hostile towards each other but now experience greater unity than ever before.
- New churches have been started, are growing, and are reaching non-Christians with the gospel. In Manhattan alone, the number of Christian residents has increased by 300%.
- Crime has dropped significantly. The murder rate is down by 70%. In fact, New York is now the safest city of over a million people in United States (Webster).

Churches from different traditions in one city coming together in prayer can have a powerful impact on the city. "In the cities that are being transformed by the power of the gospel, congregations are coming together across congregational, denominational and geographic lines to pray" (Dennison, 1999, p. 121).

Whole Body, Whole City. It takes the whole Church of a city to impact the whole city. A single local church cannot tackle all of the issues well and sustainably. A coordinated and combined effort is needed to make a real impact in the city. Roger Dewey (1974) reminds us that the image of the Body of Christ is one body and "has within it all the necessary resources for the healing and nourishment of its various parts" (p. 217). Jack Dennison (1999) addresses the necessity of unity for the sake of collaboration:

City reaching is not the domain of any particular paraministry or denominational group. There is no one event or activity that in itself can result in the discipling of a city. Each and every segment of the Body is needed to contribute to the overall objective of reaching the city (p. 97).

That the Church is a body means that each part of the body needs to know and do what it is made to do. This does not just apply to individuals in a church but to churches in a city. Some churches start trying to do it all, which leads to a number of problems. Good churches know their role in reaching the city. Erwin McManus is the pastor of Mosaic in LA. Mosaic is a well-known church with a tremendous array of resources at their disposal, but that does not mean that they try to do everything on their own. In a conversation with Matthew Barnett, the pastor of the Dream Center in LA, which excels in addiction rehabilitation ministries, McManus says they refer people to the Dream Center all of the time (Gordon, 2006). Mosaic and Dream Center know their respective purposes and complement one another's ministries in Los Angeles rather than competing for areas of impact.

Unity Does Not Mean Conformity. Unity is necessary for urban transformation, but that does not mean churches must give up their theological convictions and distinct practices. The diversity of churches will better reach the diversity of cultures in a city. This means that some kinds of citywide events advance the cause of the kingdom while other types of events may not be as suitable for a combined effort. Cooperative evangelistic events between churches, for example, have proven ineffective in promoting church growth. "Formal co-operation tends to dilute the focus on the local church to which converts must be linked" (Hinton, 1985, p. 131). Likewise, church planting in an interdenominational network can often lead to more problems and frustrations than success. Of course, it benefits the city when churches from differing denominations encourage and pray for new churches. Different churches and denominations each bless the city in unique ways which would be lost if conformity rather than unity is emphasized.

Need for Collaboration. It is not merely a matter of churches agreeing on a similar goal, but actively working together to reach that goal. CEO of the Christian Community Development Association (CCDA), Noel Castellanos (2009), speaks from personal experience when he says: "It will take the entire body of Christ working together to see the gospel truly impact our city" (p. 51).

Collaboration is a difficult work that is rarely done well. It is so hard for people to lay their own agendas aside in order to see the whole city impacted. Pastors prayer breakfasts and city-wide worship gatherings are a good start, but we need to make sacrifices toward a united effort to see God's kingdom come in the city as it is in heaven, laying aside ego, pet projects, and individualistic goals. Melba Maggay (2004) calls for this kind of sacrificial mindset: "Solidarity with others is premised on a death somewhere within us" (p. 111). This can only take place when churches begin to prioritize the good of the kingdom of God over the goals of individual churches.

Uniting in Prayer, Vision, and Action

The late missionary statesman to South India, Lesslie Newbigin, looked at the city of Madras (now called Chennai) knowing it would be too overwhelming for a small congregation of a hundred worshippers to make difference. He knew that the city's churches needed to be united in their effort (Newbigin, 1960, 1994, p. 34). Biblical scholar William Barclay (1951) noted that the impact of the church in South India coming together was like reliving the days of the early church. We hold back from collaborating because we are too busy trying to survive, when in reality working together can actually become a source of energy for congregations in a city. Jack Dennison (1999) sees how churches coming together for comprehensive city impact follows a pattern established in Nehemiah:

> In most of our cities, individual congregations alone cannot accomplish the task of citywide diagnostics. City

> transformation will come only as a comprehensive picture
> of the entire city—built in Nehemiah fashion, one part of
> the wall at a time—informs our decision making and our
> ministry. The evidence for this from around the world is
> compelling (p. 126).

If we are serious about making a difference in our cities, we need to put our own ministry ambitions aside and come together to pray for the city, develop a vision for the city, and strategize for action. In doing this, each church can find its own place in contributing as the body of Christ in the city.

Earlier in the chapter I said that unity in vision and prayer brings intangible benefits. The problem with intangible benefits is that we are not rewarded with our typical measures of success (countable things like baptisms, church membership, or churches started), and it is easy to become impatient. Also, trying to develop a unified vision when we divide over so many issues of belief and practice can be grueling. However, we must work towards unity in spite of its challenges.

I have lived in San Francisco at a couple of different times. At one point, San Francisco had a reputation as a graveyard for church plants. We knew of several failed church plants and a number of defeated church planters and pastors. Several years later, through a couple of church planting initiatives, there is a new hopefulness among church planters in San Francisco.[1] Several churches have been started and seem strong enough to last for a while. This is due to churches coming together in prayer and a vision for what God wants to do in San Francisco. The bottom line is we can't be motivated by the results. Instead, we must do it because, as Keller says, it is the right thing to do:

---

[1] Linda Bergquist with North American Mission Board coordinated the launch of a number of churches through the 10-10-10 initiative. Around the same time another Bay Area-wide group came together to see the whole metropolitan region transformed by the gospel (http://www.tbc.city/). These collaborative efforts have been instrumental in the start of new churches and a renewed enthusiasm among Christians in the Bay Area for gospel impact on their city.

It is vital for us as Christians to collaborate with one another. We must do it because theologically it's the right thing to do, and because no one person and no single church has all of the gifts. In order to do the ministry that Christ calls us to do in the world, we need each other (as quoted in Pier, 2012).

Questions for reflection and discussion:

1. What conditions must exist for a spiritual "canopy ecosystem" to be cultivated?
2. How would you describe the state of unity among churches in your city?
3. How could your church work to create the conditions that enable a canopy ecosystem to develop? With what other churches or ministries could you collaborate?

ROOT SYSTEM: Sound Theology & Healthy Missiology

ROOT SYSTEM ➡

Chapter 7
Root System: Sound Theology and Healthy Missiology

The evangelical vitality of theology will be in direct proportion to the degree to which it engages the life purpose of the church.
                                        --Wilbert Shenk (1999, p. 9)

An inadequate foundation for mission and ambiguous missionary motives and aims are bound to lead to an unsatisfactory missionary practice.
                                        --David Bosch (1991, p. 5)

A couple of years ago I was asked to consult with a group of pastors and church leaders in a Southeast Asian city. For several years they had been working hard to bring transformation to their city. They had the backing of several of the most influential churches in the city and were involved in lots of activities, but they were left frustrated. Their frustration stemmed from the fact that despite their collaboration, abundant prayer, and tireless effort, they felt as though they had not gained any traction. Some of these leaders were ready to scrap the whole effort and others were content to just continue doing what they were doing. Why was their effort failing? Why were these church leaders frustrated? It was not for a lack of passion. Nor was it due to insufficient resources. Their goal of city transformation struggled because their vision for the city was underdeveloped. They had patched together a few ideas for city transformation from some popular concepts that pop up in Christian magazines and conferences. But they had not reflected theologically on the city or on whether those popular ideas were in keeping with Scripture. With these borrowed ideas substituting for their vision, they did not have a strategy they could implement. Without a strategy, they simply defaulted to busy programs and service-oriented ministries (which tend to leave long term issues unaddressed). Vision leads to strategy. If the vision is not theologically solid, the strategy will be weak. If the vision is not missiologically informed, the strategy will remain aloof and irrelevant. A compelling vision cannot be imported, but must be crafted for its context.

A Christian model for urban transformation should be rooted in sound theology and missiology. Ed Stetzer points out the need for a missiology that is theologically deep and missiologically broad while being cohesive and focused (Hesselgrave & Stetzer, 2010, p. 80). As a subset of missiology, urban missiology must share the same characteristics.

Theologically Deep Roots

The great Roman philosopher and statesman, Cicero, diagnosed Rome's failings as a loss of justice in the Republic. His solution was to regain the virtue of justice through the political will of statesmen. Augustine, also concerned about the failings of Rome, differed from Cicero by saying that Rome had always lacked true justice. Cicero's ideal statesman was not the answer for Rome; only Christ offered true justice by invitation to citizenship in the City of God. The obstacle of human sinfulness could only be overcome by the God-man who "alone is able to heal human beings of the ignorance and weakness which prevent them both from understanding the obligations of justice and from fulfilling them" (Dodaro, 2004, p. 2). Augustine understood the vital importance of his theological moorings as he analyzed the failings of Rome.

Movements can often be ignited by a flash of passion, but passion is not a substitute for a solid grounding in theology. The movement will flag if there is not theological development. For example, one of the most incredible movements in Christian history is the underground house church movement in China.[1] These networks of many thousands of house churches in the midst of severe persecution would never have started without passionate leaders who sacrificed everything for the sake of the gospel. But friends associated with the underground church in China tell me that thousands of churches are led astray by cults and other heretical ideas every year. This is primarily because there are few leaders who have been equipped theologically to respond to the strange ideas emanating from the fast-spreading cults. Christian leaders need theologically deep roots in order to lead well over the long term.

Deep roots in theology and missiology can help the practitioner develop discernment and establish priorities, and those roots should serve as a source of spiritual vitality. A theological framework for the city establishes an eternal perspective.[2] Ultimately, it is through this foundation that a vision for transformation is developed.(Stark, 1997, p. 211) Being theologically rooted as a collective network of churches and ministries can foster unity among the churches and have a powerful impact on the city.[3] If the vision is not theologically grounded, the potential impact of transformation becomes diluted or only makes a superficial impact. Keller adds that this vision should not be simply a statement of agreed-upon doctrines, but it should move toward an

---

[1] There are a number of books detailing the expansion of the church in China over the last fifty years. Former bureau chief for Time, David Aikman, offers a nice introduction to this phenomenal work of God. (Aikman, 2012)

[2] Augustine states it well: "Since, then, the supreme good of the city of God is perfect and eternal peace, not such as mortals pass into and out of by birth and death, but the peace of freedom from all evil, in which the immortals ever abide, who can deny that that future life is most blessed, or that, in comparison with it, this life which now we live is most wretched, be it filled with all blessings of body and soul and external things?" (Augustine, 1950, p. 698)

[3] Many have attempted unity through a broad organization. Tennent suggests unity should grow out of deep theological tradition. (Tennent, 2010, pp. 47–49)

articulation of how the gospel impacts culture (Keller, 2012, p. 16). A good theological vision will continually serve to direct people to God as he is revealed in the Bible and known through Jesus.[4] Transformation that is not God-centered will be temporal and idolatrous, because genuine transformation is ultimately the work of God (Maggay, 2004, p. 135).

Not everything that can and should be said about a theological foundation for urban transformation can be said here. The first section of the book included a theological understanding of the city as well as theological considerations for understanding the good city. Everything we do has theological implications, that understanding should motivate us to clearly articulate our theological assumptions. As we saw in Chapter 3, terms like "evangelism," "kingdom," and "gospel" are used in astoundingly different ways by different theological traditions. There does not have to be complete theological agreement prior to partnership or we would never accomplish anything. However, we do need to be clear with each other about our theological positions and in agreement on the central tenets of orthodox Christian doctrine.

It may sound obvious and seem unnecessary to state, but an understanding of the gospel and its application to every aspect of ministry in the city is a vital first step in growing deep theological roots. I recently heard John Folmar, pastor of United Christian Church of Dubai say that the first generation embraces the gospel, the second generation assumes the gospel, and the third generation loses the gospel. When we go about doing church activities and programs without understanding how it relates to the gospel, we run the risk of assuming the gospel. And when churches in a city collaborate to make a difference in the city, but the gospel is not jointly understood, we reduce our impact to that of a service club like Kiwanas or Lions Club. Those organizations do wonderful work, but the transformative work of the church is to have eternal impact that secular organizations cannot

---

[4] The first chapter of Romans indicates that a general understanding of God is easily available, but this awareness of God is not sufficient for a restored relationship with him.

achieve. Real transformation must always keep the gospel in the forefront of both motivation and application.

Redeemer Presbyterian Church in New York City did what most people considered mission impossible. In 1989, Tim and Kathy Keller went into the heart of Manhattan and planted a thriving and growing church. Manhattan was a graveyard of churches and certainly was not considered fertile soil for what would become a megachurch. A few years into Redeemer's ministry, the Christian world began to clamor for the "secrets" of its success, and many asked Tim Keller to write a "how-to" book. Keller has resisted this temptation because he believes that all of the things they did—worship times, musical styles, sermon preparation, and small group training—would have meant little if the church and its every ministry were not gospel-centered.

Missiologically Broad Roots

The vision should also be grounded in sound missiology. If Christian leaders do not practice good missiological principles, then there is potential for the theological vision to be distorted as it crosses cultures (Eitel, 1996, p. 46; Sanneh, 1989, p. 30). In a similar way, if church planters are not mindful of indigenous church planting principles, the result may be churches that are not healthy enough to sustain transformation efforts (Brock, 1994, p. 58; Nevius, 1973, p. 8). Good missiology does not rival good theology; rather, they work hand in hand to ensure that the gospel can penetrate a city in a way that can be understood by its citizens and can be proliferated by indigenous churches.

For a long time, churches in the West presumed a predominately Christian society and therefore did not draw on missiology to shape the mission of the Church in their own countries. And since the majority of the international missionary force was initially from the West, missionaries planted churches patterned after the Western churches that sent them. As a result, most churches have been largely ignorant of basic missions principles and relatively unengaged with their respective communities. In contrast, when the Church has learned from missiology, it has been transformatively enriching for the global Church (D. Hall et al., 213AD, p. Location 2857).

I know a pastor who planted a church in a Southeast Asian city where Christians are an embattled minority. He told me once that when he started the church, he was actively trying to reach out to his community. But now that he is "established" and has a building, he just expects people to walk into the Sunday morning service. Missiological thinking can help us see that this church will only attract those who have a predisposition towards Christianity. If a non-Christian local has a close Christian relative or friend and they feel comfortable with the people at the church, then there is a small chance he or she might visit the church. However, the majority of the people living around the church have little or no contact with Christians and therefore will never wake one Sunday morning and decide to give a church service a try. As sincere and theologically grounded as my pastor friend may be, his church will fail to reach its community if it does not begin to think missiologically. The late South African missiologist, David Bosch (1991), speaks of the Church as having an essentially missional nature: "Just as one could not speak of the church without speaking of its mission, it was impossible to think of the church without thinking, in the same breath, of the world to which it is sent" (p. 377). Each church is God's missionary agent to its neighborhood and city.

Some of you may still be skeptical regarding the ways sound missiology can help improve our engagement with the city. We have mistakenly assumed urbanization was merely a shift in demographics. Missiologists Harvie Conn and Manuel Ortiz see urbanization more profoundly as a "sociocultural shift."[5] Missiology is an academic discipline with important implications for Christian ministry. It is my observation that many churches go about missions with a great deal of ignorance. With the reduced cost of air travel and increased mobility of

---

[5] Conn and Ortiz further lament such "little serious attention is being paid to sociology, economics or political science." (Conn & Ortiz, 2001, p. 167)

the average person, anyone who has been on a short term mission trip thinks of him or her self as an expert. Too often churches hire missions pastors who have little or no missions experience and nearly zero missiological training. If we understand the church as a missionary agent (as we see it was in Acts), we must utilize the knowledge and skills of missiology. In brief I will introduce four areas in which missiology can and should be used in the church. These four are: missional vision, cultural exegesis, indigeneity, and strategic multiplication.

Missional vision. Everything a church does should be done with the goal of gospel witness. This does not mean there are not other goals that are served at the same time, but these other goals ought to allow the light of the gospel to shine. For example, true fellowship happens because of the reconciling work of Christ on the cross (Eph. 2:14). In Acts 1, Jesus is instructing his disciples after his resurrection and prior to his ascension. This passage lays out a clear timeline for future events and the role of the church in the meantime. It goes like this: Jesus ascends, disciples wait in Jerusalem for the Holy Spirit (Pentecost), disciples are to be witnesses starting in their city and going to the ends of the earth, and Jesus returns. Clearly, we live in a time in between Pentecost and Jesus' return. According to Acts 1, the primary activity of the church is to be Jesus' witnesses.

Acts 1:1-11: The Church's Primary Task

Timeline	Event-Task	Reference
40 days after his resurrection	Jesus Ascended- Church told to wait	Acts 1:4, 8, 9
10 days after his ascension	The Holy Spirit Came- Pentecost	Acts 2
Between 1st and 2nd Coming of Jesus- **Now!**	The Church witnesses about Jesus	Acts 1:8
Unknown date	Jesus returns!	Acts 1:11

Figure 7.1 Primary Tasks of the Church Between Resurrection and 2nd Coming of Christ

A church cannot be satisfied with beautiful worship, sound preaching, and deep fellowship if it is not actively making Jesus known to those who do not know him. A missional vision keeps this primary task in front of the whole church. Maintaining a missional vision includes reading the Bible with an eye for our role in God's global mission. Old Testament scholar Chris Wright (2006) says: "Mission is what the Bible is all about; we could as meaningfully talk of the missional basis of the Bible as of the biblical basis of mission" (p. 28). Furthermore, a missional vision pushes the Church to continuously look outside the Church for witness to the gospel.

Cultural exegesis. A few years ago a church planter tried to plant a church in San Francisco using a family-oriented model. While a family-oriented model can be quite effective in many contexts, the district of San Francisco chosen by this church planter was primarily inhabited by young twenty-somethings who had just moved to San Francisco for work. Perhaps needless to say, this church plant did not take off. If the church planter had studied his neighborhood beforehand, things might have turned out differently. Missiology is interdisciplinary; in addition to sound theology, it incorporates sociology and anthropology for researching a community or city. Using tools from different disciplines can go a long way towards helping a church understand who lives in their community. When a church knows more about the people around them, they can minister far more effectively. Imagine a church situated in an area where a number of Muslim refugees have been resettled. If the church decides to hold a block party without understanding who lives around them, they might serve pork barbeque. Muslims, who stay far away from pork, will stay far away from the church and any other events it holds, and the church will be left wondering why its efforts to engage the neighborhood have failed. Missiological training can help the church with quantitative and qualitative research that can have a huge impact on how the church does missions. In terms of a vision for the city, cultural exegesis is a critical step in understanding the reality of the city. A vision of a transformed city must be formed by beginning with a clear picture of the past and current state of the city.

Indigeneity. I have a good friend who has lived in Denver for a number of years. He has seen a number of church planters from the Southeastern United States attempt to start churches in Denver. Invariably, when a new church has the cultural feel of a Southern church, it primarily attracts Southern transplants but does little to reach locals as long-standing Denver citizens conclude it is not for them. The result is that many transplanted Southerners find a comfortable church home, but the city and people of Denver remain untransformed by the gospel.

Denver is no rare example. Many would-be urban ministers do not employ sound missiological approaches because they fail to recognize their target city as a cross-cultural mission field. Church planting in a new neighborhood is always a cross-cultural endeavor. Every neighborhood has unique cultural expressions which are important to those who dwell there. Missiology centers on the task of going across cultures with the gospel. To do so effectively requires the Christian to learn the language and culture of the people. The effective church intentionally translates the truths of the gospel using language, symbols, and forms that enable a clear understanding of the gospel. Often, this means addressing multiple cultural contexts in one city: "Because urban centers are heterogeneous, no one strategy is necessarily the right one. Each neighborhood, each highrise, each squatter settlement has its own character and should be studied individually" (F. Allen, 1986, p. 11). In order for churches and ministries to thrive in a city, they must take root in the cultures of that city.

Strategic multiplication. The biblical pattern of mission is consistently that of multiplication. In the book of Acts we see the number of disciples and churches multiplied as a matter of course. The book begins with 120 disciples keeping a low profile in Jerusalem and ends with churches in most of the major cities throughout the Roman Empire. Missiologists are trained in strategic thinking about reaching a whole people group, city, or population segment. The way one church is planted can dictate whether that church will multiply itself or remain solitary. Many ministries and churches have been hampered by a lack of missiological awareness in strategic multiplication. If we acknowledge that no single ministry or church can effectively reach the whole city, then we will need to rely on missiological wisdom to multiply in order to reach the whole city.

Missional vision, cultural exegesis, indigeneity, and strategic multiplication. These four areas of missiology can be a tremendous asset to the urban church and are vital for reaching the whole city with gospel. Urban Christian leaders operating without a solid missiological awareness run the risk of either starting unsustainable ministries or failing to reach broad segments of the city's population. The values and skills offered by missiology will be brought to bear in the subsequent chapters of this book.

Equipping for Urban Ministry

The theological and missiological reflection needed to sustain transformative urban ministry requires ongoing training. At times we in the Church have been guilty of giving a theological education to middle class pastors and only practical training to ministers in working class communities. I have three brief suggestions for theological education for urban ministry. First, the theological task needs to be shared deep and wide. We cannot rely on a few theologians to think for us; we need everyone active in theological reflection in the midst of diverse ministries (Davey, 2002, p. 12). Second, we need solid theological training at all levels (from informal mentoring and workshops to formal accredited education). Susan Baker (2002) shares a lesson learned in equipping people for urban ministry and church planting. The model she used was to train indigenous leadership in Chicago, but her team "underestimated the amount of theological training necessary to prepare leaders to serve on a solid foundation" (p. 63). Third, we need theological education in the context of our cities in order to train leaders to process urban life and ministry theologically. Mark Gornik (2002) calls for innovation in how we do this: "New models of grassroots theological and missiological education that occurs in the context of ministry are vital to the ongoing development of urban church leadership" (p. 214). We make room for theologically deep roots by creating paths for education and reflection in the urban context.

A vision of what the city ought to be is a pipe dream unless it is grounded in theology that is biblical and gospel-centered and in missiology that is sound and focused on God's mission. Good theology anchors us in God's truth and good missiology gives us eyes for God's purposes. If Christian leaders in a city are unclear about what they are working towards, it can foster confusion or, worse, conflict. A clear vision can help ministries and churches discern their priorities and discover the value of networking and collaborating for the sake of God's kingdom.

Questions for reflection and discussion:

1. What are the two elements the author says make up the "roots" of a strong spiritual canopy ecosystem? Do you agree?
2. Do you feel that you and/or the ministers in your church have been well equipped for urban ministry in the ways the author describes?

3. Does your church have both sound theology and missiology as relates to the city? How could you work to strengthen your church in those areas?

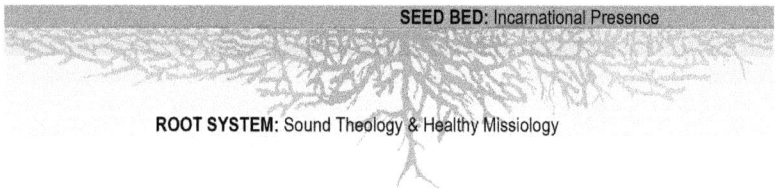

SEED BED: Incarnational Presence

ROOT SYSTEM: Sound Theology & Healthy Missiology

ROOT SYSTEM ➡ SEED BED ➡

Chapter 8
Seed Bed: Incarnational Presence

Incarnational witness is the source of the church's strength.
                                        --Mark Gornik (2002, p. 168)

*We must return to the pattern of Jesus, who chose non-destitute
poverty as a way of life, who took the time to learn language
and culture and who refused to be the welfare agency king.*
                                        --Viv Grigg (1997, p. 160)

A few years ago, for the first time in my life, I started gardening.
There was a small plot of land behind our house that was a dumping
ground for construction materials and had become a gnarly
combination of corrugated tin, broken tiles, trash, and tenaciously
twisted vines. I was absolutely drenched with sweat by the time I
cleared the land and began to dig holes for some plants we bought at a
nursery. My effort with a shovel was slow and tedious because the
ground was thick, solid, orange clay. Novice that I was, I dug a place just
large enough for the plant, packed some soil on top, watered, and
thought: "Voila, I started a garden!" Those of you who have spent time
gardening know my self-satisfied smugness was misplaced. I soon
realized those plants could not thrive in such densely packed clay. I
learned that it takes time working with the soil before it can be a place
that will foster growth and fruitfulness. In order to cultivate a garden I

needed to tend to the garden regularly. It would not be enough for me to swoop in periodically, drop some seeds, and leave again and then expect a flourishing garden.

Working with people is a whole lot like working with plants. We cannot cultivate genuine disciples of Jesus from a distance or through a quick, one-hour service once a week. Jesus modeled the importance of being present and walking with his disciples. In this chapter we will look at Jesus humbly taking on human form and the potential applications of his incarnation for ministering in the city.

The Form of God Taking the Form of a Servant

Jesus gave up a number of the benefits of being divine in order to demonstrate a love that is incomprehensible to us. Philippians 2:5-11 powerfully describes this move of Jesus who emptied himself in order to become a servant in the midst of humanity. Even if Jesus had incarnated as the wealthiest, most honored and extolled human on earth, it still would have been an unrivaled act of humility. But he chose to be born into poverty. Jesus takes this move further by being born in an animal stall, being subjected to the life of a refugee during his childhood, and taking up a working class vocation as a carpenter. Jesus really became one of us!

The astounding reality that God became human profoundly impacts theology, not only in a cognitive sense, but by dictating our missiological theology. One significant way in which the incarnation informs our theology is that it demonstrates to us that God interacts relationally with humanity. Graham Cole draws on the Athanasian Creed to say that the incarnation assumes the humanity into God.[1] God overcomes barriers between himself and humanity through incarnational presence. This move of God confirms the essential value

---

[1] This is the relevant excerpt of the Athanasian Creed: "Who although he is God and Man; yet he is not two, but one Christ. One; not by conversion of the Godhead into flesh; but by assumption of the Manhood by God." (Cole, 2013, p. 146)

of the material world and its potential for renewal. Ultimately, this overcoming of the barrier between humanity and God required the incarnate Christ to die in our stead so that we might have a more abundant life than what we knew was possible.

Imitation of Jesus

Struck by a new awareness of the dark realities of entrenched poverty and sin-induced despair in the slums of Bangkok, Ash Barker and his family moved from Melbourne, Australia to the Klong Tuey slum in Bangkok, Thailand. He did this knowing that ministering from outside the slum would do little to bring real change to the community. Although this might seem radical to many Christians, the Barkers knew it was nothing compared to what Christ gave up to become human and take up residence with us (Jn 1:14). The Barkers are not the only ones to have pursued mission in this way. Several organizations have adopted this approach. In Chapter 3, we described the "new friars" as those who have intentionally incorporated incarnational presence as elemental to their missions approach. Practitioners of this approach operate with the conviction that the best way to reach the urban poor is by living among them at their socio-economic level (For more on incarnational missiology, see: Barker, 2012; Langmead, 2004). One pioneer of this approach in our day is Viv Grigg (1997). He distinguishes the incarnational approach from the typical development worker: "We must return to the pattern of Jesus, who chose non-destitute poverty as a way of life, who took the time to learn language and culture and who refused to be the welfare agency king" (p. 160). Recognizing the bent towards a consumeristic lifestyle, Grigg even specifies the full list of belongings a single person might need to live among the poor in the slums (Grigg, 2004b, pp. 136–137).

The passage in Philippians 2, referred to earlier, appears in the context of human relationships. Paul calls on Christians to adopt the same mindset that moved Jesus to empty himself in order to become a servant among us. We are compelled to love others, serve others, and even to esteem others over ourselves (Phil. 2:3; Rom. 13:8; Gal. 5:13).[2] And Paul draws on the incarnation as the example and motivation for doing so.

In John 20:21, Jesus calls his disciples to be sent out in the same way that the Father sent him. Jesus intended for his disciples to imitate his acts of servitude and humility and his words of witness to God's glory. Philippians 2 tells of Jesus becoming a servant and the gospel accounts portray his doing so. When Jesus washed the disciples' feet in the manner of a bondservant, he clearly commanded his disciples to follow his example (Jn. 13:14-17). The incarnation of Jesus provides a lifestyle pattern that we are called to imitate.

Limitation of our Incarnational Work

In the midst of the hippy movement in San Francisco, Episcopal bishop James Pike's son committed suicide. Pike claimed to have communicated with his dead son in a séance. Here is Pike's rationale for the séance: "If Christ was resurrected, then we are all resurrected. If Christ talked to his disciples after his death, then why can't we do the same?" (Talbot, 2012, p. 43). This example demonstrates how we can overstep our theology of the incarnation by taking on the unique role of the Son of God incarnate. Extreme examples like this one along with the misuse of Scripture have caused some theologians to dismiss any use of the word "incarnational" in describing missions practice (Köstenberger, 1998). Others have pitted the model of Jesus against the model of Paul (Hesselgrave, 2005, pp. 141–165). Validation of incarnational ministry largely depends on the ways it is defined and practiced. Ash Barker has noted the different ways the concept has been appropriated for ministry (Figure 8.1). If the incarnation is understood as a continuation of Christ's incarnational presence in a place, the implication might be that mere physical presence in a community is

---

[2] The New Testament is laced with dozens of these "one another" (*allelon*) imperatives that instruct the social interactions of Christians.

transformative. Others simply adopt the pattern Jesus used as a way to enter a community. One can see the danger of being unclear about incarnational missiology.

	Method or Model for	Motif Informs and Inspires	Value as Part of	No Relevance
Key ideas and uses of incarnational metaphor in mission	Relocation, identification, movement starting, church, devotional imitation, friendship evangelism, simple lifestyle, contextualization, political liberation	Enfleshing hope, following Jesus as a pattern for mission, participating in Christ's risen presence as the power of mission, joining God's cosmic mission of enfleshment in creation	One stream to help spiritualise, one aspect of humanising, one sign for postmodern missional paradigm, one value in missional organization	Rejecting the flesh, only God can enflesh
Metaphor used...	More literally	Middle way	More figurative	Not used in Mission
Some aspects of this view can be in the writings of...	V. Grigg, A. Hirsch, M. Frost, J. Perkins, J. Hayes, D. Harris, D. Andrews, M. Duncan, R. Warren, J. Stott, C. Sheldon, Francis of Assisi, Mother Teresa, J. Rayburn, Romero, C. Boff, R. Sider, J. Bonk, J. Sobrino	D. Bonhoeffer, NT Wright, J. Moltmann, R. Langmead, A. Root	W. Wink, M. Borg, D. Bosch, R. Foster, Emerging Church, New Friars	D. Hesselgrave, W. Simson, K. Kostenburger, K. Baker, T. Chester, R. Fung

Figure 8.1: Spectrum of Four Possible Understandings of an Incarnational Approach to Slum Transformation (Barker, 2012, p. 127)

Two interrelated points might help bring clarity to a healthy theological perspective on the issue. First, the incarnation of Jesus is unique and unrepeatable. Even though we are called to imitate Christ, there should never be confusion about who Christ is. We always point others to Jesus as the Christ and not to ourselves. Second, we are called to be witnesses to Jesus. Though we imitate a pattern of Jesus' servant ministry, our actions must be accompanied by words of gospel proclamation. In other words, in the incarnation we are given a pattern for missional entry to a neighborhood, but remain a witness of the incarnated Son of God. Our imitation of Christ has limitations, but it does not mean we give up on incarnational presence altogether. We still follow the pattern of Jesus in humble presence in our cities.

Incarnational Presence in the City

Urban ministry practitioners are nearly united regarding the need to be physically present in the neighborhoods we serve. There is widespread agreement that incarnational presence in the city is a vital step in urban transformation. Even when incarnational terminology is not used, presence is a value.[3] John Perkins (1982) says "Jesus… didn't commute to Earth one day a week and shoot back up to heaven. He left His throne and became one of us so that we might see the life of God revealed in Him…. The incarnation is the ultimate relocation" (p. 92). So much of urban life is so impersonal that city dwellers build up immunity to all of the marketing and hype. Personal interaction is still the key to changing the lives of individuals and their communities and has greater impact when context and circumstances are shared. Good discipleship starts with being present with the people who are being discipled (Ortiz, 1992, p. 87). Incarnational presence can lead to transformation (Edwards, 2008, p. 97).

Incarnational presence is not the end-all of urban ministry, but it is an important first step of service. "As a servant, the degree of involvement and the place of leadership must be determined, not by the sending agency, nor by one's own insistence, but rather by those being served" (Cheyne, 1996, p. 71). Programs and methods will not change a city, cities need people living out the gospel in every neighborhood (Hammond & Overstreet, 2011, p. 106).

The call to incarnational presence applies to churches as well as individuals. Churches can operate all of their programs without ever

---

[3] For example, John Piper has placed a value on inner city proximity for all of the staff at Bethlehem Baptist Church since he began as pastor in 1980, although he does not use incarnational terminology. (Piper, n.d.)

becoming a part of the neighborhood (Davey, 2002, p. 37). However, the presence of churches is needed in local urban communities so they can minister effectively in the context of the congregants (Georgi, 2005, p. 348). Brad Smith (2008) ties incarnational presence with the importance of place: "There is a 'theology of place.' God calls us to a place to be present; totally immersed as His agent of transforming presence" (p. 127). The call to love our neighbors can be applied not only to the lives of individual Christians but to the whole church (Kauffman, 1994).

Being Agents of Change in the City

Our neighbor, Anastasia,[4] was a foreigner from Central Asia. While her husband worked, she was at home with her two small children in a strange, Southeast Asian city and no friends to speak of. All that Anastasia knew of her neighborhood and city came through negative news reports of crime and corruption. She lived alone and afraid until one day my gregarious wife befriended her. By the time we moved away from the city they were good friends, and we had come to realize that Anastasia's situation was no exception. Our neighborhood was full of people who were living disconnected, isolated lives even while residing in close proximity to others.

The isolation problem is further exacerbated by our tendency to be conditioned by the norms. The urban social norm is not to talk to the people we pass on the sidewalk, ride the elevator with, or buy our groceries from. We assume other people do not want to talk to us. Contrary to our assumptions, a recent study of subway riders showed people very willing to talk to strangers (North, 2014). But the key is that someone has to go against social norms and start up conversations. Once this happens, friendships are sparked and conviviality breaks out on the train (or sidewalk or elevator).

---

[4] Her name is changed to respect her identity.

It is natural for a neighborhood to feel cold and detached. Just as some of the effects of urbanization have spread to the village, so too the effects of suburban living have crept in on urban life. Life has become privatized to the point that two people eating lunch together may each be engaged in their own private pixelated world on smart phones. The result is minimal social interactions with neighbors.

Urban transformation requires individuals and groups who take the initial impetus in leading a movement of change. Without the presence of change agents pushing for transformation, cities move toward decline. Change does not happen automatically and without individual initiative. In other words, transformation happens through individuals who intentionally seek to make changes (Rogers, 1995, p. 369; Schaller, 1989, pp. 11–12).

An understanding of the role of change agents is best aided by three observations. First, transformation requires the injection of new ideas by individuals (Lingenfelter, 1996, p. 270). Second, and related to the first observation, the introduction of new ideas into a community also includes a challenge to the incumbent ideas (Lingenfelter, 1996, p. 273). This challenge is not necessarily hostile, but it does mean older ideas are replaced by newer ideas. Mac Pier (2008) notes the importance of leaders who see the need for change: "Leaders are discontent with the spiritual and social conditions of the world and order their priorities accordingly" (p. 34). Third, an army of change agents is not necessary to bring about change. Jane Jacobs (1993) has observed: "It takes surprisingly few hop-skip people, relative to a whole population, to weld a district into a real thing" (p. 175).

Different models of urban transformation feature different types of change agents. Robert Linthicum (1997) advocates for a community organizer who will develop networks in the community so as to empower them to have a voice on matters pertaining to their neighborhood. More about this process will be described in Chapter 11. In communities where there is minimal or no church presence, there is a need for Christian men and women to enter the communities as catalysts for movements of new churches. Outsiders to the community are needed as trailblazers in frontier territories. Grigg (2004b) sees this calling as comparable to the Irish *perigrini* ("exiles") monks whose sacrificial journeys throughout Europe were vital for the conversion of northern Europe and mirrored Paul's practice of starting new churches in the Mediterranean Basin. The goal is to establish self-sustainable and self-perpetuating churches that can introduce change to the whole community.

As churches are established in a city, they become change agents. Collectively and individually, the presence of the church is that of servant and prophet. The church actively serves the needs of the community because they embody the ultimate example of a servant, Jesus. But the church also plays a prophetic role by advocating for the poor and marginalized and calling on reform. These acts will combine to change society. In defense of this point, Tim Keller (1997) says, "The church's work of transformation and even relief will certainly change social structures.... If a ministry lifts up the poor in a community, it will drastically alter the order of things. Therefore it is mistaken to say that the church should not be seeking to change the shape of society" (p. 189). But the church must always remember that its first priority is to serve and represent Jesus Christ. As this is the case, the church is better off letting individual Christians and parachurch ministries become more vocal on issues of public policy, while the church equips Christians to think through these complex issues biblically. Even though the church exists for the community, it is ultimately in existence for God. As the people of God, however, the church needs to develop a vision for its entire community (Keller, 1997, p. 191).

Even though Linthicum, Keller, and Grigg use different terminology for change agents, they agree that change agents are needed and should not succumb to common approaches to wield power and influence. Over the centuries, the church has been tempted to use power in traditional ways (e.g. with wealth, by coercion, or through political machinations). This is not the way of the gospel. God's power is manifested through weakness (1 Cor. 1:26-31; 2 Cor. 12:9). Christian change agents are best thought of as catalysts for change as God uses our service, devotion to the ways of God, and witness to the transforming gospel of Jesus Christ.

Catalytic Presence in the City

Real urban impact will not happen unless there is a commitment to be present in a particular community. Jesus did not telecommute from heaven, he came to dwell among us. But being present is not enough on its own. Solidarity with the poor and oppressed has its place, but Christians must go beyond mere presence and become change agents. This is our vocation in neighborhoods throughout the city.

Questions for reflection and discussion:

1. What does it mean for the Church to have an "incarnational presence"?
2. Do you feel that you are able to have an incarnational presence in your current context? If not, what would need to change so that you could?
3. Does your church have an intentional incarnational presence in your city? What are some ways your church improve in this area?

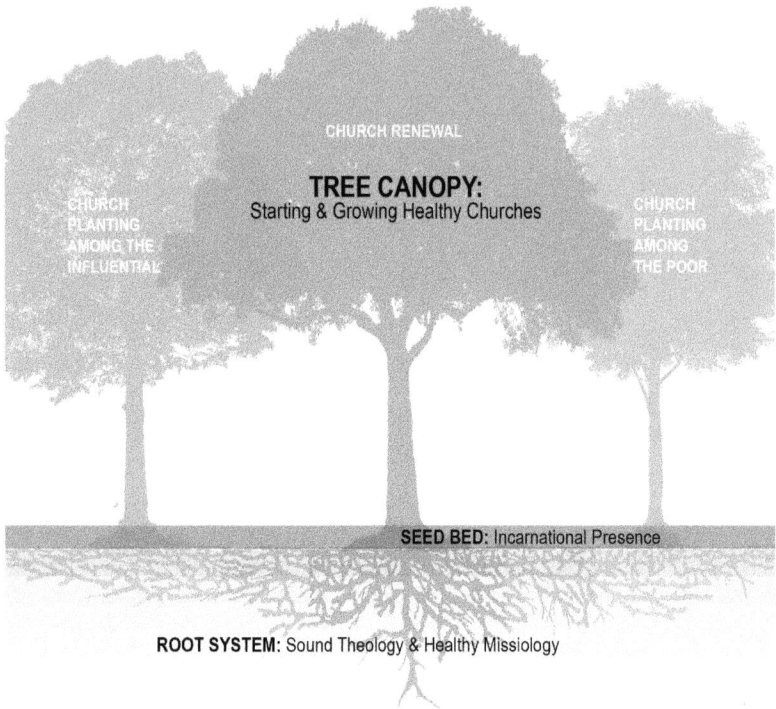

CHURCH RENEWAL

TREE CANOPY:
Starting & Growing Healthy Churches

CHURCH
PLANTING
AMONG THE
INFLUENTIAL

CHURCH
PLANTING
AMONG
THE POOR

SEED BED: Incarnational Presence

ROOT SYSTEM: Sound Theology & Healthy Missiology

ROOT SYSTEM ➡ SEED BED ➡ TREE CANOPY ➡

Chapter 9
Tree Canopy: Starting and Growing Healthy Churches

The planting and development of compassionate churches in every part of the city must be the long-term goal. This is the most effective solution to the multiple ills of the urban community.

--Roger Greenway (2000, p. 77)

In the city, a great many congregations are needed to reach all the people.

--Paul Hiebert and Eloise Hiebert Meneses (1995, p. 341)

The tree canopy supports a host of interdependent organisms. The sloth makes its home in the branches of the canopy, touching the forest floor only once a week. Each sloth is home to its own ecosystem of algae, fungi, and insects that are entirely dependent on these odd-looking, long-toed creatures who hang from high tree branches almost all of the time. One researcher discovered 950 beetles living on just one sloth. All of this life found on the body of a sloth is only possible with the presence of big leafy trees that provide a home for sloths and the plethora of life forms that depend on sloths for sustenance. Many of the most beautiful and exotic birds also find their homes in the canopies formed by trees. When trees are cut down, the survival of these birds and sloths and countless other species are threatened. Trees are the essential building blocks of the teeming ecosystems within the canopy ecosystem.

Likewise, churches ought to function as city ecosystem building blocks as they seek transformation in the city. The local church is God's primary unit of discipleship and community for Christians. If the churches are not healthy, it spells trouble for all of the other Christian entities in a city. The survival of schools, clinics, youth groups, tutoring programs, soup kitchens, counseling services, seminaries, Bible studies, choirs, advocacy groups, and workplace fellowships would be threatened if churches ceased to exist. Healthy, gospel-centered churches are critical if cities are to become more like the biblical vision of the New Jerusalem.

Given that churches are imperative to substantive transformation in cities, location-specific diagnosis is needed. Some cities have too few churches to form much of a network. The starting point for an urban missionary there is clearly church planting and evangelistic witness. Other cities have many churches but lack a vision for urban impact. In this instance, it would be more beneficial for Christian leaders to dream together as they seek the good of their city. Or perhaps it is discovered that the middle and upper-classes are well-served by the churches of a city, yet poorer communities have very few churches. This scenario calls for church planting from the bottom-up. A study of your city can help you discern the best starting point to initiate change.

Starting New Churches in the City

When I first began college studies in Birmingham, Alabama, I was overwhelmed by the choices of churches I could attend. I noticed a number of churches bearing the names of streets in downtown Birmingham that were nowhere near those streets. These churches had moved from urban Birmingham to suburban Birmingham and took their stained glass windows with them. Of course there were a lot of dynamics leading to the decision to move which we will not explore here, but the result was that the city of Birmingham was gutted of its church presence. This urban exodus happened all over the United States, and the urban cores of cities became inhospitable locations. The causes for urban deterioration are manifold and complex and certainly not solely the fault of the Church, but the Church missed an opportunity to buck the trend by serving in the midst of this difficult transition.

The Church needs to be everywhere there are people. But churches do not simply materialize. Churches need to be started in every kind of neighborhood and among every kind of people. It is not workable to simply add people to our existing churches. When Starbucks was surging in growth in the 1990s, I remember walking around Union Square in downtown San Francisco. In the eight blocks surrounding Union Square, we counted at least nine Starbucks (not to mention all of the other places one could buy a cup of coffee). If Starbucks operated like many churches do, they would have just expanded one location until it was nearly the size of the block. But Starbucks knew they needed to be everywhere there are people.

Churches have lifecycles. They grow when they are young, ideally they reproduce, and eventually become stagnant and die. This calls for the continuous planting of new churches in our cities. New churches are able to attract more non-Christians and are more able to be innovative and adaptive to reach their community (Keller, 2008a, p. 5; Murray, 2001, p. 45). Tim Keller (2008a) says "...the only way to significantly increase overall the number of Christians in a city is by significantly increasing the number of new churches" (p. 6).

Church planting is not only about adding to the number of church attendees quantitatively. The process of church planting also brings a qualitative benefit. Our understanding of what the church is and what it does is refreshed in the process of starting new churches (Chester, 2000, p. 25). The start of new churches allows for innovation and contextualization of church practices in constantly changing cities. New churches have the freedom to try new things. It is very difficult for older churches to change the ways they do things. In this way, new church plants become the "Research and Development Department" for the whole Church of the city (Keller, 2008a, p. 7). Church planting also provides the opportunity for younger Christians to grow as leaders and take ownership of reaching their generation (Murray, 1990, p. 138).

The New Testament offers a pattern of prioritizing the establishment of churches in the cities of the Roman Empire. Even when Paul was chased out of several cities in Acts 13 and 14, he returned to those same cities to encourage disciples and help establish leadership in the churches there (Acts 14:21-23). These churches were neither accidental nor incidental. Paul and Barnabas ministered in these cities with church planting as an immediate goal.

The presence of the church introduces into the city a foretaste of a transformed community and a signpost to the God who transforms. Melba Maggay (2004) says, "The church in the world, while historically ambiguous, at its best has, through the centuries, served as leaven, permeating and transforming the social order" (p. 19). Strong, sustainable, gospel-driven urban churches are essential to true transformation of the city. Keller and Thompson (2002) unequivocally affirm the need for church planting:

> The vigorous, continual planting of new congregations is the single most crucial strategy for 1) the numerical growth of the Body of Christ in any city, and 2) the continual corporate renewal and revival of the existing churches in a city. Nothing else—not crusades, outreach programs, para-church ministries, growing mega-churches, congregational consulting, nor church renewal processes—will have the consistent impact of dynamic, extensive church planting (p. 29).

These churches should grow out of the roots of theological and missiological vision.

While many are in agreement about the need for starting new churches in our cities, not everyone is agreed on the place to start. Some advocates call for starting in the center of the city among urban professionals and those who are positioned to be the thought and culture leaders of the city. Others urge a grassroots approach for the church to start with the urban poor and marginalized in a city. Each of those approaches will be explored here.

Top-down Church Planting

Redeemer Presbyterian Church started meeting in an apartment with fifteen people in 1989 (Pier, 2008, p. 140). That same year, they began a public service. Tim Keller and the church-starting team intentionally started with a group of recent believers who were actively sharing their faith. Having researched Manhattan thoroughly, he knew that the church would need to look and feel different if they were going to attract the core population of Manhattan. He says, "We also happily noted that many long-time evangelicals had stayed away from us" (Keller & Thompson, 2002, p. 15). They committed to doing church with nonbelievers in mind but maintaining rigorous exposition of the Bible. Within the year they were offering two services and soon added a third in order to meet the need for options for busy Manhattanites. The church was mostly composed of members who could walk to the church, 85 percent of whom were single (Keller, 1993, p. 37). The uniqueness of the context led Redeemer's leadership to emphasize cell groups as the primary structure for pastoral care and discipleship (Keller & Thompson, 2002, p. 16). These groups became the "nerve system" of the church, providing intense community for transient urban dwellers (Perkins, 1995a, p. 152). The church continued to grow steadily, mostly through reaching nominal Christians and non-Christians. Redeemer adapted their structures according to the people of their community. Keller and the staff of Redeemer recognize that cities continue to change and that a vibrant urban church must continue to research the city and adapt to changes (Keller, 1993, pp. 40–41).

From the very start they wanted to be a movement rather than just a church (Keller & Thompson, 2002, p. 18). With this as a part of their core vision they endeavored to launch more worship sites and churches. They began to start churches in New York and New Jersey. Keller and others at Redeemer recognized that global cities share certain characteristics; therefore, they can help church planters in these contexts (Luo, 2006). In order to expand beyond the two states, they developed the Redeemer City to City network for the purpose of assisting in starting churches in global cities around the world. They have assisted in seeing over one hundred churches started in global cities such as San Francisco, Boston, Paris, and London (Pier, 2008, p. 146). They have also prioritized mercy ministries in their city. Instead of starting ministries from scratch, Redeemer has chosen to come alongside existing ministries in New York by providing a volunteer force and other resources (Perkins, 1995a, p. 156). Redeemer Presbyterian Church has been at the forefront of church planting efforts in global cities and continues to come alongside mercy ministries for the holistic engagement of New York City. They have established regional networks of churches around the world that share a commitment to being gospel-centered.

Keller's model emphasizes the importance of starting a church at the cultural center of the city. Although there are risks and it is investment-heavy, it can prove to be a strong foothold in the city.[1] Once a church is established in the heart of the city, then it is strategic to plant churches throughout the city from the initial one (Kubiak, 2009). The Apostle Paul went into the Mediterranean cities and reached many of the influential and elite of Roman society (Aghamkar, 2000, p. 19). In the case of Keller's church and other churches in the same network, the church at the cultural center has a lot of members who eventually

---

[1] Schaller draws a comparison between the "high performance" city center churches and the three-self ideals promulgated by missionary statesmen Henry Venn and Rufus Anderson. (Schaller, 1993, p. 14)

move to other parts of the city that are more sustainable for families.[2] The kinds of people that a "center church" can draw are often educated, financially-stable, and influential. The church can gain stability quickly and then have a wide impact on the whole city.[3] A church at the center of the city is strategically positioned to launch a movement of churches and ministries that can impact the whole city region.[4]

We have many examples of this top-down approach throughout missions history. Missionaries of the past have opted to begin by sharing the gospel first with tribal chiefs or royalty. When these leaders give approval to the gospel message, the rest of society is more willing to hear it. People have a tendency to allow others they esteem to be gatekeepers of truth. Milan and New York have become gatekeepers for the fashion industry, setting the standard for each season. Trends from the city's influential people will become trends all over the city. If the church takes root among those deemed influential in the city, their influence becomes a vehicle for the spread of the gospel to the rest of the city and beyond.

Starting churches at the city center is a great beginning, but it is not enough on its own. It has proven difficult for wealthier churches to minister to the poor. Even though Redeemer Presbyterian Church wants to start churches among the poor, they have struggled to do so effectively (Keller, 1993, pp. 31–41) (Cho, 2012). For this reason, there needs to be a simultaneous focus on the marginalized and urban poor, as well as the cultural center of the city.

---

[2] In contrast, Keller says it is rare for churches that start on the periphery of the city to successfully plant churches in the center of the city.

[3] Center or flagship churches only have the influence and impact they have because of the power, centrality, and influence of cities. (Conn & Ortiz, 2001, p. 251)

[4] Urban literature uses a number of different terms to refer to the city region. It acknowledges that the municipal boundaries of a city do not accurately define the broader metropolitan area that functions as a whole. Although technical definitions exist, Richard Florida defines the city region as "somewhere you can walk all the way across, from one side to the other, carrying nothing but some money without ever getting thirsty or hungry." (Florida, 2008, p. 47)

Bottom-up Church Planting

Viv Grigg has served God by going to the slums of some of the largest cities in the world and prophetically calling the Church to minister among the neglected millions of slum-dwellers. Grigg began serving in ministry in 1969 and has continued in urban-focused ministry and training to the present ("Introducing Viv Grigg" n.d.). His incarnational ministry began in Manila, Philippines, when he realized the presence of many missionaries and churches in the large city but a noticeable void among the considerable population of slum-dwellers. He describes his discovery:

> More nightmarish than the poverty and the staggering growth of that poverty is to find no more than a handful of God's men and God's women ministering among these poor in each city.
>
> I do not mean that there are no relief and development agencies. They are many, and most of them are doing good work in their roles as diaconal agencies of the church. *But the church has given bread to the poor and has kept the bread of life for the middle class* (Grigg, 2004b, p. 12).

As a young, single man he moved into one of Manila's slums and was instrumental in starting a church there. Grigg (1997) charges, "The greatest mission surge in history has entirely missed the greatest migration in history, the migration of Third World rural peasants to great mega-cities" (p. 151). Grigg notes the paucity of churches in the slums of megacities as compared with the number of churches among the middle and upper classes (Grigg, 2004b, p. 96). This reality is troubling for Grigg because he sees the potential harvest among the poor: "The migrant poor are the largest, most responsive group on earth today" (Grigg, 1997, p. 151). He considers the urban poor to be an unreached people group. For Grigg, it is a tragedy that millions of the urban poor have been underserved by missionaries and church planters. Timothy Monsma surmises that Grigg's holistic approach to church planting among the urban poor is effective and that it teaches us that when Christian witness and economic help are combined, lives are improved (Greenway & Monsma, 2000, p. 159).

Grigg's starting point is the opposite of Keller's. Grigg believes it is best to start with the urban poor because they are more receptive to the gospel. He also believes that the movement will spread from the urban poor to the whole city because those changed by the gospel will move up the socio-economic ladder, thus impacting the whole city. Grigg is primarily concerned that the poor are underserved with the gospel (Grigg, 2004b, p. 114).

> Establishing the church is the primary objective in developmental activity for those committed to the Scriptures. Kingdom perspectives see the development of the spiritual kingdom as the central element of societal transformation. Economic, social and political development are an outgrowth of this spiritual development. They are important, but not central nor primary (Grigg, 1992, p. 335).

Estimations show that one out of every six people in the world is a slum dweller, but only one of every five hundred missionaries serves in the slums. Even fewer (1/10,000) local Christian leaders (like pastors) work in the slums.[5] Many missionaries and church planters are from financially privileged socioeconomic backgrounds. They therefore more naturally gravitate towards people like themselves, leaving the poor without an incarnational witness to the gospel.

Although there are many challenges to the planting of stable churches among populations that have known very little stability, the urban poor are a rising percentage of city-dwellers and are in desperate need of the gospel (Barker, 2012, pp. 109–112). Church planting among the poor will necessarily look different than church planting among wealthier classes. Methods and models need to be adapted according to

---

[5] The authors of this study further state that even fewer of those who do work with slum dwellers live among them. (Bellofatto & Johnson, 2013, p. 164)

level of education, decision-making culture, and types of interaction (Uken, 1992, p. 181). This adaptation will require a healthy process of critical contextualization so that the seed of the gospel can be planted among the urban poor (P. G. Hiebert, 1987). A model that does not effectively plant the gospel among the urban poor will result in the neglect of a large portion of the urban population. And when the urban poor are neglected, the whole model of transformation is rendered incomplete.[6]

There is no attempt here to pit the top-down approach against the bottom-up approach. Both are needed and each is ineffective at reaching the whole city by itself. The methods used to reach educated, upwardly mobile metropolitans will naturally differ considerably from the methods used with working class urban dwellers. These are not intended to be static and isolated strategies; wealthy churches should always try to reach out to the poor, and poorer churches should always try to reach out to the rich. While there are some churches that are trying to bring multiple socioeconomic groups together in one church, most often a church draws more readily from one group or the other.

Revitalizing Churches in the City

In addition to church planting, Viv Grigg and Tim Keller both stress the importance of church renewal.[7] The Apostle Paul also spent time strengthening churches in the cities he visited (Acts 14:22; 15:41). There is a tendency for urban churches to become parochial by closing themselves off from the rest of the city (Bakke, 2002, p. 35; Linthicum,

---

[6] The whole city suffers when one segment of the city suffers. A neglected community can have a negative impact on the whole city by draining municipal services or increasing the threat to security. By engaging every socioeconomic class with the gospel, the door is opened to reconciliation and solutions to transformation that involve the whole city. (D. W. Smith, 2001, pp. 229–231)

[7] The work of church strengthening comes under a number of different names (church growth, church revitalization, etc.). Keller and Grigg both use terminology that acknowledges the Holy Spirit's role in restoring churches to vibrancy. (Grigg, 2009, p. 156; Keller, 2012, p. 361)

1997, p. 170). A renewing through the work of the Spirit can breathe new life into older congregations. However, it is possible for a church to undergo spiritual renewal and yet remain aloof from their urban context. As churches experience renewal, they will need to learn how to engage the city by experiencing fresh expressions of the theological vision for the church's missional purpose in the city (Dennison, 1999, p. 118). The needs and the vernacular of the city are constantly changing. Urban churches need to continually adapt their language and their ministries in order to impact the city with the gospel.

Revitalizing Struggling Churches

Walter Williams was pronounced dead around 9pm on Wednesday, February 25, 2014 in Lexington, Mississippi. The 78 year old man was put into a body bag and sent to the funeral home. When Williams was on the embalming table, those preparing to embalm him noticed his feet kicking. Soon after, the once-pulseless Williams was breathing (McLaughlin, 2014). Sometimes that which appears to be dead still has life.

Most cities already have a Christian presence of some kind.[8] However, we may be deceived into thinking this presence is stronger than it actually is because we see church buildings everywhere. Many of these buildings have only a remnant congregation struggling to maintain the facility. Meanwhile, other church buildings have been sold off and serve other purposes. I've seen church buildings become a grocery store, skater store, and even a mosque. My friend JB went to pastor a struggling church inside the Atlanta urban perimeter. The previous pastor thought the church's death was a foregone conclusion and was preparing for its funeral. There are many reasons urban churches began to decline (e.g. scandal or division in the church, changing demographics of the community, or failure of the church to

---

[8] Even in most Muslim nations closed to the gospel, there is often a small, beleaguered church presence in the cities.

adapt to changing times), but no matter the reason, many churches seem to have lost their way and are already picking out funeral flowers. JB, however, found a small yet resilient congregation that was not ready to die yet.

JB and others have taken up the call to lead such struggling churches through revitalization. A few years ago this notion was met with cynical pessimism and statements like "It is easier to give birth to a baby than raise the dead." It has since been discovered that many older, struggling urban churches are worth revitalizing for several reasons. First, these churches still have pockets of believers already embedded in urban communities. Second, these churches are established in strategic places in our cities, places that are now being repopulated and revitalized. Third, these churches have great facilities that would be enormously expensive to replace. It is a matter of churches recapturing their mission as well as being willing to change in order to accomplish it.

In some cases churches have been going through the motions so long that the purpose of the church is forgotten. When this happens, missional priorities are replaced by institutional priorities. Such churches need leaders who will help the church understand their diagnosis and submit to a kind of relaunch of the church (Hanbury, 2014). At the center of this is a renewed emphasis on the gospel understood through expository preaching and teaching. An older member of a revitalizing church respond to this renewal by saying "so this is what the church is really supposed to be... I have faint memory of this kind of church from my childhood."

In Oakland, California, Rockridge United Methodist Church was destined for death and all thirteen members had accepted this fate except one older lady. She had a dream that the church was supposed keep going and grow to 45 members. Her prophetic dream compelled the church to make significant changes:

> Instead of focusing on death, they would need to focus on
> Jesus Christ as the giver of new life. Instead of a primary

ministry of compassion for the few surviving members, they would need to focus on telling the good news of Jesus Christ in their community. Instead of preaching the Scriptures as a source [of] comfort to the faithful remnant, they would need to proclaim God's call for the remnant to spread the gospel to those in their community who were poor in spirit as well as in fact (L. Y. Barrett et al., 2004, p. 16).

This church took stock of their assets and discovered a wealth of retirees with time at their disposal. In addition to prayer and Bible study, the church began to offer tutoring to underprivileged children in the neighborhood (Branson, 2003). Although some members continued to oppose these changes, the church grew in numbers and vibrancy.

Ongoing Renewal Dynamics

Times of spiritual renewal should spark ongoing changes that spill into every aspect of life. Unfortunately, many revivals have come and gone without effecting much long-term change. Often, revivals can be an emotionally thrilling experience for people, but without a plan for ongoing spiritual growth, the emotional high often falls flat.[9] In order to capitalize on the initial surge produced by a revival, new Christians need discipleship that helps them integrate the whole gospel into every aspect of their lives (Smith, p. 141-148).[10] Keller (2012) says, "We need to continually renew the spiritual remembrance of our salvation" (p. 58). Grigg suggests revivals can lead to long-term change through the development of intentional structures that encourage widespread

---

[9] Throughout history there have been revivals that have been truncated by a failure to develop structures and theological understanding that helps people move beyond the initial experience. (Pierson, 2009)

[10] David Smith observes Paul combating a Roman imperial ideology that is entirely different from the message of the gospel. Paul's letters served to help people internalize and assimilate the gospel into their lives. Smith, *Seeking a City with Foundations: Theology for an Urban World*, 222.

changes that impact the city as a whole (Grigg, 2009, p. 163). Ongoing renewal ensures the churches remain healthy and growing.

In order for a church's renewal dynamics to have multiplicative changes in a city, renewal cannot be considered in only spiritual categories. Isaiah 58 unequivocally challenges the common error of God's people to consider spiritual activities like prayer and fasting as enough to please God. This Scripture teaches that a right relationship with God must also include the fair treatment of employees and concern for the poor. Today in our churches we have allowed spiritual activities alone to pass for godly living. Churches need to be proactive in considering the ways the gospel that changes our hearts of stone also changes churches' collective impact on their city.

For those involved in specialized ministries in the city, it is important to relate to churches through awareness and education. Church members will naturally hold stereotypes gained from media and pop culture unless we help reorient understanding. For example, a ministry to sex workers may hope to help former sex workers find a church home. Ministry leaders will need to help the church understand how to welcome and disciple a former sex worker without making the person feel ostracized. The work of the urban church calls for deliberate adaptation of methods in conformity with the gospel.

Missional Postures for the Urban Church

The more urban the environment, the more competitive the atmosphere. For example, a restaurant in a world class city has to serve excellent food and market it well or it will go bankrupt, while in a small town a restaurant has fewer competitors and can get by with less effort. In the same way, worldviews are highly contested in a city. Urban dwellers have too many options of religious or ideological communities to simply attend a church casually. If a church is not intentionally engaging the people of the city with the gospel in word and in action, it will struggle for survival. The following suggestions are merely an initial foray into the ways in which an urban church should be missionally engaged with the city.

Seeking Shalom for All. The urban church should do all that it can to seek the shalom (full flourishing) of the whole city. This means the church should be available to all people in a city. At times, some churches give the impression that they are primarily for a particular ethnic group or socioeconomic class. This might be due to the congregational make up or it could be the issues addressed publicly. A church in a wealthy neighborhood of the city must resist the temptation to address only the problems of its own community. The church should use their resources to help in areas that have minimal church presence. Even when the church disagrees with the majority culture over a number of issues, it should always have and act out of love for the city.

Bridging Into the Community. One way for a church to seek the shalom of the city is by bridging into the community. One friend who consults with urban churches will walk the blocks immediately surrounding the church building and ask people where that church is located just to see if people in the area know the church or anyone from it. The number of urban churches that are virtually unknown in their own communities is a terrible indictment. We saw in Chapter 4 the advantage that density brings, but we must take advantage of that density. Churches—even active churches—can become so closed in around their own programs and needs that they cease to be a source of light to those all around them. Harvard sociologist, Robert Putnam, has popularized the idea of social capital (mentioned briefly in Chapter 4) (Putnam, 2000). Social capital is the glue that holds communities together. If the church is not part of that social glue, then the community may wonder if the church has any value at all.

There are two kinds of social capital; bonding social capital and bridging social capital (Hern, 2010, p. 90). Bonding social capital builds community within an enclosed group. Bridging social capital emphasizes linking others into the community. Evangelical churches have tended to favor bonding social capital over bridging social capital.

Putnam summarizes "…evangelicals are more likely to be involved in activities within their own religious community but are less likely to be involved in the broader community" (Putnam, 2000, pp. 77–78). For a church to make a difference in their community, they need to bridge into the networks and associations of the community and incarnate the gospel. The social capital concept is not inherently transformative; the gospel is. Social capital is simply a vehicle for the gospel to take root.

Urban Expression of the Church. The city changes the ways we process events, think, and relate to others, so churches are not only a force for change in the city, they are changed by the city (Currie, 2013, p. 1373). It stands to reason, then, that urban churches are going to have a different look and feel than non-urban churches. As a result, for example, urban churches need to be more intentional in establishing community: "In a rural society the church does not usually need to provide community, but in the city the church needs to work hard to create a conducive environment in which people can develop relationship" (Hinton, 1985, p. 93). In some ways, this is one area in which the church acts counter-culturally to the urban norms. But it does not mean that the same communal forms are operative in the city. Community will necessarily take on different forms among various urban subcultures. Identity, education, and ways of interacting will necessitate innovative ways of creating space for real fellowship. For example, Setha Low (1999), in her description of global cities, uses the term "the transnational capitalist class" (p. 13). The church in a global city may need to ask, "What does an indigenous 'transnational capitalist class' church look like?"

Urban churches will need to develop patterns of gathering and interaction that fit the rhythms and tendencies of their city. Ray Bakke (1997) notes the ways other institutions adapt to their urban context: "Like supermarkets, hospitals and police departments, churches will require day pastors and night pastors for twenty-four-hour environments in all languages, cultures and class groups, now residing in the same communities" (p. 13). Churches will need to learn how to be available to the people of a city around the clock. As it is today, a passerby of an urban church will most often find its doors closed.

Distinct Community of Christ. It is important for the church to adapt to its urban context, but it must avoid over-adapting. If the church looks exactly like the rest of the city, it fails to bring any change to the city. The Church is not naturally distinct from society, but, through repentance, can become a pioneer model for society. Stassen, Yeager, and Yoder (1995) argue that the Church is not unique in terms of human sinfulness. In their view, it is this common vulnerability that shows the potential of transformation:

> The church is part of society's vain idolatry, a recipient of God's judgment. So Yeager insists: 'the church serves as a model precisely because it is representative of the larger culture, not distinct from it. As a representative of culture, 'it repents for the sin of the whole society and leads in the social act of repentance.' In the wake of the many scandals that have rocked the churches, and in the light of the ideological captivity of much church teaching, the church can hardly be pioneer without leading in the act of repentance (p. 223).

While these authors rightly emphasize our similarity with the rest of the city, they do not point us toward a new society. The church creates a new gathering that is, in fact, distinct. The kingdom ethos should permeate a congregation (Matt. 13:33). The church becomes a city within the city: "As we are to redeem human families by spreading within them the family of God, so we are to redeem human cities by spreading within them the city of God" (Keller & Thompson, 2002, p. 45).

The way a church relates to its surrounding culture is by no means a simple issue. We share in our humanness with the rest of society (Eph. 2:12-13) and yet through identity with Christ, we become like sojourners in a foreign land (Eph. 2:19-20). However, we are not called to be aloof, but rather to do public good as engaged sojourners (1 Pet. 2). Rooy (1992) describes sojourner engagement this way:

> While the church is not absorbed into the city, it takes its place and realizes its function inside the structures of the city. Flight from the city, the place of heightened human encounter, is no longer allowable, unless it is to go to another city to teach all things commanded by the Lord. The church is still a stranger and a pilgrim looking for the Eternal City, the place of perfect communion with God and man. But the new Israel does not abandon the secular city. Instead, it becomes salt and light within urban life (p. 226).

As the Church anticipates the New City, it is an agent of transformation as it embodies and proclaims the gospel throughout the city. If the Church wants to change the city, it needs to be changed by the gospel: "But if the city is to be transformed, the vast majority of congregations that currently exist must undergo congregational transformation which will require spiritual/relational vitality, mastering change and learning again how to learn" (Dennison, 1999, p. 118). There is no other path for true transformation. It begins by turning entirely to Christ and becoming vessels of God's work of transformation in the city.

Conclusion

A network plays a significant role in starting churches strategically in a city. Stuart Murray (2001) notes the network advantage:

> Collaborative church planting is vital if new churches are to be planted in the urban and rural areas where these are most needed. Strategic planning for a city or region enables 'mission priority areas' to be identified and appropriate resources to be allocated. If church planting is left to local churches, these priority areas will continue to be neglected (p. 254).

Eric Swanson (2014) is a widely recognized advocate for churches' proactive involvement in transformation. He believes in the critical importance of starting vibrant churches in the city and understands the need for a culture that encourages church entrepreneurship. Swanson notes the contrast between the number of business entrepreneurs in the city of Boulder, Colorado and the dearth of church planters there. He suggests that we need to collaborate to create an environment for new and creative churches to thrive and have essential supports.

A canopy ecosystem is nothing without strong, life-giving trees creating the environment for an abundance of life. Vibrant, gospel-centered churches in the city provide the base community out of which transformation and mission flow. Building a strong "canopy" of churches requires church planting as well as ongoing church renewal, growing healthy churches in all sectors of society.

Questions for reflection and discussion:

1. What four missional postures does the author propose for churches in urban environments?
2. Which kind of ministry appeals to you most—church planting among the influential, church planting among the poor/marginalized, or church revitalization? How can you leverage your gifts toward that work?
3. Is your church new, revitalizing, or in need of revitalization? Who are the people it is reaching well, and who are the people it could work toward reaching? How might you implement changes to make that possible?

Part 3

Life forms for a Healthy Ecosystem

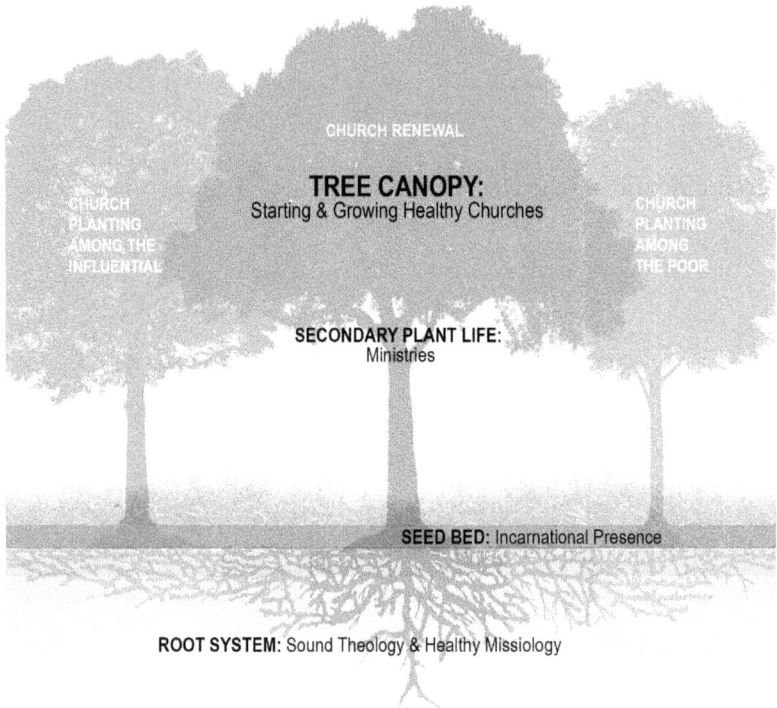

CHURCH RENEWAL

TREE CANOPY:
Starting & Growing Healthy Churches

CHURCH PLANTING AMONG THE INFLUENTIAL

CHURCH PLANTING AMONG THE POOR

SECONDARY PLANT LIFE:
Ministries

SEED BED: Incarnational Presence

ROOT SYSTEM: Sound Theology & Healthy Missiology

ROOT SYSTEM ➡ SEED BED ➡ TREE CANOPY ➡ SECONDARY ➡
PLANT LIFE

Chapter 10
Secondary Plant Life: Ministries

The movement of God's purpose always starts from the particular on its way to the universal.

--Richard Bauckham (2004, p. 47)

The cities of our world will remain largely unreached until and unless the numerous components making up the collective Body of Christ begin to work together.

--Wilbur Stone (2003, p. 86)

I have always enjoyed flying on Thai Airways. They run efficiently and have impeccable service. One added perk of flying with Thai Airways is the free orchid they give to each passenger. It's a pleasant spot of beauty on a long trip through multiple airports. But that experience is nothing compared to the joy of finding a wild orchid growing on a tree deep in the forest. Orchids come in thousands of varieties and are commonly found growing on trees, including high up in the canopy. Orchids not only benefit greatly from this position on trees, but also contribute in important ways to the whole ecosystem. Their existence in a canopy invites various insects and fungi and even helps humidify the air, which contributes to the health of other plants. Orchids are temperamental plants and require precise conditions for their growth and perpetuation. These conditions are so optimal for forest vibrancy that it is said "orchids offer a clear picture of a forest's health" ("Endangered Orchid...").

Like the presence of orchids in the forest, the presence of Christian organizations and ministries in a city can provide a clear picture of the kingdom ecosystem of the city. Just as trees benefit from secondary plant life as they grow symbiotically, churches benefit from other ministries that work in partnership for healthier and more sustainable churches. Throughout the history of the Church, these types of organizations have emerged to focus on specific needs. The city needs organizations that are focused on evangelism, discipleship, community service, and leadership development.

The Particular

When we take a step back to look at the big picture, the need for specific ministries becomes more apparent. Churches are rarely in a position to simultaneously be running ministries for single parents, special needs families, addicts, homeless, elderly, college students, business owners, and multiple language groups. If one church tried all of this it would inevitably neglect many of the ministries and likely burn out staff and volunteers. However, all of these ministries and then some are needed in every city. Therefore, there needs to be an environment that encourages the launch and continuation of these ministries. They are not to be considered a threat to the church. In some cases, a ministry will result in a new church. This is where it is important to maintain a kingdom mindset rather than being obsessed with adding members to one particular church or ministry.

Each ministry in a city develops because there are people who need focused ministry. The reality is there are people who are *not* easily ministered to by existing churches or ministries. Sometimes the isolation is obvious; there may be a large community of resettled refugees from Southeast Asia, for example. Many in the community do not speak English nor are they very well integrated into broader society. This community will likely only be served by a ministry particularly focused on their group. Then there are groups of people that are less obviously disconnected from existing churches or ministries. In my city in Southeast Asia, almost all of the churches worship on Sunday morning. But Sunday morning is also a favorite time for eating beef noodles. For all of those who sell beef noodles, Sunday is their biggest day for business, so they will never attend a church service at that time (no matter how good the music or preaching is). A ministry to these business owners and workers will have to meet at a non-traditional time. Every city has thousands of particular groups who are not naturally served by the mainstream church programs.

Taylor Field has been ministering among the down and out in the Lower East Side of Manhattan for thirty years, creating a ministry called Graffiti. Graffiti has served the homeless, addicts, at-risk children, and others marginalized by mainstream society. Over the years, Field and his colleagues saw spiritual response from their ministry and pulled this rag tag group of believers into a church. To the outsider, this church would appear to be highly dysfunctional. But underneath the arguments, interruptions, and relapses, this band of believers found community and grew as the church. It was always Field's goal to help this small and socially awkward church integrate with a more established Baptist church in midtown. After much effort, it became clear this experiment was not working. The gap between the Graffiti church and the culturally mainstream church was far too wide. He found that these new believers were digressing from any spiritual maturity they had developed through the small church. He realized they needed their own "Sanctuary of Hope."(Field & Kadlecek, 2001, p. 39) In order for this group of Christians to grow, they required a uniquely tailored church and ministry. If our churches try to appeal to everyone, we will surely miss out on remarkable walking testimonies of God's work of transformation like the ones in the church called Graffiti.

The Particular to the Whole

It is never the goal for each ministry to operate in isolation. "Good work in the city always starts with the particular (whether youth, food, housing, or employment) and then moves to the general" (Hillis, 2014, p. 23). This mirrors the God who has consistently chosen the particular in order to accomplish global purposes. New Testament scholar Richard Bauckham has shown that this pattern emerges throughout the Bible. God chose one particular individual in Abraham through whom the nations would be blessed (Bauckham, 2004, pp. 28–35). God's plan of redemption for all of humanity was ignited by calling one individual. In the New Testament, it was a few individuals chosen by Jesus who began the Great Commission movement that was to go to the ends of the earth. Although Jesus was at events with thousands of ready followers (Mt. 14:13-21; 15:32-16:10), it was the few who took the torch to pass on to the ends of the earth.

True and lasting impact in a city only takes hold through ministries that begin with particular people. Generic and broad sweeping approaches will not adequately reach a city. Ray Bakke (2006) notes the importance of focusing on the particular in evangelism: "The bigger the city, the narrower the focus; the more personal and relational evangelism must be. This is the reverse of the way folks think, which is big city, big meetings, and big strategies. But the opposite is true: the bigger the city, the smaller the focus" (p. 135). Cities are inundated with broad-based marketing that builds people's immunity to such approaches. The only way to cut through the incessant, large-scale approaches to persuasion is go small and personal.

When there are thriving ministries across the city impacting all strata of society, it will lead to stronger churches and will benefit other ministries. An effective Christian counseling ministry will help struggling marriages and families thrive. When these families are thriving it will inject life into the local church. When the local church is thriving it can more consistently and competently serve other needs in the city. The city benefits from the combined impact of ministries who are serving particular people.

An Indicator of Health

Just as a thriving orchid can be an indicator of the health of the whole forest ecosystem, a seminary can be one indicator of the health of a kingdom ecosystem in a city. When a local seminary is thriving, it tends to reveal a thriving ecosystem of churches and ministries throughout the city. Healthy churches will raise up new leaders who need seminary training. Ministries and churches that are doing well to proclaim the gospel in word and deed in each particular context indicate the seminary is training people effectively. If seminaries fail to equip well, churches and ministries suffer. When they suffer, the stream of seminary students dries up.

In order to be effective in the city, ministries must constantly assess how well they are engaging society. Urban-based seminaries and churches are often oblivious to their urban surroundings. Ronald Peters (2007) observed this trend: "In reality, churches and seminaries frequently fail to recognize that they are each merely extensions of the other" (p. 6). The idea here is that churches and seminaries can become a closed circuit, which can lead to a failure of critical engagement with the world.

The absence of a local seminary in the city is acutely felt in the ecosystem. Churches and ministries benefit from being able to hire locally trained graduates. Ministries with limited funding can benefit from student interns and student volunteers. An urban seminary also has the capability to offer classes at night and on weekends for bivocational pastors and lay church members. The theological expertise of a seminary is also an invaluable resource when doctrinal controversy emerges or when new ethical concerns arise. Seminaries are by no means the only litmus test for a thriving ecosystem. When an ecosystem is operating optimally, every part of it contributes to the whole, and in a healthy spiritual ecosystem, various types of ministry arise to meet the city's needs.

Questions for reflection and discussion:

1. How do specialized ministries fit in to the spiritual canopy ecosystem?
2. What is your experience with specialized ministries? Have you seen or been part of a successful ministry to a particular subset of your community?
3. Does your church run or partner with a specialized ministry? If so, does it seem to be effectively meeting needs and making disciples? If not, what kind of specialized ministry might your church be best positioned to start or join?

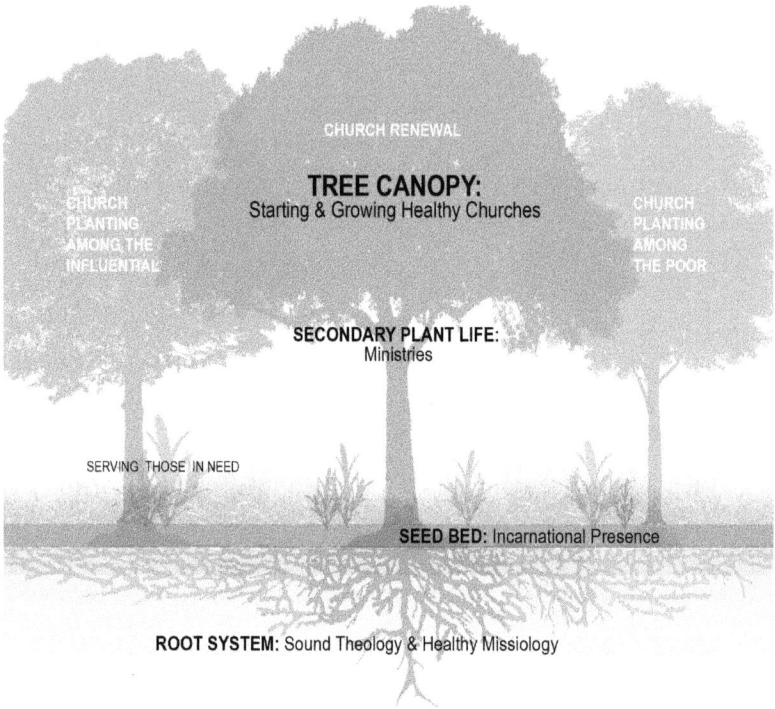

ROOT SYSTEM ➡ SEED BED ➡ TREE CANOPY ➡ SECONDARY ➡
PLANT LIFE

Chapter 11
Serving Those in Need

There were no jobs upcountry. So she came to the city.
                                        --Robert Neuwirth (2006, p. 25)

Whoever mocks the poor insults his Maker; he who is glad at
calamity will not go unpunished.
                                        --Proverbs 17:5 (ESV)

In the squalor of Bangkok's endless slums, a barefooted dentist works tirelessly to relieve poor children of their toothaches. He works extra hours among the wealthy so he can relieve the pain of more children in need. This pro bono dentistry is the work of a Burmese immigrant who is a devout Buddhist. As Viv Grigg relays the story, he adds this convicting commentary: "Elsewhere he looks upon a thousand easy-going middle class, careless Christians. They read his words about the poor but will not go. And they ask for his love. Are we not shamed, outdone by this barefoot dentist? (Grigg, 1988, p. 44)." Grigg's passion for the urban poor and the unequivocal call of Christ to serve them drives his life's work. He has been championing work among the poor for over three decades. The future of mission work is among the poor in the urban context (Grigg, 1993, p. 195).

Global statistics on urban poverty demand a response from the church. Two out of seven people in the world are counted among the urban poor (Johnson & Crossing, 2013, p. 33). More than half of the world's urban population lives in poverty. Moreover, there are an estimated one billion urban slum dwellers in the world, and the numbers are projected to increase to 1.3 billion by 2020 (Beall & Fox, 2009, pp. 27, 61). These numbers drive Robert Linthicum (1991a) to conclude: "there is no way to talk about the city and ignore its poor" (p. 173).

In this chapter we will look at the dynamics of urban poverty and a biblical response to it. It soon becomes clear that poverty is not easily separated from unjust systems and oppression. Injustice will be taken up in Chapter 12.

Urban Poverty Up Close

Subtle Yet Real Poverty

Urban poverty has many faces. Most often our understanding of poverty is derived from what we see of it. I recently had a meeting in the SOMA (South of Market) district of San Francisco. In the short two block walk from my car to the coffee shop, I was confronted by aggressive panhandlers, spotted a man urinating on a sidewalk and heard the rantings of at least two people with mental illness. These are the more obvious and familiar images of urban poverty. Yet most of the urban poor live in out-of-the-way communities, eke out a living, and struggle to raise a family. In many countries the poor are housed in high-rise apartments and offered government assistance. Today, another dynamic is occurring among the poor in some developed nations: the suburbanization of poverty. As urban real estate escalates in price, the poor are getting pushed to public housing at the fringes of the city where real estate is cheaper.

When we offer the poor these types of services, two things happen to our mindsets. First, our interactions with the urban poor are reduced. When the poor are stashed in giant chicken coops or pushed to the periphery of the city, we are no longer confronted by the realities of their poverty. Out of sight, out of mind. Second, when we hear about the government assistance the urban poor can access, we think they have what they need to thrive and even rise out of poverty. If we perceive families as failing to capitalize on these advantages, we grow frustrated and allow stereotypes of the poor to inhabit our thinking.

When a family is pushed to an apartment in a fringe part of the city, they face new types of adversity. In these low-cost housing zones, employment opportunities are rare, infrastructure is neglected, education is abysmal, safety is under threat, and transportation options are few. The poor often lack access to affordable groceries or bank loans. The lack of a safety net for the poor means they are one missed paycheck away from homelessness. Children raised in this environment may not receive adequate nutrition or educational help. They grow up to have few employment opportunities and little chance to raise their children any differently. Therefore the cycle of poverty continues. Low salaries, job vulnerabilities, health issues, and accidents prevent the poor from rising out of their situation.

Dire Poverty

When we first arrived in Bandung, Indonesia, a garbage dump in the city exploded (decomposing food creates pockets of combustible gases that explode when triggered by intense heat) spitting garbage as far as a kilometer away. That explosion took the lives of 55 people who were living on the dump site. For many who migrate to the city, survival means scavenging on mountains of decomposing garbage. Millions of people live in crude, unsafe, makeshift environments in order to survive. A billion people live in slum households, defined by the United Nations as "urban households lacking one or more of the following: durable housing; sufficient living area; access to an improved water source; access to improved sanitation, or secure tenure."(United Nations Population Division, 2008, p. 26) India has 230 million slum dwellers. Fifty-five percent of the Mumbai population lives in slums (Brugmann, 2009, p. 145). Projected estimates tell us the African continent will have

840 million slum dwellers in forty years, equivalent to 40% of the population (Johnstone, 2011, p. 7).

Life in a slum intensifies the issues of poverty. Being poor means being vulnerable. Being poor in a slum means extreme vulnerability. A normal threat is made worse in slum conditions. For example, a typical house fire is most often extinguished before it spreads to another house. In a slum, a fire whips through a whole neighborhood in 15 minutes. Ash Barker describes slum poverty:

> Rather than just being another kind of neighbourhood facing poverty, slums were like a 'perfect storm' of poverty. The various 'fronts' of poverty kept thundering together, causing misery to multitudes: evictions, fires, floods, urbanisation, vulnerable employment conditions, dangerous housing materials, sewerage inadequacies, superstitions I didn't understand, corrupt officials, language barriers, sanitation problems, AIDS and other preventable infectious diseases, premature deaths of children, the disabled and the elderly, and often no meaningful connections with Christians (Barker, 2012, p. 15).

Life is tenuous in the slum. This combination of "fronts of poverty" can overwhelm those who want to help.

In order to respond Christianly to this important issue, we need to understand the causes of poverty from a biblical perspective.

A Theological Understanding of Poverty

Politicians and pundits often paint poverty with simplistic brush strokes, saying that is due to individual laziness or caused by society. The Bible, however, addresses poverty with frequency and nuance. The topic is worthy of a book-length study, but here a summary will have to suffice. In *Companion to the Poor*, Viv Grigg (2004a) develops a theology of poverty starting with the 245 references to poverty in the Bible. Several different Hebrew words are translated as "poor." Tim Keller simplifies the biblical material on poverty by suggesting three causes of poverty.

Oppression by the rich and/or powerful. Keller, like Grigg, notes the Hebrew word "ani" is frequently translated as "poor," but is better translated as "the wrongfully disposed" (Keller, 1997, p. 100). The oppression occurs through extremely high interest charges (Ex. 22:25-27), unfairly low wages (Jer. 22:13; James 5:1-6; Eph. 6:8-9), or a biased judicial system (Lev. 19:15). The Bible often describes the gap between the poor and the rich as the fault of the rich (Amos 5:11-12; Ezekiel 22:29; Micah 2:2; Isaiah 5:8). The Mosaic laws were designed partly to mitigate against these abuses of wealth and privilege (Keller, 2010a, p. 33).

Natural disasters. Natural and accidental occurrences can also send people into impoverished situations. Circumstances like famines (Gen. 47), fires, floods, disease, and injury can either put someone into poverty or keep them there. In some cases, these circumstances are such that one is not able to rise out of poverty despite his or her personal hard work and wise decision-making. This cause of poverty is beyond the control of the individual to prevent (Keller, 2010a, p. 34).

Personal moral failures. According to Keller, the third cause of poverty is failure on the part of the individual. Slothfulness (Proverbs 6:6-7) and a general lack of self-discipline (Proverbs 23:21) can lead to poverty. The Bible clearly expects people to work hard in order to provide for themselves (Proverbs 12:11; 14:23). Those who are blessed with the ability to work and cultivate their resources have a responsibility to be stewards of these God-given gifts. In other words, individual decisions can impact one's poverty (Keller, 2010a, p. 34).

Assessing the cause of a person's poverty is not easy. In most cases, poverty has a complex combination of causes that are partly the fault of the poor individual, partly the fault of others, and exacerbated by natural causes. This leads Keller (2010a) to conclude: "Any large-scale improvement in a society's level of poverty will come through a comprehensive array of public and private, spiritual, personal, and corporate measures" (p. 35). For Keller, a complex diagnosis of the problem means a complex answer to the problem. Conn and Ortiz (2001) bid us to take all three causes into account: "To ignore any of these is to ignore the resolve of the gospel. Often all three are found together" (p. 357). We turn now to the resolve of the gospel.

A Gospel-Centered Motivation to Respond to Poverty

In biblical times, people sought to win the favor of their gods with offerings and spectacular temples, making religion more accessible to the wealthy than the poor (Keller, 2010a, p. 40). The God of Scripture called people to worship him through faith in spirit and in truth, not works or wealth-based merit. The right motivation for responding to poverty and injustice is foundational to any Christian ministry to the poor. Simply responding to the emotional tug of the plight of the poor out of pity or guilt is sure to lead to burnout, self-righteous pride, or even disillusionment. Rather, it is by embracing the gospel that the Christian can respond to poverty in the healthiest manner. Tim Keller (2008b) articulates the gospel-centered motivation well: "If it is the gospel that is moving us, our giving to the poor will be significant, remarkable, and sacrificial" (p. 2). It is in this area that Keller leans heavily on Jonathan Edwards' works "Christian Charity" and "The Duty of Charity to the Poor." Edwards saw an increase in poverty in his town of Northampton, Massachusetts. This poverty was due, in part, to injustices between long-term residents and newcomers (Keller, 2010a, p. 68). For Edwards, the substitutionary atonement is the quintessential model for ministry to the poor. One key text for both Edwards and Keller is Galatians 6:1-10. The call to do good to all people is premised on the idea of bearing each other's burdens in a manner fulfilling the "law of Christ" (Gal. 6:2). In other words, Christians should do good in a sacrificial manner because sacrifice is the ultimate way Christ did good for the world (Keller, 2008b, p. 2). As such, this demonstration of Christ-like sacrifice on behalf of others also becomes evangelistic in that it demonstrates the gospel to the world (Keller, 1997, p. 55).

Mercy is an essential part of loving one's neighbor and therefore is not optional. "Orthodoxy without social concern is not orthodoxy" (Keller, 1997, p. 114)! Micah 6:8 says to "do justice and love mercy." Keller suggests doing justice is the action, and loving mercy (*chesedh* in Hebrew) is the motive behind the action (Keller, 2010a, p. 3). Drawing from the parable of the Good Samaritan, Keller notes that the purpose of telling the parable is to describe Christian love to her/his neighbor. These extreme acts of mercy shown toward a stranger from a different ethnic group are given as the example of loving a neighbor. He says: "The striking truth is that the work of mercy is fundamental to being a Christian" (Keller, 1997, p. 39).

Jesus himself "moved in with the poor." His incarnation with humanity sets the stage for his ministry to the marginalized and poor. He ate and socialized with the ostracized (Matt. 9:13). He showed dignity to those publicly known to be immoral and raised the son of a poor widow to life (Luke 7). Jesus defied the entrenched social norms of racism and oppression in his teachings and actions (John 4; Luke 10:26ff; Luke 4:25-27; 14:12-13; Mark 12:42-43). For example, "Jesus bluntly and shockingly contradicted the spirit and practice of the patronage system of his day, telling his disciples to give without expecting repayment (Luke 6:32; 14:13-14) and, if possible, in secret (Matthew 6:1-4)" (Keller, 2010a, pp. 47–48). Keller provides many more examples demonstrating that proactive concern for the poor and marginalized is very much close to the heart of Jesus. One cannot love Jesus and ignore the plight of the poor and marginalized (Keller, 2010a, pp. 53–54). As such, Jesus' actions become a paradigmatic example for the church, not as a path to salvation, but as a demonstration of the values of God's kingdom.

In addition to Jesus' demonstration of tangible actions that lead to a just society, the church inherits the Old Testament calls to model a just society. There is a connection between the command to have no poor among them from Deuteronomy 15 and the early church practice of caring for all of the needy among the people of God as described in

Acts 4:34-35 (Polhill, 1992, p. 152). Furthermore, the early churches were instructed to develop ministries for the sake of serving and helping the poor in their midst. Keller considers "diaconal ministry" to be a crucial part of the community life of the early church. He defines the Greek word *diakonia* as "humble service to practical needs" (Keller, 2010a, p. 60). This call to serve pertains both to serving the church community as well as the neighbors all around them. Keller notes that Jesus intentionally demonstrated with the story of the Good Samaritan that there are no boundaries regarding who qualify as neighbors (Keller, 2010a, pp. 66–67). The story of the Samaritan is told in such a way that the listeners would identify with the victim, because it is ultimately Jesus who comes to rescue people in a similar state of despair (Keller, 2010a, pp. 74–77).

For Keller, mercy ministry is inextricably tied to evangelism. But he is careful to say that it is not simply a means to gain converts or church members. Mercy ministries can touch people's lives in ways that a mere verbal presentation cannot. Mercy ministry is an exhibition of God's common grace which can help the unchurched hear and understand redemptive grace. Keller states, "Mercy deeds give the gospel words plausibility (Acts 4:32 followed by v. 33)" (Keller & Thompson, 2002, p. 135). Keller describes how mercy ministry reaches those with whom most churches rarely connect and that "modern evangelism has developed few models that help churches to reach out except to the 'churchy' non-Christians. The 'webbed' and especially the 'unwebbed' non-Christian must be reached through felt-need ministries" (Keller, 1997, p. 216). (Unwebbed refers to those who have little or no natural connection to Christians.) Keller views ministries of mercy as vital to church life because they can be used by God for the demonstration and proclamation of the gospel as well as because Christians need to give of themselves to others as part of their own growth in the gospel.

Responding to Poverty in a Way that is Dignifying and Sustainable

The church will need to focus more on the ever-increasing population of the urban poor. Much of what the church does among the poor is token ministry that does little for the long-term physical or spiritual health of underserved communities. *How* one gives help to the poor and marginalized is very important if one truly wants to help them. Keller says motivation is not all that matters: "It is one thing to want to help the poor; it is another thing to go about it wisely" (Keller, 2008b, p. 6). The church needs to seek solutions that truly help the poor. In order to simplify the key ideas in responding to poverty, I will highlight five primary ideas: methods that are dignifying, ministries of mercy, movements through community organizing, maintaining focus on the message, and making holistic disciples.

Methods that are Dignifying. Often our ministries to the poor inadvertently humiliate and subjugate those we intend to help, cornering the poor into receiving whatever we offer rather than what will bring dignity and well-being. In understanding the true difficulties and heart-breaking nature of poverty, individual stories are much more telling than statistics (Linthicum, 1991b, p. 7). Statistics do not adequately describe the shame and vulnerability experienced by the poor. We must remember that everyone, whatever his or her income, race, struggle, or addiction, bears the image of God (Gen. 1:26-27). Robert Linthicum is not content with hearing sad tales about the poor; he anticipates their potential to overcome their struggles. After pastoring inner city churches in the States, Linthicum went on to lead World Vision's urban community development division. Linthicum cites Isaiah 61:3-4 to describe the dignity of the deprived in the economy of God: "In this passage, the defeated and cast down of the city will become the rebuilders of that city; their healing will enable them to assume responsibility for their city's future" (Linthicum, 1997, p. 175). Linthicum believes that a basic assumption for effective urban ministry is that all people, no matter how uneducated or marginalized, have the capacity to understand and determine a solution to their own problems. He believes that they are in a better position to do so than the benevolent outsider.[1]

For a few years I worked in disaster relief after the horrendous destruction from the earthquake and tsunami in Southeast Asia in 2004. The world responded with an unprecedented outpouring of aid through disaster relief agencies (Non-Governmental Organizations— NGOs). As our team worked in the area hit hardest by the tsunami, we saw over 800 relief agencies come in to provide aid to this devastated area. This was an eye-opening experience for me. Agencies entered with expert personnel and millions of dollars, yet I was appalled at much of their work. One agency drilled a bore well that spewed malodorous water and still put an expensive electrical pump on it. One agency bought fishermen a whole supply of new fishing boats, but bought a kind of boat the fishermen had never seen and didn't know how to use. Another agency built 500 new homes in an inaccessible area. All of these projects looked good to donors on their promotional materials, yet all of it went unused and was a waste of hard-earned donations. The basic flaw in all of these projects was the "experts" did not think to consult the local people about the water quality, type of fishing boat, or location of the houses. We restore dignity by listening to those we seek to help and including them in the solutions for improvement.

Ministries of Mercy. Also called relief ministry, the ministry of mercy is the starting point in engaging those with pressing needs. Relief ministry is most often spontaneous and informal. A sudden need confronts the church or a member of the church, and the response is usually a short-term solution. Church leaders should equip the church to respond to these types of needs, simultaneously recognizing that it is not a substitute for a long-term response.

There are differing views regarding the degree to which mercy should be provided to those in need. Some Christians advocate an

---

[1] That is, better positioned following a deep assessment and community organization. (Linthicum, 1991b, p. 44)

indiscriminate approach to mercy. In this approach, relief is provided without condition for all who have needs. Most soup kitchens and homeless shelters operate in this way. Others advocate a discriminating approach in which mercy is only offered to those who did not personally contribute to their own poverty through addictions or bad choices. Keller adopts a modified discriminating approach that offers unconditional relief at the start but then challenges the recipient to allow the church to help him or her address some of the contributing causes of his or her poverty (Keller, 1997, pp. 96–103). Keller (1997) says, "Mercy must have the purpose of seeing God's lordship realized in the lives of those we help" (p. 97).

Movements through Community Organizing. Soup kitchens and shelters provide an immediate response to one's plight, but do little to address the long-term needs of whole communities of the poor. Drawing from his experience with World Vision's Urban Advance, Robert Linthicum views the community organizer as the key to facilitating change in the community. It is ultimately the work of the community as a whole, but the community organizer acts as a "midwife in the birth of the community" (Linthicum, 1991b, p. 25). The underlying value of the community organizer is the faith in the contribution of the whole community:

> The concepts of networking and community organization rest on the belief that all human beings, however uneducated, exploited and beaten by life, have a greater capacity to understand and solve their own problems than the most highly informed or sympathetic outsider (Eph. 4:11-6:9; entire book of Nehemiah, but especially 2:17-18) (Linthicum, 1987, p. 10).

Linthicum attributes this capacity to the image of God in every individual, no matter their lack of education.

The church, operating rightly, ought to identify those in the congregation that are gifted for the purposes of community organization (Linthicum, 1991a, p. 189). Linthicum offers individuals from the Bible who exemplify this kind of role: Moses, Paul, and Nehemiah. He considers the book of Nehemiah to be the best urban ministry textbook ever written (Linthicum, 1991a, pp. 194, 198). Since these church member-community organizers are identified, equipped, and nurtured through the ministry of the church, the church and community organization cannot be easily separated. The individual change agent ministers as a result of the corporate change agent, the church.

There are two important elements that are foundational to being an effective community organizer. One is that ***incarnational presence*** is essential for connecting with the community.

> An incarnational ministry is one which casts its lot with the neighborhood's people, working among them, spending time visiting with them, walking the streets, coming to know and care about and love them. Networking is built upon this incarnational foundation (Linthicum, 1991a, p. 200).

Linthicum (1991b) also asserts that the church as a whole should have an incarnational presence: "That church becomes flesh of the peoples' flesh and bone of the peoples' bone" (p. 23). In Linthicum's view, the church should be with the community as opposed to being merely in the city or going to the city. This is an important distinction for Linthicum because it means that the church acts as a fully participating member of the community and has a humble posture toward others in the community.

The other element for effectiveness is ***emotional investment*** on the part of the community organizer. Nehemiah's love for Jerusalem caused him to risk his job and likely his life when making his request of the king for whom he was cupbearer. From this observation Linthicum (1991a) gleans: "To be effective in urban ministry, you must have a heart that is as big as the city itself" (p. 196). Feeling the pains of the community will increase personal motivation as well as grant a deeper understanding of its problems.

The organizer, essentially, follows five steps (Linthicum, 1991b, p. 25):

1. networking
2. coalition-building
3. acting/reflecting/acting
4. leadership empowerment and
5. the birth of community

First, *networking* is a vital role for the community organizer. The community organizer develops relationships with people in the community. These relationships build trust between the poor and the church community. Networking also brings essential insights to the community organizer regarding needs of the community and who is who within it. Linthicum views this as the foundation to Nehemiah's work of urban renewal and ultimately the key to his success (Linthicum, 1991a, p. 197).

Networking is a prominent concept in Linthicum's writings. Since networking is a relational activity, the focus is on people rather than problems or projects. There are a couple of reasons for this. Problem-focused development is destined for failure according to Linthicum. He says, "The natural tendency of churches, foundations, government agencies, and other institutions is to identify or define a community problem and then create a project or a program to meet that need. There is no strategy more designed for failure in the city than this approach" (Linthicum 1997, p. 179). The other reason goes back to Linthicum's value for relational power. If the primary source of power for solving problems in the community is in coalescing people, then relationships are necessarily primary (Linthicum, 2003, 2004).

Since networking is people-oriented, Linthicum (1991a) offers practical tips for knowing who some of the key people are in the community:

Of particular importance to ask of the residents are these questions: 'If you had a problem getting a service of the city that is rightfully yours, to whom would you go for help?' and 'If you had a real crisis at two o'clock in the morning, to whom would you turn in your neighborhood —outside of your family?' If these questions are asked of enough people, certain names will begin to emerge repeatedly. The repeated names given in response to the first question will reveal the implementers or 'gatekeepers' of the community (the can-do people). The repeated names given in response to the second question will give you the compassionate 'caretakers' of the community. These are the pivotal people you and your church leaders will need to know, those with whom you will need to build strong and trusting relationships, who will be the people most critical to the redevelopment of that neighborhood (p. 173).

Knowing who the gatekeepers and caretakers are in the community is exigent in building community coalitions and ultimately accruing relational power. The stakes are high in this step because "networking then becomes the means to enable an oppressed, exploited, or alienated people to discover each other and to mobilize successfully" (Linthicum, 1997, p. 176). Even though these key people may not have official leadership positions in the community, functionally, they operate as the true leaders of the community (Linthicum, 1991b, pp. 48–51). If the community organizer falters at this point, the rest of the steps are pointless (Linthicum, 1991b, p. 51).

Second, the community organizer engages in *coalition-building*, bringing the poor and the church together in order to address the concerns of the community. Coalitions are important for building the capacity of the community's relational power in order to confront other power holders. Confrontation can sometimes imply violence, but Linthicum is clear that violence is actually an indicator that healthy confrontation failed (Linthicum, 1991b, p. 81). Although violence is sometimes a response in opposition to a community coalition, it is important for the community organizer to prepare the community to respond with integrity, peace, and non-violence while not relenting

(Linthicum, 1991b, p. 87). Linthicum himself was threatened with his life when a community he worked with opposed a prostitution ring in the neighborhood (Linthicum, 1991b, p. 88). Although there are risks, coalitions help reduce the risk to individuals.

It is important for the community organizer to encourage the coalition to prioritize the concerns identified by the whole community. This inevitably involves a confrontation with the status quo, but it needs to be done in a healthy manner. Healthy confrontation is issue-based and not character-slandering, because the point is to change the status quo, not create enmity. Linthicum views confrontation as a biblical value demonstrated by Nehemiah (Neh. 4:1-23; 5:1-6:19) and Paul (Gal. 2:11-14; 6:1) (Linthicum, 1991b, p. 85).

Third is the step of *acting/reflecting/acting* with the coalitions. Linthicum describes this as a dynamic process, meaning it continues to change as the circumstances do. The reflection process should be spiritual as well as structural and should continue to reflect and act on the community's own sinfulness. If this process is done well, root problems are addressed and action is taken. The process of identifying root problems is complex and will require several rounds of acting/reflecting/acting. Each step of the way, the level of trust within the coalition increases.

This step of acting/reflecting/acting is where Linthicum sees evangelism playing a significant role. Gospel-centered reflection will create natural avenues for Christians to share their faith with others in the community. Linthicum suggests evangelism is best done through the key leaders that the community organizer discovers through his or her extensive networking (Linthicum, 1991b, p. 50). Prior to this time, the community organizer has not really earned a hearing. Once the community sees the love the church has for the poor, they are more open to hear the gospel (Linthicum, 1997, p. 180). By this time, the community has seen the gospel lived out, and it is now time to put words to it.

Fourth, *leaders from within the coalition are identified and empowered.* Both church leaders and community leaders emerge during this step. These new leaders need to be equipped and encouraged and provided with opportunities to grow as leaders. This was Nehemiah's most glaring mistake, according to Linthicum (1991a), resulting in "a near-disastrous power vacuum which, upon Nehemiah's return to the court of the Persian king, almost destroyed that noble experiment (Neh. 13:4-31)" (p. 207). A vision for a new and empowered community begins with the emergence of these leaders. Leaders are necessary to continue to address the problems in their community, but these leaders must be from within the community and committed to the needs of it. Both the lack of leaders and the improper development of leaders can result in the community being subjected to evil powers and principalities once again (Linthicum, 1991b, p. 92). Hasty leadership development derails the whole process.

Fifth, *the community is reborn*, which is the goal of community organization. At this stage, the community is born as a viable, sustainable urban community fully capable of addressing further concerns. This rebirth of the community can be marked by a time of celebration to provide a symbolic point which the community can all acknowledge as beginning a new era and a solemn putting away of the old community. They can look back on the symbolic point should they go off course in the future (Brueggemann, 1978, p. 49). The community is now organized and the poor now have a voice. With this kind of organization, the community experiences an improvement in their quality of life (Linthicum, 1991b, p. 26). Failure to reestablish the community can undo all of the hard work the community organization has done. The community is re-established in such a way that the whole community has ownership rather than just a few (Linthicum, 1991b, pp. 100–101).

Linthicum sees the role of the community organizer as an empowering role. The change agent does not make changes alone, but catalyzes the community to make changes. He argues that this is a biblical posture for helping new communities gain independence. Isaiah 61:4 depicts the poor and downtrodden actively rebuilding from their ruins and renewing devastated cities. Another example is offered in Paul's letter to Titus. Paul initiated the work there and provided training, but then Titus and the new believers are given the responsibility to work things out and even select their own leadership (Titus 1:5). Linthicum asserts that this approach is necessary; otherwise the poor will conceive of themselves as helpless (Linthicum, 1991a, pp. 175–176).

When the community has taken full ownership of the process of overcoming their problems and they establish their own leadership, it is time for the church and the community organizers to move into the background. The church continues to be involved as part of the community and as the conscience to the community (Linthicum, 1991a, p. 228). In this way the church continues to act as prophet, but no longer takes the lead. By stepping back, the church ensures that it does not abuse power, but uses relational power as the avenue of change. The community members are fully equipped and empowered to introduce necessary change to their community.

Maintaining Focus on the Message. The physical needs of the poor can be so overwhelming that we become too exhausted or distracted to proclaim the life-giving message of the Messiah. However, "To reduce our definition of people's needs to physical and material needs is to undercut the work of Christ in the city" (Ortiz, 1992, p. 88). Viv Grigg maintains the right perspective on the need to keep gospel proclamation in the forefront of our ministries. Proclamation of the good news of the kingdom is Grigg's priority when it comes to addressing the poor (as well as anyone else). He does not believe this somehow puts "word" over "deed" because the good news of the kingdom immediately addresses the holistic issues plaguing the individual. Economic programs and community development are good things, but they come secondarily to proclamation. Additionally, preaching the good news is also a direct confrontation with the prevailing demonic influences that impose themselves on a community.[2] In Grigg's ministry, this confrontation sometimes included the burning of idols and charms that held influence over peoples' lives. There are immediate ramifications to proclamation, as it leads to disciple-making (Grigg, 2004a, pp. 103–104).

Making Holistic Disciples. Discipleship should cover every aspect of the Christian life, including the handling of finances. There is a Seinfeld episode where George Costanza discovers he has $1,900 from an interest account he invested in when he was a kid. Jerry Seinfeld tells George he ought to put the money in the bank. Incredulous, George answers: "The *bank*? This is found money. I want to parlay it. I wanna make a big score!" It is common for Christians to use God-given resources foolishly instead of stewarding for the common good. Viv Grigg identifies the evangelical wholesale adoption of consumerism as unhealthy. It exploits the innate human proclivity towards greed and covetousness (Grigg, 2010, pp. 34–35). He points out that early Calvinism actually emphasized the "just use of resources for the common good, frugality, diligence and their relationship to the emergence of capitalism." Grigg points out the effect of the rise of wealth and the middle class upon the developed-world church; we have abandoned biblical principles of stewardship, generosity, and remaining debt-free (Grigg, 2009, p. 112). In this observation, he draws from Weber's *The Protestant Work Ethic and the Rise of Capitalism* (1980). The status quo among Evangelicals is an unhealthy approach to financial issues.

Addressing this issue is not as simple as just giving away a percentage of earnings or periodically giving away things stored up in our closets. Grigg sees a fundamental worldview tension in this. When the Christian's default approach is to accumulate material possessions, even to the point of accruing debt, then he or she is not prioritizing God's kingdom. This is a discipleship issue. In response, Grigg has

---

[2] Grigg speaks both of the demonic societal structures as well as literal accounts of demon possession. For one vivid account see (Grigg, 2004a, pp. 124–125)

developed a manual that challenges Christians to transition to a kingdom-oriented view of economic issues that touches on debt, financial management, and intentional generosity with wealth (Grigg, 2010).

This type of discipleship is for all believers. The poor have to work through any habits developed while enveloped by a culture of poverty. But the wealthy also have to address any habits that have perpetuated patterns and structures of oppression that come with having wealth. In other words, the discipleship process should lead both the wealthy and the poor to address personal sin as well as structural sin (Grigg, 2004a, p. 46).

The Ifs, Ands, and Buts of Working with the Poor

Urban poverty is not a simple matter and has no quick solutions. It is easy enough to lay out the basic steps of community organizing, but that is entirely different from actually doing it. The truth is many humanitarian development organizations (nonprofits and NGOs) have been much more successful in rural villages than in cities. Programs that have worked so well in rural settings (i.e. child sponsorships and micro-financing) have not worked well at all in urban areas. Ash Barker notes a survey of large NGOs indicates that all work primarily in rural areas, with as little as 5-15% of their budgets allocated for work with the urban poor (Barker, 2012, p. 95). He quotes World Vision's David Kupp summarizing International NGO (INGO) work in urban contexts: "INGOs have a clear history of rural activity and, many would argue, a bias against working in urban settings... on the whole, INGOs are primarily rural organisations playing catch-up in the face of rapid urbanisation" (Barker, 2012, p. 95). There are many factors that complicate community transformation in cities. These include:

- Less cohesive communities as compared to rural areas
- Multiple stakeholders outside the church
- Difficulty of project tracking and follow-up

- Sin compounded by urban density

Communities are less cohesive in cities. The community organizing described by Linthicum and many associated with the Christian Community Development Association (CCDA) relies on a community in which members are connected enough to know each other and who see themselves as a community. Different languages, distrust for each other, and the anonymity of city life make it difficult to bring a community together.

In the urban context, there are multiple stakeholders outside the church. One organization can work exclusively in a village with no one else interfering. Cities have a number of different groups vying to "help." Micro-financing works best in rural and cohesive communities where accountability and community-driven support are in effect. In cities, local mafias, loan sharks, and even big-box retailers are quick to swoop in to offer loans to the urban poor (for a price).[3] Attempts at micro-financing loans in the city have had abysmal payback rates.

Project tracking and follow-up with individuals are complicated in the city. For example, child sponsorship relies on working with the basic support systems in the child's life (education, family, health). In a rural context, there is a minimal number of aid providers to work with and few other avenues of assistance for the child. In the city, on the other hand, there are many more levels of government, non-profit, and for-profit bureaucracy, and most services to the poor are rendered impersonally. In cities, there are endless possibilities and institutions, which makes a sponsorship program administratively unworkable.

In cities everything is intensified. This means sin is compounded by the density. Viv Grigg (2004a) reminds us "Some poverty is caused by sin. But poverty also causes sin" (p. 34). Our innate sinfulness forces us

---

[3] I have been told that multinational retailer, Tesco, offers small loans to slum dwellers in Bangkok. When the need for cash arises, one will get a loan from Tesco. If the borrower cannot repay the loan when it is due, they turn to a loan shark. All of these loan options make it difficult to create a healthy micro-lending community, a strategy that has worked well in rural areas.

to seek God as the true source of transformation. These challenges of serving the poor in cities force us to rely more heavily on God's grace and find satisfaction in serving faithfully.

Conclusion: Looking to the Early Church

Greco-Roman cities were the incubators of the early church. Rodney Stark describes the squalor of the cities in the Roman Empire. The density of Rome far exceeded any modern day city. Tenement housing more likely resembled slums and were under constant threat of collapse or combustion. Soap did not yet exist, water was mostly contaminated, and waste was dumped into open sewers on narrow footpaths. The stench of the city was unavoidable. Crime was near constant, more prevalent than the most crime-ridden cities of today. Diseases festered in the midst of human density and open sewers, spread by insects and rodents (Stark, 2011, pp. 106–112).

These miserable cities were a priority for Paul's missionary work and the launching pad for the rapidly growing Christian church. Tragically, the plague ravaged the empire during the second century, killing between a quarter and a third of the population. It became so bad that family members pushed their own relatives out of the home if sickness was discovered. It was in the midst of such dire times that Christians, knowing this life was only temporary, risked their own lives to care for the sick, including their pagan neighbors. The survival rate among Christians was far higher than the rest of the populace because they nursed those who fell ill. Stark (2011) makes a point to say that their actions during the plague merely highlight the everyday mercy and charity shown by Christians. In another work, Stark (1997) summarizes the transforming impact of a persecuted and embattled church on the cities of the empire:

Christianity revitalized life in Greco-Roman cities by providing new norms and new kinds of social relationships able to cope with many urgent urban problems. To cities filled with the homeless and impoverished, Christianity offered charity as well as hope. To cities filled with newcomers and strangers, Christianity offered an immediate basis for attachments. To cities filled with orphans and widows, Christianity provided a new and expanded sense of family. To cities torn by violent ethnic strife, Christianity offered a new basis for social solidarity.... And to cities faced with epidemics, fires, and earthquakes, Christianity offered effective nursing services (p. 161).

Christian history is filled with examples like this of Christians offering care and love even when no one else does. God's love and mercy was demonstrated for us in the greatest sacrifice of the Son of God on the cross. In our embrace of a gospel-centered life, we have the courage and love to demonstrate God's great love to the poor, marginalized, and forgotten. Or as Randy White says: "ministry to the poor is at the heart of the gospel" (White, 1996, p. 14).

Questions for reflection and discussion:

1. According to the author, what are the three possible causes of poverty?
2. Have you participated in a ministry of justice or mercy? Was that ministry both "dignifying and sustainable," as the author puts it?
3. What issues of poverty or injustice are endemic to your church's city? How can your church make holistic disciples in a way that leads members to overcome patterns contribute to those problems?

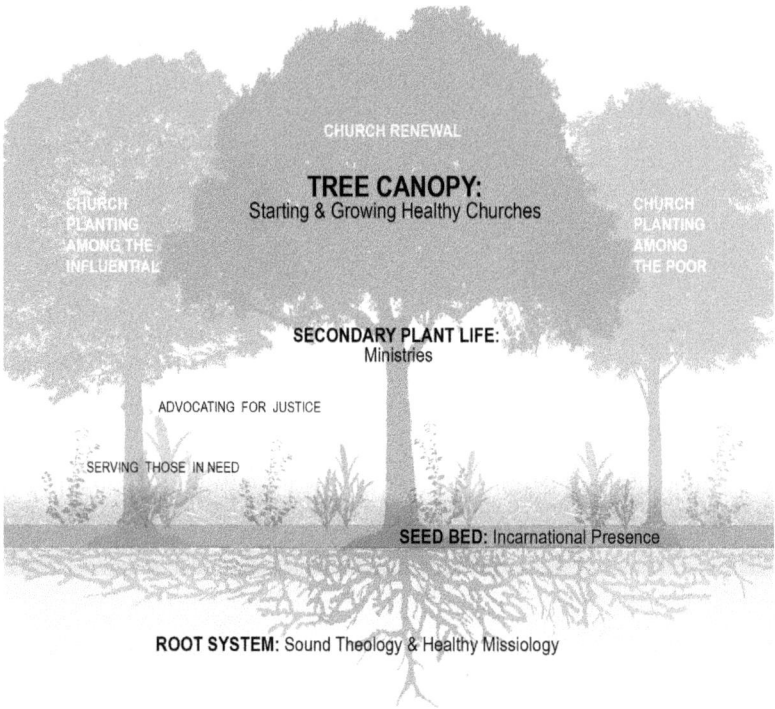

CHURCH RENEWAL

TREE CANOPY:
Starting & Growing Healthy Churches

CHURCH PLANTING AMONG THE INFLUENTIAL

CHURCH PLANTING AMONG THE POOR

SECONDARY PLANT LIFE:
Ministries

ADVOCATING FOR JUSTICE

SERVING THOSE IN NEED

SEED BED: Incarnational Presence

ROOT SYSTEM: Sound Theology & Healthy Missiology

ROOT SYSTEM ➡ SEED BED ➡ TREE CANOPY ➡ SECONDARY ➡ PLANT LIFE

Chapter 12
Advocating for Justice

But the fact is, true justice has no existence save in that republic whose founder and ruler is Christ, if at least any choose to call this a republic; and indeed we cannot deny that it is the people's weal.

--Augustine (1950, p. 63)

We have failed to fight for right, for justice, for goodness; as a result we must fight against wrong, against injustice, against evil."

--Abraham Heschel (1997, p. 256)

Mary was living in a slum in Bangkok. Her family had sent her to the city to earn money to help pay off family debt. With her humble upbringing she could not find a job, so as a last resort she sold her body to earn a little cash. A friend told her about a real job opportunity, in a highly developed global city in another country that would pay off her family's debt in a couple of years. Arriving for her new job, she soon found herself locked in a basement brothel. Once she saw the boots of policemen outside her basement window. Seeing an opportunity for escape, she knocked until she got their attention. The policemen came down and raped her and then left her in her slavery. If only Mary's story were an exception. Every day people are trafficked and forced to work against their will, many in the sex industry, but also in brick making, garment manufacture, construction, and countless other labor intensive industries. Over 20 million men, women, and children are currently enslaved around the world. They labor in obscurity, hidden beneath layers of paperwork and shadowy links in the supply chain, part of a complex system in which we are all connected in some way.

Many injustices in our cities have systemic causes. Systemic issues are ones that are caused collectively rather than individually. In this chapter we will take a closer look at systemic causes of injustice in our cities. Blighted urban neighborhoods, homelessness, unemployment, crime, and inequitable access to municipal services are among the injustices in the ever-growing urban centers of the world.

Many in the Church have been operating from places of privilege and relative comfort. When a family has always been able to rely on consistent municipal services, entrust kids to quality schools, and enjoy the security of police protection, they do not realize what life is like without those privileges. With those needs consistently met in ways unrelated to the church, middle class Christians are able to develop a theological worldview that minimizes the importance of meeting these physical needs. In other words, our life situations impact our theology:

> The identity between the church's theology and patterns of urban ministry and the dominant ideology of secular society also presented an obstacle to mission amongst those who continued to experience the shadowside of secular progress. The irony was that in the secular city the church thrived in the suburb, in the places where the rewards and securities of the new order were greatest, while in the new housing areas the church struggled to establish and maintain strong churches, in a complete reversal of the mission of the early Church (Northcott, 1998, p. 283).

Bakke (1997) frames it this way:

> Those who say, 'Let's just preach the simple gospel,' usually live where good, working social systems are in

place. Their plea for unadorned evangelism proclamation will have greater credibility when they live incarnationally alongside the people they wish to evangelize. And when these Christians do enter urban communities, they inevitably see that it is not a simple thing to evangelize (p. 86).

The Church's response to the plight of the poor and oppressed comes in the forms of mercy and justice. As discussed above, acts of mercy hone in on meeting human needs whether "deserved" or not. Acts of justice address the prophetic calling of the church to amend global realities that are out of line with God's just kingdom. Defining views of justice can be just as complex as understanding the causes of poverty. Tim Keller (2010a) acknowledges differing views of justice,[1] and he gives a broad picture of what doing justice entails: "To 'do justice' means to go to places where the fabric of *shalom* has broken down, where the weaker members of societies are falling through the fabric, and to repair it" (p. 177).

Society is not simply a collection of people. It is an intricate tapestry of interrelated individuals. Every individual is responsible to weave themselves into this fabric, not just in terms of money or volunteerism, but sacrificially integrating one's life into the fabric for the sake of repairing it. This means each individual, those in positions of influence in particular, are called to work for justice in society. The Bible calls on rulers, even pagan ones, to act with justice and mercy to the poor and oppressed (Keller, 1997, pp. 123–127).

It is time for the church to come alongside the downtrodden as ambassadors of the supremely just God. A failure to act against systems of injustice means tacit approval of these systems (Harden, 2013, p. Location 2019). It is only as we enact the truth of justice that the church is able to speak the truth of the gospel to people and communities suffering from injustice.

---

[1] Keller recognizes that opinions vary widely and says, "I propose that readers remember that the Biblical concept of justice is very comprehensive and therefore it should be possible to glean great ideas from all kinds of sources." (p. 214n120).

Not Just...the Facts

The statistics are staggering! There are more than 50 million refugees and internally displaced persons (IDPs) in the world ("World Refugee Day," 2014). According to Compassion International, an estimated 3.4 million children under the age of 15 are living with HIV. Three billion people live on less than $2.50 per day. Every day, nearly 16,000 children die from hunger-related causes ("Hunger Facts," 2014). We could go on and on with statistics. And the facts become even more egregious when they are compared with the wealth and waste of the richest five percent of the world. Forty percent of all food produced in the United States ends up in landfills. We do not just have injustice in the world, it is the norm!

We can hear these statistics and feel justifiably outraged and yet live somewhat detached from the day-to-day realities of poverty. We feel no connection to the major injustices we know exist, yet these global realities have local causes. Employers who choose to offer the bare minimum in wages and health benefits while enjoying a large profit contribute to injustice. The one shopper who purchases goods from a store sourcing merchandise from sweatshops because they have lower prices advances injustice. Choosing to eat at a restaurant that is known to treat employees abusively is a choice in support of injustice. Pride, greed, and selfishness spur injustice on to the point that it is all-pervasive. Even those who have been oppressed become oppressors when it is the only system they have known (Conn & Ortiz, 2001, p. 357). Injustice is the social outworking of sin. Nicholas Wolterstorff (2013) describes injustice simply: "to wrong someone is to treat that person unjustly; it is to deprive him of something to which he has a right" (p. 85). Randy White describes the compounding of sin: "when simple, run-of-the-mill human sin, corruption, favoritism or sheer laziness enters the systems of a city, the effect is the same. Filipina theologian and activist Melba Maggay rightly calls these the 'depersonalized forces of evil at work in the social climate...or entrenched in structures of the created order'" (White, 2006, p. 66). This idea of systemic injustice is worth looking at more closely.

Systems of Injustice

Accurately assessing the power of systems in a city is vital to urban transformation. Linthicum believes that cities are inhabited by systems that are so strong and given over to evil that an individual cannot experience full transformation without some degree of piercing through the systemic strongholds. His perspective is worth a closer look.

Linthicum tells a story from his days working with youth in the inner city while in school. One young black woman, whom he calls "Eva," had become a believer in Christ and matured physically into a beautiful woman. Before he left for his summer vacation, Eva came to Linthicum concerned about pressure from a gang in the neighborhood which pulled girls into prostitution for wealthy white men in the suburbs. He gave her what he would now refer to as typical church advice: resist evil and it will flee from you.

When Linthicum came back at the end of the summer, he observed that Eva was no longer involved at the church. When he went to find her at her apartment, she wept, saying, "They got to me, Bob, I've become a whore!" Linthicum asked her unsympathetically why she did not resist them. She then told him that the gang beat her father and brother in an effort persuade her to become a prostitute. When she didn't relent, they threatened to gang rape her mother. She finally gave in, and it destroyed her faith. Linthicum asked why she did not just go to the police. Linthicum records her response: "'Bob, you honkey, who do you think are in that gang? It's the police—the police are running the prostitution ring!'" (Linthicum, 1991a, pp. 45–46, 1991b, pp. 5–6, 2003, pp. 20–21).

This event was paradigmatic for Linthicum. He (1991b) describes his further realizations about this urban system that was supposed to protect the citizenry:

> The police—the very people entrusted by society with the task of protecting and defending the people—were, in reality, the worst exploiters of the people. I eventually discovered that what the police were doing in that one precinct was only the tip of the iceberg in that city. The entire legal and political system of that city was arrayed to protect a mass betrayal of the people to enable police, judges and politicians to enrich themselves at the people's expense (p. 10).

The experience was a powerful demonstration of the power and pervasiveness of these systems in a city. It also showed Linthicum that effective urban ministry could not limit focus to individuals, but must address the systems of the city. He concludes, "We cannot simply save individuals in the city and expect that the city will get saved. If the church does not deal with the systems and structures of evil in the city, then it will not effectively transform the lives of that city's individuals" (Linthicum, 1991a, pp. 46–47).

The source of the dominating power of these systems is evident in the Bible. Linthicum is influenced by the Old Testament scholar Walter Brueggeman on this point (Linthicum, 1991a, p. x). Both the Old Testament prophets and Jesus had to go up against systemic powers. The call for God's people was always to have compassion on the least of these, which was a direct confrontation to the controlling systems which operate without compassion (Brueggemann, 1978, pp. 85–86).

Linthicum (Linthicum, 1991a, p. 47, 1991b, p. 11, 2003, p. 23) draws on other urbanologists when he notes that the primary systems of a city are economic, political, and religious.[2] He believes these systems to be intertwined and integrated and have many subsystems, such as education, arts, health care, etc. (Linthicum, 1991b, p. 11, 2003, p. 23). An understanding of these systems is important for understanding how God intended society to be as well as for diagnosing where society went off track.

---

[2] Although Linthicum states this claim derives from urban sociology, he does not provide any references from which he makes this assertion.

- First, the political system is the system by which a society agrees on decisions about common life. Society is governed by these decisions in order to seek the common good. The essential question about the political system is, "How do we as a people determine to live together?" (Linthicum, 2003, p. 23).

- Second, the economic system is the society's system for producing and distributing goods and services. Economics, according to Linthicum is essentially about an agreed upon method of wealth generation and distribution. The essential question is, "How do we as a people choose to create and distribute our wealth? " (Linthicum, 2003, p. 23)

- Third, the essential question for the religious system is, "what do we, as a people ultimately value?" (Linthicum, 2003, p. 23). Understanding this system is complicated by the fact that the term "religious" is mired in presupposed meanings. I'm employing Linthicum's definition of the term, which points out that this value system does not necessarily include belief in the divine. [3]

These systems are evident in the Bible as well. Deuteronomy 6 serves to demonstrate God's intention for society in all three of these systems. As the people of Israel took possession of the pagan-inhabited Promised Land, they needed to order their lives as God's people. The foundation for Israel was relationship with the one God (Deut. 6:4-6, 14-16), which was crucial for the religious system. The political system in their newly organized society should be a sustained politics of justice (Deut. 6:6-9, 17-19). And the economic system needed to rest firmly on the reality that what they had was given to them by God and they were merely stewards, not owners (Deut. 6:10-12) (Linthicum, 1991a, pp. 48–51). In contrast to blueprint visions of a perfect society generated throughout history by the likes of Plato, Karl Marx, or Thomas More, Linthicum explains that, "The new society that Moses prepared the

---

[3] "By "religious" I mean the system that gives the city its reason for existence (the word's original sense, from the Latin *religio*, means 'to bind fast' or 'to structure'). A religion is that which structures or brings ordered meaning to life. With such a definition, we can readily see that even the most secular and materialistic city has a religion, because it uses a commitment to modernity to bring order and structure to its existence." (Linthicum, 1991a, p. 47)

Israelites to inaugurate in the Promised Land was not...a utopian state. The commandments, stipulations, and decrees that formed the fiber of that new society were all laws and covenants, not of perfection, but of justice!" (Linthicum, 1991a, p. 49). Deuteronomy offers a plan for society that recognizes humanity's fallen state. Faithfulness to God, justice, and stewardship marked this new society.

This plan did not last, unfortunately. The Bible offers an analysis of the nature and repercussions of corporate sin. Ezekiel 22 gives insights into all three systems, conveying a message that is consistent throughout Scripture. The root cause of systemic sin is the withholding of vital information by priests or other power-holders (Ezek. 22:26). The priests could control the people by withholding information, and therefore began to dominate the people (Linthicum, 2003, p. 43). In Ezek. 22:25, we see the political powers oppress the people rather than stand for justice. In Ezek. 22:27 there is a shift in the thinking of the economic leaders from viewing themselves as *stewards* to viewing themselves as *owners* (Linthicum, 2003, p. 46). These three systems intertwine in such a manner as to collaborate for "greater exploitation" (Linthicum, 2003, p. 49).

As we work toward urban transformation, our task is to incorporate Linthicum's exposition of systemic injustice into our broader understanding of societal evils and their causes. Linthicum concludes that evil is as social as it is personal. The depth of this evil is best understood by tying it to a theology of power, which we will discuss briefly in Chapter 13. This social evil is more difficult to address in many ways because it has become system-wide. The Evangelical church has largely assumed evil abides primarily in the individual. Linthicum offers a needed corrective, noting the ways evil operates through social structures. However, the case can be overstated and remove the biblical emphasis of individual sinfulness. Systemic injustices are rooted in the reality that every individual has an innate bent towards evil. The gospel of Jesus Christ addresses our individual sinfulness as well as systemic injustice.

Breaking the Chains of Injustice

The ubiquitousness of injustice presses on us from every side. What does the Bible say about justice? Will injustice simply have its way until the return of Christ? In the previous chapter it was clearly established that while poverty is rooted in a number of causes, the most common cause is oppression. One person's poverty most often benefits/profits someone else. The Bible attests to this fact again and again. The people of God perpetually fell into a treacherous pattern of oppressing others. Isaiah 58 illustrates this clearly. Even when God's people are worshipping enthusiastically to please God (for selfish reasons) they are still oppressing employees, withholding food from the poor, and seeking pleasure for themselves. In the next chapter of Isaiah, the human predicament is stated in unequivocal terms. Humanity is incapable of justice. Our default actions are to oppress others and indulge in wickedness. This has been true of humanity since the fall, and we are hopelessly bent towards injustice against one another unless God intervenes in our lives.

As we noted earlier, our wickedness seems to be compounded when we settle in greater numbers. The city was intended as a good gift but has now become an amplifier of evil. Even the model city of Jerusalem succumbed to this pattern of injustice. There was nothing but oppression in that showcase city (Jer. 6:6).

The law was not designed for the upright, but for the sinner. Knowing humankind's proclivity for oppressing the weak, the law given in the Pentateuch makes provisions and reparations for inevitable inequalities. Laws requiring generosity and restoration (i.e. instructions on generosity to the poor in Deut. 15 and for practicing the jubilee in Lev. 25) show that God knows the condition of the human heart. But even these laws were distorted or outright ignored and injustice went unchecked.[4]

God's just nature and our unjust nature can only be reconciled by one who takes our hearts of injustice and gives us true, godly justice. The arrival of the Messiah signals the arrival of God's kingdom reign. Entrance to this kingdom requires a radical reconfiguring[5] in the pattern of the Messiah. This is the phenomenal work of God that transforms the vilest of hearts. With the dawn of God's kingdom also began a new era of justice. Jesus ushers in this new era as the one who begins the reversal of the bondages of captivity, blindness, poverty, and oppression (Lk. 4:18-19). Jesus calls us to die to ourselves and place our lives in his. As we (the Church) are now his body, we carry on his work of reversing injustice.

Christians are usually tempted either to understate or overstate the implications of this passage in Luke 4. Some have chosen to interpret this passage as metaphorical and teach that it refers only to a spiritual reality. Jesus is certainly speaking of the spiritual reality of releasing us from bondage to sin. But we cannot reduce the scope of the kingdom and exclude tangible acts of undoing the impact of evil on our world. When John the Baptist was trying to verify whether or not Jesus was the long awaited messiah, the confirmation from Jesus in Matthew 11:4-5 was this: "Go and tell John what you hear and see: the blind receive their sight and the lame walk, lepers are cleansed and the deaf hear, and the dead are raised up, and the poor have good news preached to them" (ESV, 2008). The work of Jesus can be seen publicly in his acts of justice and his words of spiritual release. Jesus went beyond healing

---

[4] Chris Wright offers an outstanding description of Israel's oppressive practices and the ways jubilee was intended to correct those practices. "The primary purpose of the jubilee was to preserve the socioeconomic fabric of multiple-household land tenure and the comparative equality and independent viability of the smallest family-plus-land units. In other words, the jubilee was intended for the survival and welfare of the families in Israel." (C. J. H. Wright, 2010, pp. 290–297)

[5] I am here referring to the biblical notion of *metanoia*, often translated as repentance. The Greek term *metanoia* communicates a radical shift that addresses life comprehensively. Too often we have allowed the term "repentance" to be a religious mea culpa.

and feeding individuals; he questioned injustices, confronted the privileged, and even physically protested those profiting off of people desiring to worship God in the temple. Wolterstorff (2013) says, "justice runs like a scarlet thread throughout the New Testament" (p. 87).

As the body of Christ, we extend the ministry of seeking justice to our neighborhoods and cities. One cannot love Jesus and ignore the plight of the poor and marginalized (Keller, 2010a, pp. 53–54). As such, Jesus' example of justice becomes paradigmatic for the church, not as a path to salvation, but as a demonstration of the values of God's kingdom.

A Just Response

God's people are called to act in ways that are just (Mic. 6:8), and without the inner life-transforming work of God, we would be incapable of cooperating with the God of justice. Likewise, as David Smith (2004) says, "Evil cities are best changed from within" (p. 20). There are a plethora of ways in which the people of God can work towards kingdom justice, and these vary somewhat from community to community. Since we cannot explore every possible response for every kind of situation, a few brief categories will have to suffice to move us in the right direction. Just response may fall into one of these four broad categories:

- Advocacy
- Activism
- Economics
- Reconciliation

Advocacy. Help for the poor and marginalized can come in many forms. One the church often overlooks is the need for Christian lawyers and legislators to lead the city in becoming more equitable and just. Urban blight is in part the result of individual decisions, but systemic sin can also contribute to poverty and breed injustice. "If the church does not deal with the systems and structures of evil in the city, then it will not effectively transform the lives of that city's individuals" (Linthicum, 1991b, p. 11).

Whether we realize it or not, we have been trained to think and vote according to what helps us individually. For the past few months we have been living in Marin County on the other side of the Golden Gate Bridge from San Francisco. The people of Marin County are outwardly very environmentally concerned. They buy organic and recycle and drive low-emission vehicles. However, these bedroom communities of San Francisco regularly stop any development proposals that would allow for greater density in local neighborhoods. The lack of development in Marin County is creating greater sprawl in towns much further down the highway. In other words, those in these small communities near the city want to avoid minor inconveniences that would result from higher density, and the impact is longer commutes, greater congestion, and worse pollution in the greater Bay Area. Every day, people are making decisions that serve the individual but cause harm to the whole community.

It is no accident that freeways built through cities are built in the middle of poor neighborhoods. People want the convenience of freeways that drop suburbanites right down into cities, but no one wants a freeway over their own home. Wealthier neighborhoods are able to find lawyers and legislators who will prevent such construction in their own backyards. By doing so, those lawyers and legislators smooth the way for bulldozers to tear right into poor neighborhoods. The people who lived in those areas are displaced but not justly compensated. Jobs, schools, and support networks are disrupted for thousands. But their voices are rarely heard.

Our cities need advocates who can speak on behalf of the poor and oppressed, advocates who can address important issues of justice long ignored by society, advocates who will hold accountable those who have neglected their duties in carrying out justice. When policies and laws are unjust, advocates must call for change no matter how daunting the opposition or intractable the injustice, William Wilberforce labored for 18 years before finally persuading parliament to abolish the slave trade (Metaxas, 2007). Every generation, every city, every community needs advocates who will speak on behalf of those who are not heard or heeded.

Activism. We are quick to extoll charity in our society. Charity is great, but it does nothing to address the root causes of poverty and oppression. "Alleviating the symptoms of urban decay has proved for most local churches a more manageable and less contentious task than tackling the wider causes of poverty and inequality" (Garner, 2004, p. 28). Consider the hypothetical scenario of a poor community where people keep getting extremely sick. A charitable church offers free clinics or donations of medicine. Some congregants jump to conclusions about what is making people sick. "Those people are eating too much junk food." Or, "their apartments are too dirty." It is later discovered that a big factory is dumping illegal waste into the water supply for this community. The factory has made sure local authorities will ignore their pollution violations, and this injustice can only be overcome with activism. All the church's free clinics and medicine will not prevent people from getting sick. Charity is not enough; justice requires vocal action against the causes of injustice.

In 2006, Bono addressed the National Prayer Breakfast in the United States with these words:

> This is not about charity in the end, is it? It's about justice. . . . And that's too bad. Because we're good at charity. Americans, Irish people, are good at charity. We like to give, and we give a lot, even those who can't afford it. But justice is a higher standard. . . . Preventing the poorest of the poor from selling their products while we sing the virtues of the free market, that's not charity: That's a justice issue. Holding children to ransom for the debts of their grandparents, that's not charity: That's a justice issue. Withholding life-saving medicines out of

deference to the Office of Patents, well that's not charity. To me, that's a justice issue (as quoted in Monsma, 2008, Kindle location 531–535).

When poverty is rooted in injustice, charity is insufficient by itself. We must actively pursue justice.

Economics. In a village setting one can survive without money. Food is grown or scavenged, shelters are built where there is space, and work is collaborative and informal. In a city, however, one needs money to survive. Everything is owned by someone. Goods are sold or rented by the owner. This means everyone, including the poor and the marginalized, need jobs with sustainable wages in order to survive. In many countries, children have to pay for school books and uniforms. Children of poor families often miss out on an education because of these demands. Without an education, these children will not be able to get a formal or stable job, and they will not be able to provide books and uniforms for their children. These and other costs, negligible to most in the developed world, are so great that they prevent the poor from being able to escape poverty.

A powerful, and often overlooked, way to pursue justice is helping the poor find employment. Around the world there are organizations that are doing good work by teaching people valuable job skills. What is lacking are benevolent employers who are willing to take a risk on hiring the poor, the recovering addict, or the ex-convict and pay them fair wages. We need entrepreneurs who will start businesses with a social conscience. The poor and marginalized are in such desperate situations that they cannot negotiate for fair wages or working hours. In our work with refugees who are desperate for any kind of stable work, we have seen employers who demand they work 12-hour days, 7 days a week for a meager wage. If a worker is unwilling to comply, these employers know they can find someone else who is desperate enough to work in those conditions. This is particularly devastating for families with young children as parents cannot work those hours without neglecting their children.

Nicholas Wolterstorff calls for "theologically faithful economics" (Gornik, 2002, p. 37). This is a different side to the economics issue. My wife was reading a book by a well-known personality touting financial wisdom. His advice has helped many get out of debt. But he told a story of waiting to buy a car until a struggling used car lot at the brink of bankruptcy dropped its prices under the market value for the car. Of course one person managed to get a cheap car, but at what cost? Another man's business went bottom-up, leaving him, his family, and his employees with no job. Many Christians interpret stewardship as getting the lowest possible price for something, but that often means the products we're purchasing were made by people working for pennies. Cut-throat bargain hunting is completely legal, but that does not mean it is just. The ways we choose to spend our money can either encourage injustice or justice. We need to be willing to pay a little more for a product at a store who treats its employees well and deals honestly with its suppliers.

I once had a professor who spent a lot of the class time promoting free market capitalism as the most biblical economic theory. But human greed pushes any economic theory beyond what is just. While free market capitalism has its merits, if left unchecked, it can lead to poverty and oppression for many, as can any other system created by sinful humanity. The Old Testament law recognized the tendency for humans to accumulate wealth even when doing so causes suffering for others. In that time period land was the primary means for livelihood (C. J. H. Wright, 1990, p. 110), and God's jubilee laws called for restoration of land rights to each family. Whatever the laws of our land, we must strive for a lived theology of economics that is just for everyone.

Reconciliation. John Perkins (1982) is an African American who grew up in Mississippi during an era of intense racial segregation. He left for California to escape what was sure to be a life of destitute poverty. After coming to faith in Christ he felt called to return to his home state to help communities living in poverty. He tells of one experience where he was driving a van down a state highway. When white policemen pulled him over, he was assertive in asking for civil rights. The officers then beat him to the point that he had to be hospitalized. In *With Justice for All* he reflects on this experience:

> Demanding our rights had not softened the white community as we hoped it would. Instead it stiffened their opposition. Lying there on my bed, I was able to see that confronting white people with hostility was only going to create war. If there was going to be any healing it would have to take place in an atmosphere of love. I had been trying to demand justice. Now God was opening my eyes to a new and better strategy—seeking reconciliation.
>
> I could not bring justice for other people. As a Christian, my responsibility was to seek to be reconciled. Then out of reconciliation, justice would flow.
>
> Affirmative action, integration, and so on might be useful, but they alone were not justice. True justice could come only as people's hearts were made right with God and God's love motivates them to be reconciled to each other (p. 102).

Superficial measures will not fix issues of injustice like racism or prejudice. As we experience true reconciliation brought by Christ, we then become conduits of reconciliation in our world. One constant I have observed everywhere I have lived in the world is the pervasiveness of racism and prejudice. In every cultural context, if there is a robbery, the blame is cast on whichever group is despised by the rest of society.

The New Testament church was born in the midst of racial division. Antioch of Syria was a city of ethnic division. Due to its location at a crossroads, the city was ethnically diverse. Even at its founding, the city was divided in two parts—one for the Greeks and one for the Syrians—and had a wall dividing them (Stark, 1997, p. 157). Antioch was estimated to have had 18 ethnic enclaves or quarters within it, and was noted for continual ethnic tensions (Stark, 1997, p. 160). The church did not abide by these cultural norms. In Acts 13:1-3, we catch a brief glimpse of the church's leadership team. This multiethnic church body included Jews and Gentiles. From the names of the leaders we can deduce they included black Africans, brown Africans, and olive-skinned men from the Mediterranean. "The leadership of Antioch," writes David Rutt (2003), "was a microcosm of the diversity of cultures, languages, and origins of church" (p. 40). The churches started in the New Testament could easily have remained ethnically homogeneous. Instead, their multiethnic composition was in itself a statement of Christ's work of reconciliation.

Conclusion

The injustices that are so prevalent in our world can overwhelm us. We must remember that justice does not depend on us. God's just kingdom has dawned and we are assured of a New City where God will bring absolute justice. Mark Gornik (2002) captures the hope of the church:

> Urban hope is based not on any notion of human progress but on the Lamb that was slain, the one who in self-giving life and death redeemed the world (Rev. 5:6, 12; cf. 1:1).... Christ is 'the hope of glory' (Col. 1:27), the promise of the new creation. For this reason, the hopes and cries in the face of urban oppression are hopes and cries for Christ, the coming of God who will make all things urban all new (p. 27).

The church lives in this future reality, hope-filled, that small acts of justice point us toward the one who justified the church.

Questions for reflection and discussion:

1. What biblical texts and examples does the author cite regarding the Christian responsibility to work for justice?
2. What systems of injustice exist in your city? Have you experienced any first hand?

3. What system(s) of injustice is your church in a position to combat? Does the situation call for advocacy, activism, economics, or reconciliation? Or some combination of these?

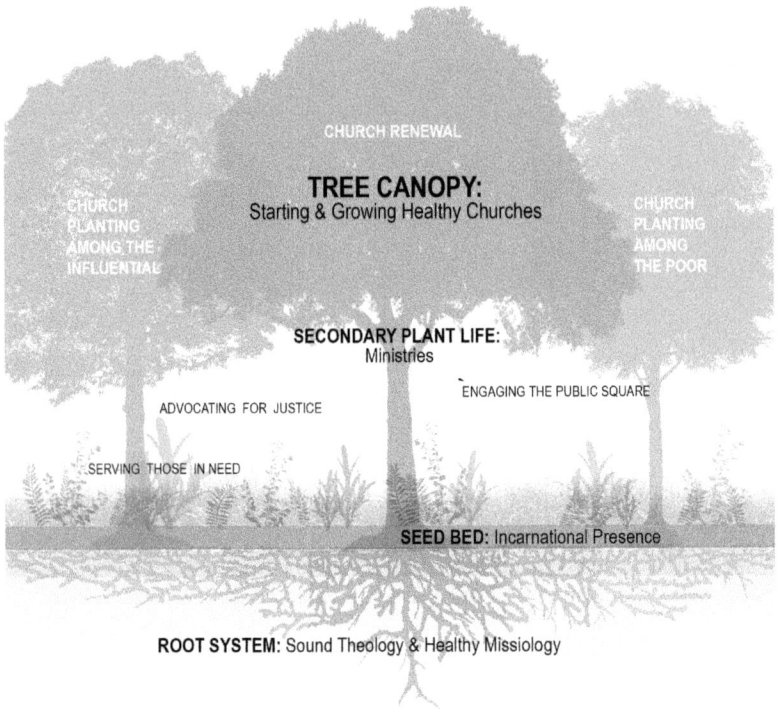

CHURCH RENEWAL

TREE CANOPY:
Starting & Growing Healthy Churches

CHURCH PLANTING AMONG THE INFLUENTIAL

CHURCH PLANTING AMONG THE POOR

SECONDARY PLANT LIFE:
Ministries

ENGAGING THE PUBLIC SQUARE

ADVOCATING FOR JUSTICE

SERVING THOSE IN NEED

SEED BED: Incarnational Presence

ROOT SYSTEM: Sound Theology & Healthy Missiology

ROOT SYSTEM ➡ SEED BED ➡ TREE CANOPY ➡ SECONDARY PLANT LIFE

Chapter 13
Engaging the Public Square

The dynamism of the gospel and its relationship to culture must be understood and lived out on its own terms, whatever the challenges today.

--Os Guinness (2014, pp. 21–22)

Why is power a gift? Because power is for flourishing. When power is used well, people and the whole cosmos come more alive to what they were meant to be. And flourishing is the test of power.

--Andy Crouch (2013, p. 13)

Following the Protestant Reformation in the 16th century, religious practice became privatized. Almost without knowing it, the Church has accepted this privatization of religion and is now nearly completely absent from the public square. Churches need to reenter the public square as a prophetic voice calling the city to justice and righteousness. They need to publicly give witness to the message of God's kingdom. Churches have the potential to offer a visible foretaste of the New City (Newbigin, 1954, p. 143). "The church must first be a new society for it to contribute meaningfully to the peace of the city where it dwells. We must think creatively about how to imagine and construct the life of the Church so that it can more faithfully embody Christ within culture" (Friesen, 2000, p. 126). The Church has been content to remain aloof from society and yet has expected society to adopt biblical morality.

If we hope for change in our cities, we must go deep into the culture of the city. A city "cannot be transformed without a significant cultural transformation" (Jardine, 2004, p. 261). Cultural transformation cannot be achieved through an occasional Christian event or periodic evangelistic crusade. The Church must engage culture at a deeper level, the worldview level, in order to impact the culture of a city. And the Church must participate in cultural production.

Get to the Public Square

If we could gauge society by our statements on Twitter, we would come across as revolutionary and sacrificially compassionate. If we could gauge society by our involvement in local-level politics, we might come across as apathetic and resigned to the downward spiral of society. I see a lot of comments complaining about presidents, past and present, but see almost nothing about local elections and issues. In a TED Talk, Eric Liu (2013) of Citizen University challenges his listeners to engage in civics at the city level, because he believes "cities can be the seat of the solution." Change begins locally.

It is a challenge for the Church that it has been relegated to the private sphere in society. Lesslie Newbigin (1954) highlights the relative insignificance of the Church in public life:

> The Churches in most of the countries of Western Europe take it for granted that by far the greater part of the secular affairs of their members are conducted without any direct relationship to the Church. Education, medicine, art, music, agriculture, politics, economics, all are treated as separate spheres of life, and the Christian who plays his part in them does so as an individual, looking for guidance in them not to the Church but to acknowledged masters in each sphere who may or may not be Christians. It is no longer expected, nor would it be generally tolerated, that the Church should control these activities directly (p. 14).

Of course, the church should not attempt to control these activities, but to influence them toward implementing kingdom principles. As it currently stands, the Church is largely absent from most of secular life.

When it comes to political involvement, the Church has tended toward one of two extremes. Throughout the centuries the Church has been drawn to a Christendom model which seeks to make society more Christian through political power (Shenk, 2005, p. 127). In reaction to the abuses of the power-seeking approach, others have withdrawn as much as possible from politics. Both alternatives are at best unhelpful and at worst destructive to society. As a societal body within the larger body of the city, the church needs to be a voice in the public square:

> God calls on Christians who seek the peace of the city where they dwell not to withdraw from participation in government simply because it is the will of God that governments use the sword (as some Mennonites have done). The church should not try to impose a utopian vision on the world (as Marxism does). Rather, it should be a creative witness to government and within governmental structures for justice, and it should work to resolve conflict nonviolently (Friesen, 2000, p. 237).

The voter most naturally votes for that which gives a personal advantage. In contrast, the Church is called to vote with orphans, widows, and foreigners in mind. The Church should support legislation and public servants who seek the good of the city. For the Church to offer a ministry to the poor and yet as individuals vote in favor of legislation that hurts the poor is hypocritical. The Church must be present in civics, in the venues of debate, and in the conversations that concern the people of the city.

Gaining Perspective on Power

One of the major obstacles to a healthy engagement in the public square is a misunderstanding of power. Many have equated power with control and believe that in order to exert power, one must be the top leader or be in league with a majority of decision makers. This was the dominant narrative for the "Christian right" or "moral majority" in the 1980s. There were several problems with this approach. The model was untenable without a majority of the voting population, it placed Christians in an adversarial relationship with those of different political views, and it would sometimes succumb to an "ends justifying the means" approach to politics. This is not a new phenomenon, in the fifth century Augustine (1950) saw the ways politicians blinded the public:

> For just as the demons cannot possess any but these whom they have deceived with guile, so also men in princely office, not indeed being just, but like demons, have persuaded the people in the name of religion to receive as true those things which they themselves knew to be false; in this way, as it were, binding them up more firmly in civil society, so that they might in like manner possess them as subjects (p. 140).

At various times throughout history, some Christians have misused political and religious power for selfish ends. Seeing Christians involved in power-grabbing politics drove other Christians to run away from all civic engagement. How does the church avoid the two extremes of abuse of power or apathy towards power? A healthy theological understanding of power is instructive for us.

Robert Linthicum has written a great deal on a Christian understanding of power. Central to Linthicum's theory is his understanding of different kinds of power and the importance of using the right kind of power in catalyzing increased opportunities for the community. In his book *Transforming Power* (2003) he seeks to "present a theology and practice of power that is transformative" (p. 22). Linthicum establishes that power is ubiquitous and is a "reality of human existence;" the Church needs to recognize this reality. Power has both a dark side and bright side (p. 3). He defines power as "the ability, capacity and willingness of a person, a group of people or an institution to act" (p. 81) and goes on to say that there are two main types of power. *Unilateral power* is a power over a people, the kind used by governments or other authoritative institutions. Unilateral power draws authority from position. The other type of power is *relational power*, which is less obvious (Linthicum, 2004, p. 5). This power is participatory in nature and is "power with" rather than "power over" (Linthicum, 2003, p. 82). Relational power opts for persuasion over coercion. While Linthicum maintains that both kinds of power can be used for good or for evil, it is relational power that is primary in the Bible. God prefers to use relational power with people. Jesus employed relational power routinely in his ministry.[1] Andy Crouch (2013) arrives at a similar conclusion using different language in *Playing God: Redeeming the Gift of Power*: "The power to love, and in loving, to create together, is the true power that hums at the heart of the world" (p. 53). The truest relationships are woven together by love. It is, in its own way, the purest renewable source of power.

Unilateral Power	Relational power
• Power "over" • Influence from authoritative position • Coercion	• Power "with" • Influence from relationship • Persuasion

Figure 13.1 Two Types of Power

Here Linthicum (2003) gets to what he considers to be the root of the issue: "In the final analysis, the ultimate problem is not the people or the churches or the poor themselves. The problem lies with the way the political and economic systems organize to amass and maintain power. And such misuse of unilateral power is, at its root, a spiritual problem" (p. 88). Power used in the right way is biblically legitimized (1

---

[1] Linthicum sites several examples from Matt. 21:23-22:46. (Linthicum, 2003, pp. 83–84)

Cor. 4:20). Thus, restoring and leveraging relational power is a central premise in Linthicum's model.

Linthicum's categories of power are helpful for the Church in the city. When the Church becomes consumed with unilateral power, there is a tendency to distort the gospel message. The church that uses power in this way is relying on systems for their authority.[2] On the other hand, the Church should not abstain from all types of power. Although God's power is unlimited, the biblical record consistently shows a preference to working through relational power. Jesus overcomes rival powers through a position of weakness. From 25 years of working with the down and out of New York's Lower East Side, Taylor Field gleans, "that weakness is the envelope of God's power" (Field & Kadlecek, 2001, p. 8). The Church's path to influence and change must be through concern and service to the whole city. When a church is seen as being concerned for the welfare of the whole city, rather than only their own, they are more readily heard when there is opportunity to speak on public issues.

Grassroots Involvement

When my family and I lived in a large Indonesian city, we attended a local church that met in the middle of a residential neighborhood. We enjoyed worshipping at this vibrant and welcoming body of Christians. Not long after we moved to another city, the neighborhood surrounding that church began to voice their displeasure at the church's presence. They claimed that the church members took up all of the parking on Sundays and had loud singing too early in the morning and did not add to the neighborhood in any positive way. The church members were really only concerned about the programs and activities inside the walls

---

[2] This is where the "7 mountain mandate" goes wrong. In an effort at influencing the seven mountains of society, advocates of this model become overly concerned with moving their own people into positions of unilateral power in each sphere of society. This quickly turns into an us-against-them power struggle and no longer communicates God's great love for all people.

of the church and did not see themselves as a tangible part of the neighborhood. If the church had engaged with the residents of the neighborhood and actively sought to address the issues of the community, their presence might not have been protested.

There are thousands upon thousands of churches in cities all over the world going about church life in a similar manner. The lack of community engagement is a tacit acknowledgement that faith is an easily compartmentalized private issue, and worse, that it has no significant bearing on public life. In Chapter 4, we established that cities are made significantly better by an engaged (vibrant) citizenry. Matt Hern (2010), an advocate for urban welfare, states the matter bluntly: "cities need engaged citizens" (p. 10). The people of God can seek the shalom of the city by engaging in its issues, vibrancy, and sustainability. It is at the local level that we can really make a difference and do so using relational power rather than unilateral power.

As the Church, we need to think twice before we throw our hands up in despair because of frustrations with bureaucracy, schools, or politics. Change takes time, intentionality, and sacrifice. Withdrawing from our cities only further tears at the fabric of society. Public schooling is in trouble in many cities. Families that can afford to do so tend to switch their children to private schooling options, leaving fewer families with the time and ability to help at the public schools. When this happens, schools end up in deeper trouble. Robert Lupton (2005), who has served in inner city Atlanta for many years, writes about the choice their family made in moving to that long-neglected community. Like any of us, they had been concerned about their children's education. He describes what happened after only a few years:

> By the time Jonathan, our younger son, took the battery of standardized scholastic achievement tests administered to all fifth graders in the public school system, a remarkable amount of learning had taken place at Slaton Elementary School. The average test score had risen to the seventy-first percentile in four years. This was an achievement of monumental proportions given that the demographics of

the school had changed little during that period—still mostly low income and minority. And at least two middle-income parents had learned some important lessons as well. First, a little leaven causes the whole loaf to rise. Second, where your treasure is, there will your heart be also (p. 175).

It was a step of faith for the Luptons to enroll their children in a struggling school, but by deciding to invest in the local public school rather than avoid it, they helped to improve the education of many children. Just a few Christians actively investing in declining neighborhoods can trigger change for the better. This only happens when the church sets aside their lofty agendas for hot-button issues, and turns to their communities in love and patience, always ready to speak prophetically within their communities.

Global Consciousness

One of the great marks of the Church has always been its universality. From early on, the churches have been concerned with the welfare of the Church in other cities, as when the churches of Galatia sent relief to impoverished Christians in Jerusalem (1 Cor. 16:1-3). In the same manner, Christians are called to be aware of needs and afflictions around the world. With the rise of globalization, this responsibility only increases. "In constructing a theology of mission for the city, we can no longer divorce global issues from local ones, or macro analysis from micro encounter" (Van Engen & Tiersma, 1994, p. 275). There is a direct relationship between issues of poverty in Southeast Asia and human trafficking in North America.[3] This means the citizen of an American city is impacted by what is going on in Southeast Asia. Moreover, urban people more readily move from one city to another. Therefore, people from cities in different countries may

---

[3] There have been many cases of impoverished women in Southeast Asia looking for jobs and then falling prey to human traffickers who force them to work in illicit massage parlors in the United States.

share more in common culturally than people from a city and a village in the same country (Keller, 2012, p. 155). As we seek transformation in our cities, we must leverage these connections for the sake of city transformation worldwide.

The domain of the Church's mission has always reached to the ends of the earth (Matt. 28:18-20; Acts 1:8). As such the church is to be continually praying for the nations and actively responding to global concerns. David Bosch describes how Evangelicals in the late eighteenth century, renewed by the gospel, rose up against injustices all over the world.[4] It is said that Evangelical Christians of the day were among the most educated about the world because of their concern for peoples in distant lands. Churches based in global cities today are uniquely positioned to continue with the legacy bequeathed by those feisty Evangelicals of the 1700s. Global networks require urban nodes where people and issues converge for greater impact. Ministries and churches in one city can connect a Christian who's relocating to ministries and churches in the destination city.

---

[4] Bosch (1991) is worth quoting at length here: "It is important to note that evangelicals —whether in the United States, Britain, or the continent, and whether Anglicans, Lutherans, or members of non-established churches—were nonconformists in the true sense of the word. The 'official' churches were, by and large, indifferent; they showed little interest in the predicament of the poor in their own countries or the detrimental effect of colonial policies on the inhabitants of Europe's overseas colonies. It was those touched by the Awakenings who were moved to compassion by the plight of people exposed to the degrading conditions in slums and prisons, in coal-mining districts, on the American frontier, in West Indian plantations, and elsewhere. William Wilberforce, who launched a frontal attack on the practice of slavery in the British Empire, was an avowed evangelical. William Carey protested against sugar imports from West Indian plantations cultivated by slaves. Christian Blumhardt, one of the founding fathers of the Basel Mission, challenged the first group of Basel missionaries never to forget 'how arrogant[ly] and scandalous[ly] the poor Black people were for centuries...treated by people who called themselves Christians'. Many, many more similar examples could be added. Small wonder that the chartered companies administering the colonies did everything in their power to keep the missionaries out! At the same time these evangelicals had no doubt that soteriological emphases had to take precedence that they were not proclaiming mere temporal improvement of conditions, but new life in the fullest sense of the word. As such the burgeoning evangelical movement, particularly if compared with the bulk of Western Christianity and ecclesial life which by and large had succumbed to the spirit of Rationalism, represented a fairly effective opposition, in some respects even an alternative, to the Enlightenment frame of mind" (p. 281).

Another dimension to the global consciousness of urban dwellers is the impact on the culture of the city. When there are acts of injustice in one place in the world, we see protests in major cities throughout the rest of the world. People living in cities are more aware of, moved by, and involved in global issues. News media in the most global of cities delivers the most globally informed news. Andrew Davey (2002) says "…the culture of the city is increasingly global…" (p. 6), which means the church in the city needs to be also. In order for the urban Christian to engage the people in her/his neighborhood, she/he needs to be well-informed of global current events. The urban church needs to be acutely aware of diverse cultural differences because the nations are represented locally in that city.

Generating Great Art, Science, and Thought

Presence in the public square is not only about civic engagement. Society thrives with great art, science and thought. However, the Church seems to have forgotten its legacy of artistic, scientific, and philosophical innovation.

Right after college I worked in a Christian bookstore. A Christian music label sent us a poster that listed their artists, and next to each artist was a comparable secular artist. Music promoted this way did not feel like art; it felt like a gimmicky sales tactic. I have never gone to Tower Records and seen a poster that told me I should like Coldplay because they sound like U2. Resembling something popular doesn't make great art. Rather than producing Christianized versions of current pop culture trends, the Church ought to join with the city in creating organically, contributing to the generation of great art, science, and thought.

Unfortunately, many Christians who strive for great art or approach other disciplines creatively become marginalized by the Christian community. Urban churches and ministries should be spaces where art thrives because nothing is more deserving of creative expression than the gospel! Christian scientists should bring knowledge and application to new heights because they know the Creator. In our unending struggle to understand ourselves and our significance, we desperately need thought-leaders who think in light of the hope we have in Christ.

Although the Church has a rich history of great artists, scientists, and philosophers, such creative endeavors are no longer a priority in most churches today. We have within Christian subculture an environment that favors a herd mentality and bumper-sticker-thinking. We prefer the scientist who defends a "Christian" belief over the scientist who, compelled by her/his belief in the Creator, seeks to understand creation as objectively as possible. The philosopher who smartly defends the status quo is more valued than the philosopher who challenges our shallow worldviews. The musician with mediocre ability and happy Jesus lyrics is prized over the musician with honest faith questions and truly beautiful music. We, the Church, have settled for shallow, mediocre, and bland, while the city rejects such lukewarm offerings in favor of the stimulating, creative, and beautiful. This apathy towards creativity diminishes an opportunity to reflect the Creator God. N.T. Wright (2008), seeing the missional potential of artistic expression, says "Genuine art is thus itself a response to the beauty of creation, which itself is a pointer to the beauty of God" (p. 223).

Cities are amalgamators of culture. "Cities compress and unleash the creative urges of humanity. From the earliest beginnings, when only a tiny fraction of humans lived in cities, they have been the places that generated most of mankind's art, religion, culture, commerce, and technology" (Kotkin, 2005, p. xx). In far too many cases the Church has scoffed at the ideas of others and great art has gone unappreciated or scorned by people of faith. It is as if we are threatened by the ideas and expressions of others. By engaging with creative art and thought, the Church tangibly contributes to the wellbeing of the city. Churches tend to have spaces with good acoustics that could be used throughout the week as spaces for rehearsals and practice and the exchange of ideas. "Cities with a vibrant cultural heart and lots of performance space, both inside arts buildings and in open squares or wide pedestrianized streets, are more livable, and have a higher quality of life" (Northcott, 1998, p. 34). The church can contribute to quality of life in the city just by opening its doors to give space for creativity.

Art has a way of penetrating past our exterior facades and allowing for deeper human interaction. We lived in San Francisco during the terrorist attacks on September 11, 2001. A friend organized and curated an art show with diverse entries that allowed artists using a variety of mediums. It was not only an expressive outlet for the artists but also became a valuable place of contemplation, prayer, and conversation for all of those who went through the exhibit. "When artistic communication expresses our deepest values and commitments, the arts function in a way similar to religious language. In fact, the expression of religious truth and meaning is almost always integrally connected with artistic form" (Friesen, 2000, p. 178).

Aesthetic expression is a basic human value. One thing I notice as I have visited some of the poorest communities on the planet is residents displaying beauty with what they have. I visited a family in one slum community who had a beautifully arranged garden and scavenged pictures hung on the wall. Northcott (1998) notes the value of art in such communities, saying, "Creativity in art and in crossing boundaries and building on personal relationships and networks provides a model of the church as catalyst and partner in inner city regeneration" (p. 35). Unfortunately, artistic expression tends to be more accessible to the wealthy (through lessons, concerts, museums, etc., which all require money). One way in which the church can serve the city is by providing opportunities for artistic expression to poor and working class communities.

Los Angeles-based Mosaic Church has made artistic expression an integral part of their church. In a city brimming with aspiring filmmakers, actors, and other artists, Mosaic has used various forms of artistic expression as paths to creating community. Creative expression, participant inclusivity, and innovation are valued to such a degree that people from diverse ethnic and socioeconomic backgrounds come together as one body. Gerardo Marti (2009) captures the importance of what Mosaic does:

> In short, Mosaic is attracting an ethnically diverse group of primarily young adult urbanites who are open to artistry, creativity, and change, and who ultimately act on a mission-driven theological framework. It interacts with the ethnic fluidity of the Los Angeles region, coopts creative arts as a base of influence, strategically leverages culture by embracing and pursuing innovation and change, and reverses the typical age hierarchy of churches by giving young adults power and influence. Mosaic appeals to an emerging culture and younger age base, giving young adults an opportunity to respond to the church's mission and mobilization. Mosaic attracts an ethnically diverse population because it captures an emerging culture concentrated in young adults who have fluid personal identities, are open to artistry, and wish to both embrace and effect social change" (p. 3).

Indeed, surmises Marti, "Mosaic is an organization crafted for Los Angeles" (p. 3).

We also have to give permission for urban people to think and ask hard questions. I have met a number of people who left the Church or never entered because they felt as though the Church preferred to remain intellectually ignorant and isolated. Perhaps the Church has held onto vestigial anti-intellectual tendencies from a bygone era. But this will not work in our present era of urbanization and globally disseminated information. Redeemer Presbyterian creates space for hard questions by having a time of questions after the sermon in one of their services.

Instead of indulging mediocre art and thought separately from society, the church needs to seek fresh and creative ways to express faith in the public square. We need to make space for creative expressions of our faith and theology as well as open conversations to engage the world of ideas and the ideas of the rest of the world.

Generosity and Welcoming that Leads to Reconciliation

Cities are deeply fragmented among ethnic groups, classes, and even vocations. It only takes one high profile racially sensitive case to bring this fragmentation to the surface. These points of difference and exclusion are furthered by our physical environment. "Urban exclusion takes place through the construction of walls that divide, control, and ultimately injure the poor and the vulnerable. These 'walls' may actually be a street, a river, or a railroad track, but their mortar is the power of exclusion" (Gornik, 2002, p. 53). While the Church may have had nothing to do with constructing the walls, and whether or not the walls were constructed as an intentional means of exclusion, these points of division and exclusion must become unacceptable for the Church. We are called to work toward reconciliation.

The Church must become a city within the city, a home for all people. Humankind has proven to be incapable of true reconciliation without the gospel of Jesus creating a new family that includes every language, culture, subculture, and vocation. Via the cross, Jesus Christ removed our innate alienation and hostility. Through faith in Christ we join in a ministry of welcoming, holding arms open to all who turn to Christ.

This reality of reconciliation makes the nature of the Church unlike any other human institution. And as such, the Church should intentionally become a place of welcome to all people. While cultural norms and the news media urge us to be safe and lock ourselves away from crime, the Church is called to risk everything for the sake of others. While "the economy of this world is one of scarcity," Geoff and Sherry Maddock (2014) remind us that "God's people are empowered to manifest an economy of abundance" (p. 29). The New Testament shows that the early Church considered hospitality a distinctive mark of true Christian community. Mortimer Arias (1982) argues that a posture of welcoming is essential to the faithful church: "The biblical imperative of hospitality reinforces the church's calling to be a welcoming community..." (pp. 69-70, 80). The church, then, becomes the starting point of truly diverse people unified through Christ's work of reconciliation so that they become the New Humanity.[5] Gospel-centered renewal within the Church can move the Church to a more faithful representation of the people of God. The Church then becomes a visible demonstration to a divided city that God-given ethnic distinctions do not necessitate ethnic exclusion.

Conclusion

Every day we make decisions that have a bearing on the public square. Withdrawal from the public square sends a message contrary to the message of the gospel. God the Father sent his Son into a world without hope and brought redemption. We, the body of Christ, are sent into the world as heralds of that redemption. This is a public message that we must proclaim and with which we must live in accordance.

We established in Chapter 4 that a good city is marked by a vibrant and active citizenry. A positively engaged citizenry requires that the Church put the good of others on par with our own good. Christians should not only be involved in this, they should lead the way. "The citizens of God's city are to be the very best citizens of their earthly city, working not just for their own prosperity but for the common good of their neighbors and the whole metropolis" (Keller, 2005, p. 15). As the Church engages the public square it does so with a prophetic challenge and a message of grace.

Questions for reflection and discussion:

1. The author says that before engaging the public square, the Church needs the right perspective on power and describes

---

[5] David Stevens, in *God's New Humanity*, offers a thorough and sound exegesis of the "New Humanity" passages in Eph. 2:15; 4:22-24; and Col. 3:9-11. These passages are best understood in the collective—rather than individual—sense and encompass a vision of multiethnic inclusion. (Stevens, 2012, p. 176)

two kinds of power. What are those two kinds of power and which does he say is the biblically preferred one?

2. What is an area of need in your city that you could engage at the grassroots level? What personal sacrifices and challenges might that bring for you and/or your family?

3. How can your church recapture the Church's legacy of engagement with art, science, and thought? Are there needs or opportunities in these fields that your church is equipped to meet?

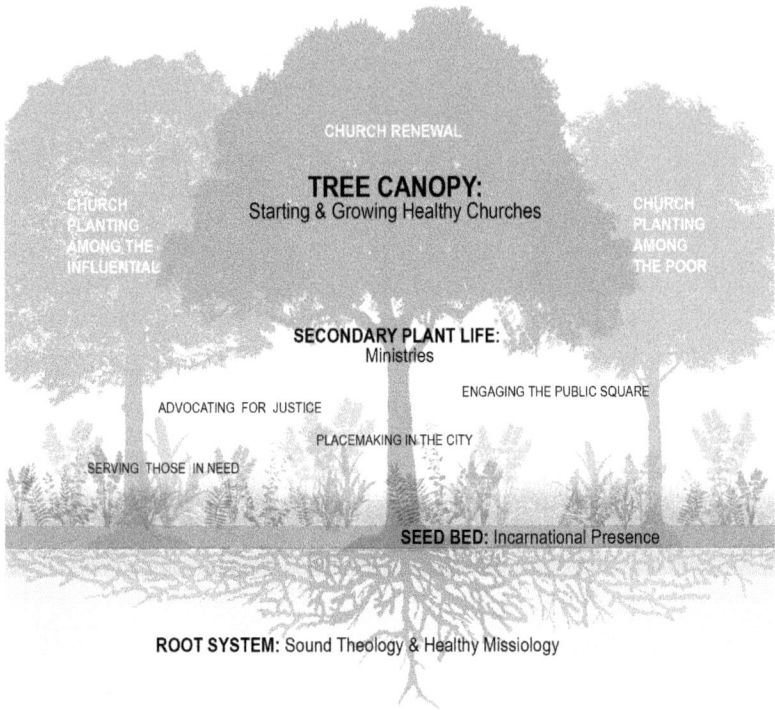

CHURCH RENEWAL

TREE CANOPY:
Starting & Growing Healthy Churches

CHURCH PLANTING AMONG THE INFLUENTIAL

CHURCH PLANTING AMONG THE POOR

SECONDARY PLANT LIFE:
Ministries

ENGAGING THE PUBLIC SQUARE

ADVOCATING FOR JUSTICE

PLACEMAKING IN THE CITY

SERVING THOSE IN NEED

SEED BED: Incarnational Presence

ROOT SYSTEM: Sound Theology & Healthy Missiology

ROOT SYSTEM ➡ SEED BED ➡ TREE CANOPY ➡ SECONDARY ➡ PLANT LIFE

Chapter 14
Placemaking in the City

Places are important in the Bible. Places can be holy. One of the root meanings for the word salvation in the Hebrew is "to make a space for."

--Taylor Field (2003, p. 58)

There is a need to rediscover the spirituality of place in the potential of urban life, through its vibrancy, diversity, and conviviality, as well the possibility of interaction and change. Those engaged in urban theology must be active new communities built on the visions and imagination of ordinary urban people, as part of the healing, redeeming, and transformation of our neighborhoods and cities, and our urbanizing, globalizing world.

--Andrew Davey (2002, p. 125)

Places matter. Cities intensify the use of space for the sake of economics, but do little in terms of building the environment in ways that foster community, social interaction, and public engagement. As cities continue to build and expand as in no other time in history, the Church needs to play a more assertive role in advocating for a built environment that is good for the whole city.

Theology of Place

Evangelicals have overlooked the importance of place and the built environment. We have aimed merely for buildings that are cheaper and bigger rather than building places that are connected meaningfully to the city. This oversight has led to churches that are as emotionally disconnected from their city as they are spatially disconnected. It has also (inadvertently, I hope) led to Christians who consume their city rather than live in a way that promotes flourishing.

A Christian reflection on space is an important topic of its own, deserving a more complete treatment than can be offered here. T. J. Gorringe (2002) argues for the "eminent spatiality of God." He says that God is the creator of all space and yet distinct from space. He builds on Karl Barth's view that divine spatiality is explicitly Trinitarian and that God, motivated by love, chooses to be present among us. An understanding of God as the author of all space is important, because it means that our use and production of space is due to God's grace (p. 20, 42-24).

The Bible indicates that place is important. Walter Brueggemann (2002) says, "Land is a central, if not *the central theme* of biblical faith" (p. 3). While he might overstate his case, it is clear that place plays a major role in the biblical narrative. John Inge also develops this idea by noting that place plays an important role in the Old Testament narratives. In the more obvious sense, the Garden of Eden and the Promised Land held special importance as divinely chosen places. But there is also the less obvious sense that the wilderness and mountains play important roles in the spiritual journey of Israel (Inge, 2003, pp. 36–38). Even our destiny is place-oriented: "I would want to say that the fact that this heavenly Jerusalem is central to the identity of Christianity is confirmation of the recognition of the New Testament that *it is very difficult for us to imagine salvation in terms of anything other than place*" (Inge, 2003, p. 57). There is significance in place.

In *A Christian Theology of Place*, Inge traces the underdeveloped theology of place in our current understanding to the Greek worldview.

The Greek view described place as simply a container that holds things, "So it does not really matter whether I live in Glasgow or Beijing, and what kind of buildings surround me will have no significant effect on me" (Inge, 2003, p. 5). Philip Bess is more specific, saying that Plato's ideas in particular have perpetuated the notion that the only place that matters is the ideal place in the afterlife (Bess, 2006, pp. 4–5). This results in an essentially agnostic view of place that persists to this day.

The New Testament is more ambiguous about the importance of place than the Old Testament but offers a more holistic understanding of place than Greek philosophy. The sacredness of specific geographical locations is sublimated by Jesus Christ. Inge (2003) proffers, "space has been 'Christified' by the incarnation...the incarnation implies that *places are the seat of relations or the place of meeting and activity in the interaction between God and the world...*" (p. 57). Jesus' approach to place is demonstrated clearly in John 4 when Jesus encounters the Samaritan woman at a well. In the conversation, Jesus plainly states that a specific location (e.g. a mountain or Jerusalem) is no longer central to worship, that worship of God can happen anywhere. From this account, we can deduce that specific locations are no longer considered more sacred or efficacious for worship than other places. But this does not minimize the importance of place.[1] This exchange with the Samaritan woman occurred in a place, as do all of Jesus' incarnational encounters. When Jesus took on flesh, he did so in a place. The well was not made holy because Jesus had a conversation there, but the conversation was enabled by the place. God works in and through places.

Urbanization has had a negative impact on the connection between place and people: "It is now clear that a sense of place is a human hunger that the urban promise has not met" (Brueggemann, 2002, p. 4). Urbanization has had an uprooting effect on city dwellers. Living and

---

[1] Timothy Gorringe concurs with this view and adds, "This passage does not mean, as it has sometimes been taken to do, that henceforward there is worship of an undifferentiated God undifferentiatedly omnipresent." He quotes from Karl Barth to say that this passage directs the reader to worship God "mediated through Jesus as the One who makes everything known to us." (Gorringe, 2002, p. 39)

working high-rise buildings, long commutes, and the globalization of franchise stores have diminished our unique connection with specific places. Given that cities are so naturally attached to a place, this disconnect between people and place in the cities is odd (Armitage & Roberts, 2003, p. 95; J. Jacobs, 1993, p. 6). Rather than being complacent about space, the Church would do well to leverage its spaces for the welfare of the city and its citizens.

The Value of Placemaking in a City

Placemaking has become a buzzword in the new urbanism movement and, more recently, tactical urbanism.[2] The idea behind placemaking is that space can be used badly or it can be used well. We have all seen token benches or playgrounds that remain empty most of the time. Those are examples of urban planners fulfilling a quota without concern for creating spaces for social interaction or public engagement. We want places that make a difference in real life.

The person who helped lead the charge in thinking this way was a feisty activist and author by the name of Jane Jacobs. When she took the train one day from Scranton, Pennsylvania to Grand Central Station in New York City, she had a life-changing experience. Jacobs, then a young single woman, made her way to Washington Square Park in Greenwich Village in lower Manhattan. At once, she was taken in by the vibrancy, the diversity, the activity of this small urban park surrounded by densely built cafes, stores, and apartments. She knew immediately that this was the place for her. Several years later, after Jacobs married and became a mother to two young children, an urban

---

[2] New Urbanism is a movement seeking to recover urban design that leads to a greater quality of life for all city citizens. From the main page of their website we see the emphasis on placemaking: "New Urbanism is the revival of our lost art of place-making, and is essentially a re-ordering of the built environment into the form of complete cities, towns, villages, and neighborhoods - the way communities have been built for centuries around the world." In "New Urbanism,")Tactical urbanism is a term referring to grassroots efforts at changing/altering the built environment to improve well-being in a neighborhood.

planner named Robert Moses was overhauling New York to make it more efficient for private cars to get in and out of the city. His master plan included running a highway right through the middle of Greenwich Village. Jacobs knew this meant certain death to the beauty of this quirky yet quaint, densely packed urban neighborhood. Robert Moses had already built expressways, tunnels and bridges in other places and had thousands of homes displaced in order to do it. He was a political juggernaut holding all the cards, that is, until confronted by Jane Jacobs. When she heard of the plans that would destroy her neighborhood, she launched a savvy grassroots campaign to put a halt to Moses' plan and save the place she loved. The battle went on for years, but eventually, Jacobs not only saved Greenwich Village, she also saved West Village. Today these communities are teeming with life, artistry, innovation, and social engagement.[3]

What Jacobs discovered, using the simple power of observation, was that streets, sidewalks, and storefronts each performed more than one function. A good sidewalk did more than transport you from point A to point B, it was a place to see neighbors, buy a newspaper or cup of coffee, or window shop. The streets and storefronts could make the sidewalk better or worse depending on how they interact with each other. The various parts of the city were best when they served multiple purposes. When sidewalks and small urban parks allow for leisure and social interaction, they become valuable places.

Private Space: Reneighboring the City

Christians, who are called to seek the *shalom* of the whole city, (Jer. 29:7) are also called to build their own houses in the city and live in them (Jer. 29:5). Citizens of a city need a place to call their own, a private place to dwell. To dwell is essential to humans (Illich, 1985, pp. 8–11). In Chapter 4, I listed security as an important characteristic of cities. A private place is one that provides security as well as offers the

---

[3] The whole story is told well by Anthony Flint in *Wrestling with Moses*. (Flint, 2009)

citizen an opportunity to shape their own space according to cultural preferences and personal taste. At the same time, a private place impacts the whole community as well as how its inhabitants can relate to others.[4]

Over the years I have had the joy of being able to live in close proximity to my neighbors, and I would not trade it for any other way to live. My children have been able to play with neighborhood children without having to schedule a playdate. We have neighbors that look out for our safety when a storm is on the way. By contrast, some friends of ours in the suburbs of Birmingham, Alabama lamented to us that each house was built in such a way that they could hardly catch a glimpse of their neighbors. They do not know their neighbors nor do their kids play with other kids in the neighborhood. We were not intended to live in such isolation.

Most Americans have bought into the idea that the large, private residence is a wonderful thing. Yet it has placed people in isolation, comforted only by mindless entertainment that is ebbing away at our humanity. We are created as social creatures and we are called to love our neighbors (Lev. 19:18; Mark 12:31). For too long we have conceived of love for our neighbors as a generalized command to want the best for others, passively. But the love to which we are called is not a passive well-wishing, as we see from the parable of the Good Samaritan. We are called to an active love for those we might otherwise pass right by. Robert Lupton (2005) posits, "The best thing we can offer an urban neighborhood is good neighbors" (p. 173). It is through these informal interactions that we, as a church, have our best opportunity to demonstrate our love for those around us. Mark Gornik (2002) describes how the early Church did this, saying, "Unlike many other first-century social groups, Christians focused not on their own privileges or status but on the benefit of the neighbor and the

---

[4] For example, architecture and proximity of a private dwelling can help or inhibit interaction with the community. (Jacobsen, 2012, pp. 139–156)

neighbor's relationship to God (10:322-33; cf. Rom. 15:2; Gal. 6:10)" (p. 107).

By living in a medium density neighborhood, we have been able to know our neighbors. As I walk to work, I get to know them as friends. We have come to realize that there are people living all around us who are hurting. Even with people all around, people become painfully lonely. When the Church begins to recapture the calling to be loving neighbors we can show these countless millions our friendship, and in the midst of many human failings, we can point them to Jesus who never fails us.

Public Space: Parishes without Borders

Public spaces are invaluable to great cities. Public space is that which is considered open to all people of the city. City parks and squares, and even sidewalks, are places where people can gather, stroll, and enjoy the interaction with the whole city.

> The denser one's social network, the more important the public space becomes as a space for leading one's life. Coincidental meetings between locals occur in every urban space where their paths cross; at crossroads, in front of grocery stores, in backyards or, of course, at the playground, that societal crystallization point of any locality (Mikoleit & Pürckhauer, 2011, p. 62).

The public, which includes the Church, should play an active role in the development and maintenance of public spaces for the sake of the whole city.

The Church has retreated to private spaces. A church near my old apartment in Birmingham, Alabama built a state-of-the-art "Family Life Center." The millions of dollars required to build this grand edifice were raised by explaining the project as something that would benefit the whole community. I soon began to doubt the church was very interested in the welfare of their community, however. Gaining entrance to their facility required the company of a card-carrying church member. And a half mile down the road was a public community center that already offered all of the same facilities. If this church really wanted to engage the people of their community, they would have done better to join the programs at the community center. The millions of dollars raised could have helped underprivileged children join in the programs already on offer.

Before the Church split into thousands of denominations, there was organizational unity of the Church in a city. A city would be divided into smaller geographical areas that were walking distance from a local church. These areas, called parishes, then came under the care of that particular church. If there was a fire in a tenement building, a pastor of that parish would respond. With the fragmented and spatially disconnected nature of the Church today, a fire can occur and no church may feel responsible to extend aid. The late Lesslie Newbigin challenges the idea that parishes are no longer relevant today:

> I do not think that the geographical parish can ever become irrelevant or marginal. There is a sense in which the primary sense of neighborhood must remain primary, because it is here that men and women relate to each other simply as human beings and not in respect of their functions in society (as quoted in Maddock & Maddock, 2014, p. 35).

It is time for urban churches to reclaim the ministry of serving a whole neighborhood.

In the previous chapter, we were challenged to engage the public square. The best way to engage the public square is through active engagement with the local neighborhood. Conn and Ortiz (2001) show this to be sign of vitality for urban churches, stating that "Today churches that have taken the challenge of parish evangelism and justice seriously are growing rapidly in multiethnic communities" (p. 298). In some cases, a church may even be able to use its own space as a public place. "Churches remain the largest voluntary association in the nation and their buildings make possible assembly, conversation, public discussion and forum for dialogue" (Garner, 2004, p. 129). Neighborhood watch meetings, theater troop practices, arts festivals, you name it; the church can deliberately become an integral part of the urban fabric. "Rebuilding community is our focus and can only be done if the local church has a parish mentality." (Kehrein, 1995, p. 173).

Sacred Space as Missional Place

A friend of mine served on staff at a church in Tennessee that was growing so fast they were looking at building a new facility. The church, influenced by the church growth movement, held fast to their priorities: cost, cars, and comfort. In order to build a large, comfortable facility with adequate parking they would need to build on cheap "undeveloped" land beyond the suburban ring around the city. What was once farmland then became sprawling asphalt with an all-in-one church campus facility in the middle. This was clearly a church only for middle-class, automobile-owning, committed Christians who would drive out of their way to attend services at this church. The church was no longer connected to any neighborhood nor would it be even if the suburbs sprawled around them. The building was built in a manner that would make it obsolete in thirty years. It was a building built only for the members of that church. It is the kind of church that replaces a sanctuary with a worship center. The new church building—and many others built like it—managed to avoid any feeling of the transcendence of God or his immanence in the world.

We have sometimes considered the presence of religious structures in a city to be neutral. This is a false conception. The presence and visibility of religious symbols and ongoing activities changes the urban environment (Daniels, 2008, p. 370). Symbols and architecture communicate something. In the Old Testament we see that there are certain places (the tabernacle and the temple) where God is present in a special way. There is a sense of awareness of God's presence in a confined place that differs from our awareness in other places (Bokser,

1985, p. 280). This is not to say that sacred space has a sacramental quality to it, but space devoted to the glory of God can be a conducive meeting place between God and his people.

"Being God's people in the city means that new spiritual, social, and material space is created, challenging the structures of the inner city" (Gornik, 2002, p. 95). A church's physical presence should mean change in society, or at the very least their presence is noticed. It is so often said that the church is irrelevant in society, meaning that the church has not had this kind of noticeable presence (speaking in generalized terms). The church needs to take their presence seriously, and this includes building location and design.

A few years ago I led a group of college students on an urban immersion experience in San Francisco. During our time of debriefing I asked when the students felt the safest and least safe. They agreed that the street that they felt most vulnerable on the street lined with three church buildings. The churches were grand edifices built off the street with at least a dozen steps leading up to large doors that were shut. Although the students did not understand why they felt uncomfortable on that stretch of sidewalk, it was the lack of human interaction and accessibility that made it feel that way. The streets that felt the safest had lots of people as well as storefronts with large clear windows and cafes with sidewalk seating.

What if churches were designed to be inviting and assuring rather than cold and intimidating? Could churches be designed so that people can easily wander in, meditate, pray, or perhaps even speak with someone about something on their heart? Issues of building design are not frivolous. The church has an opportunity to make the most of urban space by turning it into a place where passersby might meet God.

Place and Poverty

Those of us raised in middle class neighborhoods do not realize the issues of inequality that exist when it comes to shelter or even access to public places. As more and more people squeeze into our cities, land rights will become a more significant issue. Churches of all socioeconomic levels will need to be biblically conversant on these issues and prayerfully consider how the church should respond. Viv Grigg notes that although humanity was given responsibility for the land, it has always been God's land. The purpose of the land was to provide for all, and thus laws were created to maintain this perspective. Land was not intended to be owned "in perpetuity" by any one person (Lev 25:23) (Grigg, 2010, p. 17). Grigg harkens back to the Jubilee commands as an imperative for the church to manage, steward, protect, nurture and make productive the land. Grigg's biblical concern for the land is related to his concern for the poor and the opportunity for everyone to participate in this land stewardship (Grigg, 2010, p. 27). Grigg lived in Manila, where Spanish colonizers gave the majority of the land underneath Manila to three prominent Filipino families. Is this land rightfully owned by these three families, or is it stolen land that needs to be restored to previous ownership? I do not pretend this is a simple issue, but it is one that the Church needs to understand in order to be a voice for the cause of justice.

Worship space for the poor is another important issue. Most missiological literature eschews an emphasis on church buildings when planting an indigenous church. Grigg counters this conventional wisdom in the case of urban slum dwellers. He notes, with some understanding, Donald McGavran's reservations about new urban churches too quickly acquiring buildings.[5] Instead, McGavran promotes cell churches as a viable option. In Grigg's experience, however, the urban poor do not function well with the cell church and often do not have homes that can accommodate much of a church gathering. In urban slums, having a place where the church can gather freely can go a long way in helping the church become more deeply rooted in the community (Grigg, 2004b, pp. 196–197).

---

[5] McGavran's "Eight Keys to Church Growth in Cities" can be found in (McGavran, 1980, pp. 314–332).

I went to a seminar on placemaking where I heard three engaging speakers talk about the ways they have designed or transformed spaces to become great places of social interaction. It became clear to me that all of their ideas were cash-intensive and were primarily relevant to those with disposable income. During the time allotted for questions I asked about placemaking for the poor. After fumbling for some answers, one of the speakers mentioned a soup kitchen he was familiar with. There was something terribly incongruous about a discussion geared towards making the city better with great public spaces while giving little thought to half of the city's population—the poor. The Church needs to look beyond its own community and seek the good of the whole city.

Conclusion

I had a student, Sam, who served as a pastor to an ethnic minority congregation in a large Southeast Asian city. They met at a very strategically located church building in the shopping district of the city. The area was always brimming with foodies, shoppers, clubbers, and tourists from all over the world. The church building stood five stories tall with a beautifully lit cross. But there was no access except for the Sunday morning service times. Sam told me that he saw people wanting to go into the church for prayer or counseling or spiritual guidance every day. He lamented that tourists from countries with little or no gospel witness wanted to ask questions about Christianity but had no venue to do so. The church leadership was not open to innovative ideas on reaching such people. This church is missing an incredible opportunity to be a public witness in a city and country where Christ is known by only a small minority.

Whether it is in the places we dwell or our shared spaces, we make decisions that can help or hurt our engagement with the city. Places are important for everyone. As we grow in our understanding of the impact of place and the importance of the built environment, our churches can transform spaces to become places of missional connection with our cities.

Questions for reflection and discussion:

1. How do the Old Testament, New Testament, and Greek/
    Platonic understandings of place compare with one another?
2. Think about the built environment of your home, work, and
    church neighborhoods. What influence do those built spaces
    have on the people who also live and work there? Do those
    places foster community or discourage it?
3. Think about your church's building. Does its exterior invite
    people in? Does the interior of the church feel like a place for
    community? For meeting with God?

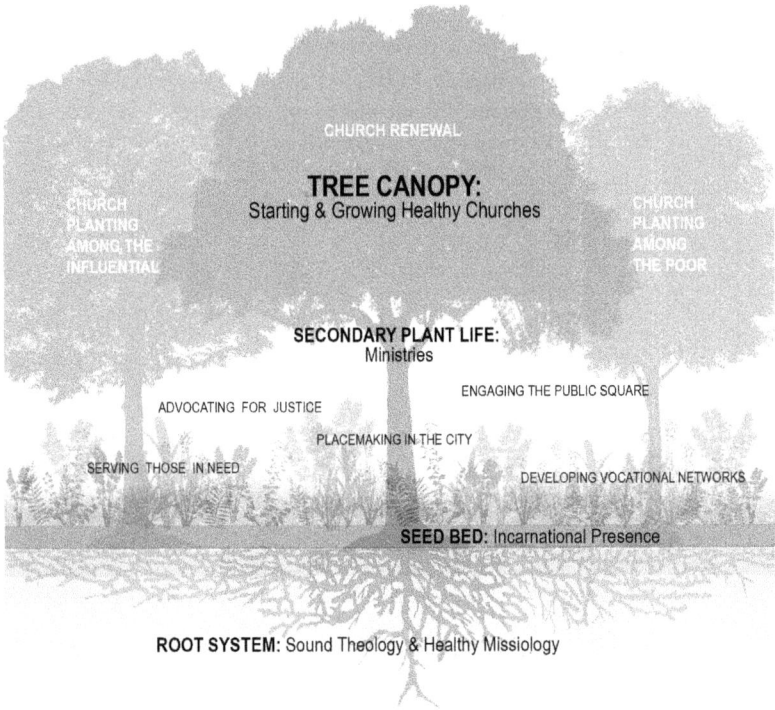

CHURCH RENEWAL

TREE CANOPY:
Starting & Growing Healthy Churches

CHURCH PLANTING AMONG THE INFLUENTIAL

CHURCH PLANTING AMONG THE POOR

SECONDARY PLANT LIFE:
Ministries

ENGAGING THE PUBLIC SQUARE

ADVOCATING FOR JUSTICE

PLACEMAKING IN THE CITY

SERVING THOSE IN NEED

DEVELOPING VOCATIONAL NETWORKS

SEED BED: Incarnational Presence

ROOT SYSTEM: Sound Theology & Healthy Missiology

ROOT SYSTEM ➡ SEED BED ➡ TREE CANOPY ➡ SECONDARY ➡ PLANT LIFE

Chapter 15
Developing Vocational Networks

All members of the ekklesia have in principle the same calling,
responsibility and dignity, have their part in the apostolic and
ministerial nature and calling of the Church. Because they live
by the same divine grace, all as children and servants of God.
--Hendrik Kraemer (1959, p. 160)

If Christians live in major cultural centers in great numbers,
doing their work in an excellent but distinctive manner, that
alone will produce a different kind of culture than the one in
which we live now.
--Timothy Keller (2006, p. 39)

In the Asian city where I live, most people live in places that are restricted only to residents and many go to work in buildings with pass-card entry. Even low-cost apartments have guarded entrances. Urban life is increasingly privatized and pass-protected. This means that pastors and other ministry leaders do not have a natural means of connecting with the people of the city. The work of ministry is shared by lay people ministering to neighbors and coworkers. "If our urban social analysis is correct, most of the city will not be reached without many gifted and empowered lay folks weaving the gospel into the fabric of their lives, delivering it personally to places and persons of greatest need" (Bakke, 1997, p. 92). In this chapter we will focus specifically on making an impact through vocation.

Real change in the city cannot happen through a few church programs or even through advocacy for policy changes. The most fruitful churches in urban centers around the world have both solid teaching from the pulpit and a laity who take their faith into the world (Ellison, 1997, pp. 100–101). Inner transformation in the lives of believers, then, must be worked out in every vocation and work environment in the city. Due to the complex division of labor in cities, a pastor cannot easily guide each member of the congregation through all of these decisions. Therefore, we need networks of believers in each vocation that can actively help other Christians work out their faith in the work place and even contribute to changes in vocational practice that help others reduce ethical compromises they face daily.

Equipping Laity

Churches that rely on pastors to do all of the work do not tend to grow or thrive (Hinton, 1985, p. 167). This is even more true in the urban context. Urban pastors must lead differently than they might have done in a more rural setting. Pastoral authority does not have the same currency as it has had in traditional small towns. City dwellers need a share in the ministry of the church. And this resonates with the biblical organization of the church described in Ephesians 4:11-12. Biblical scholar Harold Hoehner (2002) comments that leaders in the church are primarily preparing the whole church for service, therefore "every believer must do the work of the ministry" (p 550). The whole body of disciples is called to active participation in the formation and multiplication of disciples in the city.

Historians of Christian missionary movements have long noted the critical role of every Christian's empowerment for service both in the church as well as in their lives (Bosch, 1991, p. 472; Walls, 2002, p. 17). Regarding the early church movement, Bevans and Schroeder (2004) capture the idea nicely:

Christianity was neither an elite movement nor overly dependent on its leadership. Government authorities often made the mistake of thinking that they could destroy the church from the top by killing its leaders. Rather, "because Christianity was a mass movement, rooted in a highly committed rank and file, it had the advantage of the best of all marketing techniques: person-to-person influence" (p. 79).

If the "rank and file" are commissioned with the ministry of the gospel, they need to be equipped as such. They are already positioned for incredible impact in the primary social networks of society as Ray Bakke (1997) notes:

The only way we will evangelize the city is to recruit, equip, and encourage laymen, -women, and -youth to identify and penetrate their respective worlds with the gospel. It will never happen by professional evangelism and 'come-structured' strategies. Urban laypeople usually stand at the center of four distinct worlds in their primary relationships—family, neighbors, work, and play (p. 91).

The church must have a mindset of sending its members into the world and must structure themselves accordingly. Urban laypeople simply need a way to theologically integrate faith with life in such a manner that they bring light into workplaces and neighborhoods. Sydney Rooy (1992) says, "Theological training must be given to the whole church. Here it would be well to cite what is called the Strachan theorem: 'The expansion of any movement is in direct proportion to its success in mobilizing its total membership in continuous propagation of its beliefs'" (p. 238). Every Christian is a disciple called to make disciples in every avenue of life.

Church Culture

One of my colleagues at the seminary where I teach in Southeast Asia is actively involved in her church. She leads the student ministry and helps organize the worship services. Her pastor keeps asking for a larger time commitment from her. When she has commitments related to her work at the seminary, her pastor gets frustrated, saying that work at the seminary is not as important as work at the church. If this is the attitude of a pastor regarding work at a seminary, we can imagine what the pastor's sentiments about work at a secular company would be. Many in the Church hold the assumption that church work is sacred and all other work is profane. This assumption is a distortion of Scripture. Throughout the Bible, we see God commanding and commending various "secular" vocational acts from working the land (Gen. 2) to trading goods (Prov. 31). Paul made tents and Jesus was a carpenter! All aspects of life are sacred acts of worship (Col. 3:17; 1 Cor. 10:31).

Equipping the laity with a "go" mindset rather than a "come" mindset requires an overhaul of the popular conception of church life. Too often church-goers have the perception that the only valid type of ministry is involvement with church programs and that really serious Christians must go into fulltime Christian service. Rooy (1992) asserts the sacred nature of all of life: "Congregations and pastors must be trained to eliminate the elite, professional concept of the full-time ministry. All members of the church community have a sacred function" (p. 239). Pastors must preach about the sacred nature of honest work, no matter what kind of work (within the parameters of that which is legal and ethical). The Church needs to place a higher value on Christians serving in a wide variety of contexts and in the full range of spiritual gifts. "It is critical that this leadership not be clerical in the traditional sense of the word or focused on a select few. What we need are non-hierarchical structures that recognize the widest range of gifts, abilities, and callings of the Spirit of women and men" (Gornik, 2002, p. 213). When the church recognizes and commissions the whole body of believers for mission in their city, it can become an answer to the prayer of Luke 10:2. Perhaps the Lord of the harvest has already provided laborers and they are sitting in our pews waiting to serve.

Vocational Identity

In a village community, your identity might depend on who you are related to, whereas in an urban community, your identity is more dependent on what you do. The fact that identity is wrapped up in occupation has implications for ministry. "Urban people generally undergo identity shifts. Ask them who they are and they will tell you what they do. That should tell us evangelists that the most fruitful evangelistic urban world is the factory, school, or office" (Bakke, 1997, p. 92).

In times past, the pastor once had more authority because he knew your parents and aunts and uncles. In many urban settings, such ways of relating are replaced by the pursuit of extended education and career advancement. Bakke (1997) describes the impact this often has on churches that have been slow to adjust to a different world: "Meanwhile, increasing numbers of those coming to the cities come for higher education and professional employment options which can propel them to successful careers. What happens when the village parsons and evangelists confront this urban challenge?" (p. 89). It is important for the church to identify the impact of occupation-based identity and how it effects church life and discipleship.

Most urban dwellers share more contact time with coworkers than neighbors or even family members. At times this is painted as a western issue resulting from individualism. This is not the case; it is a consequence of urbanization. Evangelism and discipleship need to be adapted to reflect this reality. Lesslie Newbigin, serving the Indian city of Madras (now Chennai) noted the importance of the working community as the primary place of discipleship (Hunsberger, 1998, p. 24). One survey observed that 25% of the Christians in Singapore were part of an occupational-based spiritual group (Bible study, prayer group, etc.). The presence of these groups has proven effective for legitimizing Christianity as a viable worldview option for the professional (Hinton, 1985, p. 98). Such groups are definitely an important aspect of reaching global cities and are successful only with a mobilized laity. Ray Bakke and others repeatedly point out the fact that pastors do not have access to offices, schools, and businesses, but other believers do. We need to implement more "occupational groups."

In order to best provide leadership in an urban church, pastors need to understand the realities of work life. It is wisely suggested that: "Urban pastors should visit people where they work in factories, offices, or schools to enable members to see their ministry potential in these worlds closed to pastors" (Bakke, 1997, p. 92n22). I mentioned this idea to a businessman taking one of my classes held on Saturdays. He promptly told his pastor, and they made an arrangement for the pastor to visit the businessman at his office. The pastor is now better able to disciple this Christian businessman and can more effectively preach to a church full of similar people. The businessman is now more apt to hear the pastor knowing that he has a better understanding of the businessman's daily reality. It can be easy for pastors to lose sight of what life is really like for most of the people in his church. Small steps like this one can help the pastor lead in a way that empowers this group of Christians already placed in offices, factories, and stores all over the city.

Work that is God-Glorifying

Work existed before the fall of humanity (Gen. 2:15). Work is not punishment; rather it is ordained by God. We are created to be creative and productive. We see this modeled by God from the beginning. Ray Bakke (1997) notes that the "God of the Bible works with dirt at the beginning, and at the ending of the Bible resurrects real material bodies of Christ and us. Christianity is the only religion in the world that can integrate spirit and matter or the salvation of souls with the development of sewer systems for the city" (p. 81).

Work is one way to glorify God. This means our work has inherent value and that it should be done excellently. Good work brings dignity and fulfills, in part, God's purposes for us (Witherington, 2011, p. 4). God creates us with diverse talents and gifts to creatively make manifest his creativity. In other words, we do not join a coerced assembly line of the kingdom. Rather we are given the opportunity to cultivate our resources and produce excellence that brings God glory. And because of the fall, good work becomes a participation in God's purposes of putting the world right again (N. T. Wright, 2008, p. 112). Opportunities for good work can reverse the downward spiral of declining communities and restore one's sense of being human. Good work has the potential to inject change into a city.

As with most good things, we have the potential to distort work in a way that robs God of his glory. If we are not careful, work can become a path to idolatry, greed or oppression. Our work becomes idolatrous when we prize our work or position over our identity as a child of God. Greed takes human nature, designed in God's image, and distorts it. If we allow our job to rule us, we can treat others oppressively, whether it be employees, employers, customers, or competitors. In all of these ways we allow work to control us, to dominate our desires, and to drain our emotions. This is why Sebastian Traeger and Greg Gilbert (2013) say that "work is a terrible God" (p. 29). Work is valuable when it is correctly understood as one way in which we live for God, provide for our family, and contribute to the wellbeing of our city. But if we allow it to rule us, our work can be a detriment to our relationships with God, family, and city.

Earlier in the chapter, I indicated that our vocations give us evangelistic access to the people of the city. But it is more than merely an added place of evangelism, it is a place of worship. Ben Witherington (2011) says, "Work is not a secular activity; it is a sacred one originally ordained by God, and so it must be undertaken in holy ways" (p. 15). As Christians take this calling seriously, we will directly and indirectly point others to our Father.

Blending Gifts and Vocations

Given the value of our vocations and the importance of Christians doing their work well, there is a need for something that brings

Christians in similar vocations together for the sake of impacting that particular field. For instance, a new doctor, fresh out of medical school, may have many questions regarding how to best navigate ethical situations in a hospital. Christian doctors would do well to come together to reflect on those ethical issues theologically. But they may also join together in order to challenge each other to faithfully share the gospel in their context. Just like a missionary team might bring together gifts of evangelism and mercy, so will a group of Christian doctors as they collaborate. The hospital then benefits from seeing the body of Christ, rather than isolated individuals, at work there.

In Auckland, New Zealand, Viv Grigg brings different types of leaders together on a citywide scale in order to work for transformation. He believes the prophets and apostles need to be brought together to have a more comprehensive approach to the city. He gives an example from the First Great Awakening where God used a prophet, George Whitfield, an apostle, John Wesley, and a poet, Charles Wesley as a team which catalyzed wide-spread change through revival (Grigg, 2009, p. 187). As he states: "the fullness of revival may well result in entrepreneurial structures; the biblical terminology is perhaps prophetic and apostolic structures modeling or calling out in the public square for repentance. These then require responses of repentance by the leaders of city structures for the culture to move into cultural revitalization" (p. 182). Grigg draws on sociological studies that indicate a higher level of drivenness following religious revival. He further suggests that new entrepreneurial structures (businesses, organizations, and communities) with biblical values might develop that have a ripple effect on the incumbent structures of the city. In the same manner, Grigg (2008) hopes to recruit leaders in each city with a similar passion for urban transformation:

> The objective is the full declaration of the Word of God into each sector of the culture, resulting in individual salvation (entrance to the Kingdom), and societal and cultural transformation (reflecting the values of the

Kingdom). I would suggest that this can be measured by the emergence of new covenantal structures in each sector of society...

It starts with these big conversations, but is worked out in small forums, consultations, and ongoing cell groups so that every sector is touched. There is no sweeping way to bring transformation into each vocation, but through small intentional networks, incremental changes will add up.

Conclusion

Since vocation is so heavily intertwined with an urban dweller's identity, we must emphasize the importance of vocation-based transformation. Work becomes the place where we practice our faith, grow as Christians, and have opportunities to bring about changes in peoples' lives and in the city as a whole. In Chapter 4 we discovered that economic opportunity was important for good cities. A good theology of work helps us see the value of work and the importance of employment for all people.

All the while, we must keep it all in perspective. The urban dweller defines him/herself by vocation, but the believer must learn to draw identity foremost from Christ. Even with our identity properly centered on who we are as children of God, work can easily consume the attention of our hearts and pull us away from God's deep and abiding love for us. Ultimately, our work will fail to overcome the most critical problem, that we have hearts inclined away from God. We must turn to the work of Christ who has done the work of changing us from within so that we might now work only as a reflection of his great glory.

Questions for reflection and discussion:

1. According to the author, how does the identity of an urban dweller differ from that of people in rural areas? What is the biblical foundation for a person's identity?

2. Do you know other Christians in your workplace? Are there groups or networks to help you connect with other Christians in your profession?

3. Is your church's theology of work more of a "go" and minister or "come" and serve? How can your church better encourage and equip members to go and minister in their workplaces and/or schools?

Part 4

A Flourishing Ecosystem For the Whole City

Chapter 16
Canopy Network(s)

Networks constitute the new social morphology of our societies, and the diffusion of networking logic substantially modifies the operation and outcomes in processes of production, experience, power, and culture.

--Manual Castells (1996, p. 469)

Partnership is not just a project, not just a committee making decisions and sending some money. Partnership is expressing the very nature of the Trinity, the Godhead himself. Partnership is expressing Koinonia, the way in which we, as those who are made in the image of God, live together. That is the high challenge we have. That is the expression of the kingdom.

--Vinay Samuel (as quoted in Sugden, 1997, p. 423)

Cities are intricately cohesive. When one seemingly small part of the system breaks, the whole city can be crippled. I watch morning traffic reports in San Francisco and see how an accident on a minor traffic artery impacts the rest of the city. I was living in an Indonesian city while the sanitation workers went on a strike. In a matter of days, the city was desperate for a resolution to this strike. Trash was spilling into roadways, trash was clogging waterways, and the smell was nearly overwhelming. I would not have imagined that over just a couple of days our discarded stuff could have such a debilitating effect on the city. This is the intricately interwoven nature of our urban world.

Complex cities have complex problems that require complex solutions. Addressing the immigration issue in the United States, Christian statesmen Leith Anderson uses the analogy of a car with multiple problems simultaneously. The owner cannot decide to fix just one problem and delay fixing the others because the car still will not work. The only way to get the car functioning again is to address all of the problems comprehensively (Anderson, 2012). Cities are infinitely more complex than a car and similarly require a comprehensive solution. One church or ministry will not be able to singlehandedly transform the city. Neither will the city be transformed by all the churches tackling one particular issue. This is why the whole Church of the city must collaborate to seek the *shalom* of the whole city. Charles Van Engen (1994) observes the dangers of working for transformation in isolation:

> It seems that especially in urban Missiology, people have found it difficult to deal with the whole system of the city. On the one hand, there are those involved in micro-ministry who deal with individuals and their needs in the city—but they are often burning out in the process, in part because they are not dealing with the entire system (p. 246).

Networks of churches and ministries have the potential to respond to a complex city with a comprehensive approach to transformation.

The coming together of churches in a city for the good of the city points to the tangible impact of the gospel:

> The connecting structures of the church, for their part, should express and implement the mutual interdependence of all the parts of Christ's body. They should do this both in relationship to the particular communities that make up their constituencies (e.g., the congregations of a denomination) and in relationship to

other structures. They should foster dialogue, enable contacts, provide resources to their communities, and encourage the public witness to the Lord who is the Prince of Peace and who breaks down walls of separation.... The practice of unity and unifying ministry are ethical expressions of the radical newness of the life made possible by birth from above (John 3:3-8) (Guder et al., 1998, p. 261).

In broad terms there are two different kinds of Christian networks: informal networks and formal networks. Multiple networks of both sorts are needed in a city and the networks work collaboratively for the good of their city.

Informal Networks

Once a month we meet together to discuss, dream, pray, and eat. We are an informal collection of pastors, church planters, ministry leaders, and seminary professors. We have no officers, no budget, and no minutes from the meetings. We gather because of a mutual concern for gospel impact in the whole city. There is a kind of comradery in that room that is hard to match in other ministry situations. We are mutually encouraged and challenged in our respective ministries as we continue faithfully making disciples in our city. When a new church planter came with plans to start a church downtown, we readily listened, encouraged, and prayed over the venture. I believe the city is better off because of this gathering.

Eric Swanson and Sam Williams say "less is more" when it comes to networks. They explain:

Many citywide movements have split and fallen apart because they have tried to over organize activities or have created a litmus test (attendance at a weekly leadership prayer meeting, commitment to quarterly all-church worship events, participation in a joint evangelistic event, adherence to detailed doctrinal statements) that determines who is 'in' and who is 'out'—who is committed or not committed to city transformation (Swanson & Williams, 2010, p. 111).

Strangely, an over-zealousness in collaborating can lead to conflict and division.

The more decentralized and informal the organization, the greater the potential for innovation. Long-time advocate of organizational culture of innovation, Everett Rogers, studied the source of corporate innovations. New ideas were most commonly spread and adapted along peer networks rather than along chains of command: "Such decentralized diffusion systems usually are not run by technical experts. Instead, decision making in the diffusion system is widely shared, with adopters making many decisions. In many cases, adopters served as their own change agents" (Rogers, 1995, p. 365). In order for the church to make a difference in the city, we need increased innovation: "People are generally accustomed to and more comfortable with incremental change that can be managed and easily absorbed. But incremental change will not close the widening gap between the Church and the city" (Dennison, 1999, p. 8). Informal networks can become hives of idea exchange, experimentation, and mutual encouragement, facilitating the often drastic changes necessary for transformation to take place.

A friend once told me that being a pastor was one of the loneliest things he has ever done. The way many (thankfully not all) of our churches are structured, the pastor is constantly battling everyone. Informal networks can be safe places where pastors and ministry leaders draw encouragement and openly discuss challenges. When Christians network with a missional vision for the city, such gatherings can become incubators for innovation and collaboration.

Formal Networks

I recently attended an annual associational meeting of Baptist churches in California. Among the events at the meeting was an open and frank discussion on church planting within the association. Formal networks have budgets and officers and business meetings. While this may sound like a headache, formal networks can achieve goals that informal networks cannot. It is difficult for informal structures to fund joint projects, but this association of Baptist churches is able to collaboratively fund church planting efforts. A little institutional baggage also brings benefits.

When the Presbyterian Church of America (PCA) had the vision to plant a church in Manhattan, it was immediately clear that a sizable investment was required. It would take hundreds of thousands of dollars to get a church started in some of the most intensely sought out urban real estate in the world, and there was a high risk of the project failing (Keller & Thompson, 2002, p. 9). Few churches could take on that kind of investment on their own; only a formal network could invest enough to help the church plant succeed and absorb the fiscal punch in the gut if it did not work. From this vision came Redeemer Presbyterian Church, which has now "paid it forward" by assisting the launch of many more churches in global cities around the world through their Redeemer City to City Network.

While there are certainly challenges to formal networks, there are some initiatives that require a degree of formality to achieve success. Both formal and informal networks run the risk of becoming stiflingly traditional or dysfunctional. For both kinds of networks, remaining mindful of a few key points can keep networks moving forward. These keys to networks that make a difference are:

- Common vision for the city
- Common commitment to the gospel
- Common practice of love for our neighbors
- Maintaining organic movement dynamics
- Allowing structure to develop as needed

Networks That Make a Difference

Common Vision for the City. If the stakeholders in a network each maintain different visions for the city, the collaborative effort can be futile. The importance of vision was stated in Chapter 6; network formation is where it is essential. The vision must be common or shared. One person cannot impress their vision on everyone else. The network must work to develop a shared vision for their city, even if the process is tedious (Keller & Thompson, 2002, p. 12). This vision must look to Scripture to understand the kind of city that honors God and look toward the city with an honest appraisal of its current state. The value of the network emerges when different members of the network contribute to a more complete picture of the city as it currently is. Our network in Southeast Asia benefited greatly from having pastors from churches composed of foreign migrant workers and refugees. They were able to inject a much-needed perspective into the discussion, which led to a more compelling vision for the whole network. Just as the local church has multiple gifts that are occasionally at odds, networks can also be faced with these conflicts. One organization might be adept at mercy ministry while another is focused on verbal proclamation of the gospel. While their unique emphases might introduce tension during vision-development, it is a healthy and necessary tension.

Common Commitment to the Gospel. Networks that thrive are the ones who keep their eyes on what is important. Each ministry in the city can be so demanding and straining that it is difficult to see beyond that particular ministry. A healthy understanding of the gospel can help each participant in the network see how the gospel informs and guides each ministry. A common commitment to the gospel also provides a helpful filter for projects and initiatives. Sometimes churches settle for doing a lot of good things without evaluating whether those things point people to the gospel. For example, youth groups sometimes do activities just to keep kids out of trouble rather than stimulating their growth in Christ. The principles articulated in Chapter 6 can provide parameters for remaining mindful of the gospel. Without a commitment to the gospel, we may end up with cities that deflect glory from God or become mired in legalism. The gospel of grace reconciles God's holiness and God's love through Jesus. Transformation strategies that fail to point the city in the direction of the gospel will fail to bring transformation.

Common Practice of Love for our Neighbors. Everything Christians do should be soaked in God's love. The oft-quoted 1 Corinthians 13 passage reminds us that if we do the most amazing things in our cities without a deep and abiding love for the people of the city, it is worthless. The rubric of love helps set the attitude of the network and reminds us to look back to the gospel. Armed with conviction, we can become triumphalistic, arrogant, or obsessed with quantifiable results. Any grand plans of a network are pointless without a love for all people, including those who oppose our efforts toward transformation.

Maintaining Organic Movement Dynamics. Throughout church history there have been times of exponential growth among a people. We see this spontaneous growth in the earliest church in the book of Acts and periodically over the centuries in manifold lands. Those who have studied these movements all acknowledge factors that are catalytic for perpetuating the multiplication of the church (Addison, 2011; R. Allen, 1997; Garrison, 2004; Hirsch, 2006). A movement ethos is tied to vision, as we see in the example of the Redeemer City to City movement: "Though we had always said, 'We are not just a church, but a movement,' we had never had any concrete way of realizing that vision. Now we began to see how it could be done" (Keller & Thompson, 2002, p. 18). Unfortunately, the movement ethos can easily be lost, and a once vibrant movement becomes loaded down in bureaucracy and institutional management. The antidote to institutionalism, says Alan Hirsch (2006), is "maintaining a movement ethos" (p. 190). Networks should do their best to draw on movement dynamics in order to start churches and ministries for the sake of a gospel movement in the city.

Allowing Structure to Develop as Needed. In an urban setting we can tend to rush into increased levels of structure and institutionalism, which then slows down the movement dynamic. There is a time and place for refining and adapting our network structures, but we do so only as it fosters missional engagement. "All structures change. Our concern is that this change in missional structures be intentional and evangelically shaped" (Guder et al., 1998, p. 267). In other words, we should avoid embracing formality for the sake of formality; rather, our networks should be committed to structural minimalism as long as it serves the vision of the network. When structures are established, every effort should be made to avoid excessive politicization. A good network should serve the cause of the gospel, facilitate love for our neighbors, and continuously drive the collective vision of the group. As networks grow and increase the scope of their work, levels of structure will need to be adapted accordingly.

Conclusion

As churches mature and multiply in the city and as diverse ministries become established, it is important for these to be networked with each other. Just as an urban neighborhood only thrives when it is integrally connected to the rest of the city, so must churches and ministries be connected with one another. If the networks are developed well, then they can be a benefit to each of the individual churches and ministries.

Questions for reflection and discussion:

1. According to the author, why are networks important for transforming our cities?
2. What formal or informal networks do you know of among Christians, churches, and ministries in your city? Have you seen any noteworthy successes or failures within such networks from which you can learn?

3. Does your church participate in any ministry networks? Do you feel those networks observe the key principles the author describes here?

Chapter 17
Perpetuation through Organic Multiplication

A church (or group of churches) with movement dynamics generates its own converts, ideas, leaders, and resources from within in order to realize its vision of being the church for its city and culture.

--Timothy Keller (2012, p. 337)

First, we have to ask whether it is fair to expect a movement to survive only as movement. Either the movement disintegrates or it becomes an institution—this is simply a sociological law. Every religious group that started out as a movement and managed to survive, did so because it was gradually institutionalized: the Waldensians, the Moravians, the Quakers, the Pentecostals, and many more.

--David Bosch (1991, p. 52)

How do we implement ongoing transformation in our cities? As we established in Chapter 2, transformation will not be completed prior to the return of Christ. This means that no matter how much public good we do, there will always be more work to be done. We must actively develop new leaders and plant new churches. Each generation will need to carry on this work, which means each generation needs to be equipped and empowered to take up the work of urban transformation.

Returning to the canopy ecosystem analogy, the ecosystem only thrives when everything is reproducing healthily by design. Churches, ministries, and leaders all have lifespans. This means a healthy model of transformation must include a strategy of perpetuation. Perpetuation must be built-in at all levels. We need deep discipleship that produces disciple-making disciples of Christ. Churches, ministries, and other institutions all need leaders with character, vision, and resolve to build up the next generation of leaders. As the different parts of the ecosystem grow to maturity, reproduction can lead to a movement that spreads beyond our typical expectations. And, because we live in a globalized world, individual churches have the potential to impact many cities by what we do in one.

Discipleship

Cities are awash with buzz and hype. It is normal to see a restaurant become so popular that people are lined up around the block to get in, and soon the restaurant has branches all over the city, each one busier than the last. A year later, though, the restaurants are empty and on the verge of bankruptcy, the result of fad-based expansion. The Church may be tempted to covet the initial popularity of that restaurant, but chasing popularity creates a short-lived ministry. There are large megachurch buildings so empty on Sunday morning you can hear your echo bouncing around the cavernous sanctuary. We can do Christianity on the cheap, provide light and breezy programs, keep everyone entertained enough to keep coming to church. These models, low on expectations for attendees, are doomed to fade. They are built on what Dietrich Bonhoeffer calls "cheap grace"(Bonhoeffer, 1995).

The kind of discipleship Jesus calls us to is one that demands everything from us (Luke 9:23). For too long we have been content to "make disciples" through neatly packaged programs, passive church attendance, and fill-in-the-blank workbooks. We were successful at gaining church attendees who knew the right answers, but we failed to make true disciples who integrated belief in the gospel into every aspect of life. Viv Grigg (2004a) saw this reality clearly as he lived and ministered in a slum community in Manila:

> Disciplemaking is the transmission of life to life. It is caught, not taught. It is a fire that breeds fire. It is not a method, a program, nor even the teaching and preaching of the word of God—though all of these are involved. Disciplemaking is God's love being poured out through one life into another, until the second life catches that love (p. 62).

It is easy to read Grigg's words and feel them resonate and yet do nothing. We must alter our patterns of church life so that we begin to truly transmit the life of Jesus-followship to others. City people have become acculturated to a life of busyness, impersonal interactions, and the constant tug of other people and things vying for their attention. Church approaches that require going to a centralized location four times a week for various programs are not going to work in cities (or most anywhere) anymore. This is why Eric Jacobsen (2003) urges us to "figure out how to work out our discipleship to Christ in the specific context of our cities" (p. 67).

We need to innovate paths of discipleship that move every Christian from being a passive church attendee to a proactive disciple maker. First, our discipleship must be personal in nature. In the New Testament era, Paul was not always able to stay in a city for very long, yet he discipled new Christians in such a personal way that they could imitate his life (1 Thess. 1:5-6), and he expected his disciples to continue this pattern from one disciple to the next (2 Tim. 2:2). We must invest personally in a few others, who will invest personally in a few others and on and on. This model requires a sacrifice of time, a willingness to be vulnerable, and an intentional approach to addressing urban life issues.

If we relegate the Christian life to the reciting of a sinner's prayer to secure eternal life, we miss the calling of Jesus to truly repent and begin to walk in a Christ-formed life. Roger Greenway (1992) points out the wide range of issues good discipleship must address: "Urban discipleship means getting serious about issues like good schools, responsible government, sanitation and clean streets, fairness in the marketplace, and justice in the courts. It means working to eliminate squalor, slums, and every depressing condition that dishonors God by degrading human life" (p. 46). These issues rarely enter the consciousness of most suburban evangelicals, because they are less visible in daily suburban life. Sanitation issues are rarely noticed (garbage dumps are well hidden from the suburbs), schools are more homogeneously middle and upper class, and shopping takes place in generic chain stores. Uncontrolled by the struggles that dominate the lives of the poor, suburban believers go about much of their lives without being cognizant of how their faith should be impacting their daily routine. And when suddenly issues spring up, we are not spiritually/theologically ready to respond from our Christian worldview.

As we develop patterns of multiplicative discipleship, we need to create communities that foster a culture of gospel-centered living. We cannot rely solely on trained pastors and Christian counselors to address all of the issues we sinners bring into the church. In the early days of Redeemer Presbyterian in Manhattan, the majority of the congregation was single. Tim Keller and Allen Thompson (2002) speak to the ways that impacted their pastoral care model:

> The young single attendees had a surprising (to naïve me!) number of moral, psychological and ethical issues about which they were confused. They were almost impossible to communicate with, keep tabs on, or shepherd by traditional pastoral models of visitation. There was a desperate need for a high quality small group ministry (p. 16).

Urban pastors have to release their desire to be at the center of church's discipling ministry. In order for a pattern of discipleship to take root among the whole body of believers, the pastor must do two things. First, the pastor must trust the process of reproducing discipleship and the work of the Holy Spirit to inhabit the lives of all Christians. Second, the pastor must be proactive in multiplying leaders for service both in the church and out in the city. But we will not see good leaders surface unless we begin with intentional, holistic discipleship.

Leadership Multiplication

Society more easily flourishes with good leadership but struggles under leadership that is weak, corrupt, or too authoritarian. One of the unfortunate consequences of an over-reliance on professional clergy has been the failure to develop leaders within our churches. Churches thrive when a higher percentage of the members share in leadership. The most successful ministries I have come across during twenty years of ministry are those in which the leader(s) intentionally find promising young Christians and disciple them as leaders. A church or ministry that does this well not only helps its particular church or ministry flourish, but provides capable, well-discipled leaders for other ministries in their city and others. In addition, the development of solid leaders in our churches prepares them as good leaders in their communities, workplaces, and perhaps even larger stages.

As we look at multiplying leaders, it is important that we equip leaders to thrive in the urban context. Urban Christian leaders need to understand the issues of urban life. A pastor of a city church that lives in the suburbs is not as likely to understand the demands and realities of urban living. Christian leaders in the city need to learn how to minister in the midst astonishing diversity. My home church in San Francisco sits right at the crossroads of a thriving business district and a community of those who have remained from the hippie movement in the 1960s. This means the church requires leaders who are equally comfortable addressing the needs of the high-level businesswoman, the homeless guy, and the person struggling with gender identity. In ethically diverse cities, leaders need a high level of cultural competency. In other words, leadership in the city requires a wide skill set not traditionally associated with ministry. Glenn Smith, a principle writer for the Lausanne working group on urban transformation, writes of the need for urban leadership training:

> We affirm that all forms of training must expose the leader to several foundational, biblical components related to carrying out an effective ministry in cities.... Each leader must be grounded in a holistic understanding of urban transformation, and an image of what reconciliation might look like between classes, the races, the castes, and the sectors or systems of the city. Urban training must ground the leader in a theology of shalom, which pursues wholeness, completeness, righteousness, justice, reconciliation and flourishing of all that God has created in all of its remarkable diversity. This includes placing all material, physical, social, and spiritual systems under the lordship of Christ (G. Smith, 2004, p. 21).

Well-trained leaders can foster healthy, urban-oriented patterns of discipleship in the churches and collaborate for city-wide impact.

Movement

I have long been fascinated by social change, how it happens, and how people respond to it. My father-in-law speaks of throwing empty Coca Cola bottles out the window on the side of the highway as being quite normal not more than sixty years ago. Today, throwing a glass bottle out the car window is almost unthinkable. How is it that within a generation or two, societal norms regarding litter changed so significantly? The answer is change came through a movement. The campaign against littering swept across the United States and resulted in a change of culture. Changes in modern society have primarily occurred in response to movements (Sztompka, 1993, p. 279). Christianity has grown primarily through movements throughout its history.[1]

---

[1] If we were to plot the numerical growth of Christians in different countries we would see uneven growth due to times of awakenings or revivals among the people.

When Christianity undergoes a spike in numerical growth, there is potential for social change at a societal level. Viv Grigg (2004a) offers an example in the extraordinary society-wide changes instigated by the Clapham Sect in 18th century England:

> First, mass movements from the grassroots eventually produce changes in the top of society. The members of the Clapham Sect were the direct descendants of the Wesleyan revival. McLelland, in a significant study on entrepreneurs, shows that the two great waves of achievement in England were associated with Protestant reform or revival (p. 184).

Change in society does not always follow in the wake of a numerical surge in Christians and churches in a society. But a multiplicative increase in Christians and churches necessarily precedes gospel-centered transformation in a city.

I recently spoke at a church located on the perimeter of Richmond, one of the smaller San Francisco Bay Area cities. A while back the city's development plans included moving churches out of the city's center in order to make room for big businesses. As the churches were marginalized, crime rose dramatically.

Christianity, in its earliest years, was an urban movement, and it brought change to the cites of the Roman Empire (Meeks, 1982; Stark, 2006). More recently, however, Christianity has not thrived in cities. Research has shown the North American Church to be significantly stronger in rural areas and minimally present in the cities (D. Barrett, 1986, p. 11; Conn, 1994, p. 142). Researchers have observed similar trends in the cities of Asia, Africa, and Latin America (Conn & Ortiz, 2001, p. 26; Murray, 1990, p. 62). Even the relatively recent occurrence of church planting movements has been markedly more successful in the countryside than in cities (Garrison, 2004). There are a number of obstacles to the multiplication of the Church in our cities. At times it is due to systemic prevention as in the case with Richmond, California. In many cases, the Church has simply failed to plant churches in the urban core. More recently in China, the underground house church network has flourished in rural China but loses momentum as it enters the city. The Church must adapt ministry methods to meet the differences in city life and culture.

What will it take for a movement to take root in your city? While more research needs to be done on this topic, there are some consistent factors that are important in catalyzing movements: prayer, understanding and proclaiming the gospel, incarnational presence, planting churches, deep discipleship, kingdom-minded collaboration, and working out the faith in all of the diverse vocations, cultures, subcultures, and geographical corners of the city. If that list seems familiar, it's because those are the primary components of the model of urban transformation I propose in Part II of this book. The presence of these factors does not guarantee a movement, but a movement rarely happens without them. Ultimately, a movement is the work of God stirring the hearts of men and women for the sake of his glory. God uses our obedience and service to bring change. Movements have an amazing way of fostering change on a massive scale. They have the power to change people without them even realizing it.[2] The forces of change brought about by urbanization have primed the pump for a movement of citywide change if only we dare sacrifice to reach our cities (Sztompka, 1993, pp. 276–277).

Movements are an amazing phenomenon to behold. But humans are fickle creatures. This means great movements can fizzle out as fast as they were ignited. We are not looking for flash-in-the-pan movements; rather, we hope to see long-term presence and impact in our cities. Movements are exciting because they buzz with unifying energy and bring about tangible changes. But movements are also a bit wild. Just as protests can devolve into a riot, church multiplication movements can also be out of control. If it is left for too long, it can become anarchic or simply dissipate.

---

[2] Urban anthrolopologist George Gmelch observes, "social change is of such a nature that it is not usually perceived by the general populace" (Gmelch, 2002, p. 27).

I come from a generation that has been highly skeptical of institutions. Institutions have been viewed—sometimes for very good reason—as stale bureaucracies or corrupt systems of injustice. But institutions are far more necessary than we realize. We take for granted all of the institutions that make life livable. In fact, institutions "are essential for flourishing" (Crouch, 2013, p. 169). Movements are not sustainable over the long run. "Urban life is impossible without [institutions]. Even the church in the city must be formally organized if it wishes to carry out large projects such as missions" (P. Hiebert & Meneses, 1995, p. 283). We need a healthy process of developing structures that maintain some elements of the movement ethos but provide needed infrastructural support for churches and ministries to serve without burning out. Church historian Glen Hinson (1981) observed, "History teaches, I think, that religious movements cannot do without some kind of institutions" (p. 27). Movements that resist institutionalization become causalities of history. The early church gradually developed systems of leadership and decision-making that provided important theological consistency and stability for the ever-expanding church.

There is an evident tension in holding onto a movement ethos while embracing the development of healthy structures. Tim Keller (2012) recognizes this tension and refuses to give in to one or the other. He maintains the church is to be an "organized organism" (p. 344). The importance of institutions is critical in the urban context as urban dwellers rely on institutions far more than their relatives in the countryside. A movement ethos is aided by a firm belief in the gospel and the knowledge that our service is for God and his kingdom. A firm trust in the gospel can help maintain a balance in movement and institution.

Movements do not just spring up overnight. Good movements start slow and build gradually with the right people. Most people will shift with the winds of popular opinion. Movements begin with people who have conviction. "Students of social change tell us that it is better to aim at consensus within a strategic minority rather than to waste time and breath at soliciting the conformity of the majority" (Maggay, 2004, p. 121). Jesus started with a small number of people who had unimpressive resumes, but when threatened by the authorities, they were resolute (Acts 4 and 5).

The goal of the movement is to reach a critical mass or tipping point in the city. Maggay (2004) notes, "Sociologists tell us that it takes only five percent of a country's population to turn society around and put it on course. Social renewal begins when a strategic minority hears the call of a new order, catches a vision of what is possible and gives their all to the birthing of the coming world" (p. 124). A movement reaches the tipping point when the number of "gospel-shaped Christians" reaches ten to twenty percent of the population. Keller draws on the theory that ten percent is a sort of watershed point for social change in the broader community.[3] This kind of movement does not happen overnight; Keller notes that over the last twenty years, Manhattan's church-attending population has risen from one percent to three percent and the number of churches has doubled. While they have not reached the tipping point yet, they are moving in the right direction.

For a movement ethos to take effect, the church needs to intentionally multiply at every level. All Christians will need to take their role of making disciples seriously. Church planting should become the norm rather than a rarity. Churches should put their individual financial and numerical stability on the line in order to send out planters. Most church planting movements are halted by an inability to multiply leaders. In particular, there is a need for lay leaders. Hiebert and Meneses (1995) say, "In most of the world there are not enough seminary graduates to plant and pastor new congregations" (p. 343).

---

[3] Keller acknowledges that there is nothing magical about ten percent. Every culture and context is unique. He believes strongly, however, that the church should aim for that point of critical mass in which the culture of the city is positively impacted by the presence of Christians. Keller's church has used ten percent as a kind of target to reach. (Keller, 2012, p. 376)

This means urban churches need to start now in aggressively training and equipping lay leaders who are adept at explaining the gospel, discipling new Christians, and interpreting the Bible. When multiplication is working at every level, the canopy ecosystem is primed for a reproducing movement.

Globally Networked

Now that the world is so linked through the forces of globalization, churches can no longer be content to think only in terms of their own city. "The gap between 'local' and 'global' is narrowing" (Hillis, 2014, p. 34). Some friends of ours have immediate family members (speaking of only one set of parents and their grown-up children) living in Tehran, Toronto, Singapore, Kuala Lumpur, and Bangkok. Each family member is in a global city. This kind of global dispersal has become common, and churches and ministries in such cities need to be proactive in leveraging their place to connect the church together globally.

There are several ways for urban churches to be globally connected. One way is to be a community of welcoming for people arriving from origins both near and far. Rural, suburban, and urban networking is important. When so many are migrating to cities and shifting back and forth between places, it is important to recognize the value and even strategic importance of transfer growth. Conn (1987) notes that when many who come from the countryside to the cities are already believers, urban churches need to be poised to take in and disciple these transfer members. And now, as people go from one global city to the next for studies, work, or to seek political asylum, churches need to be tapped into a global network of churches so that discipleship can continue.

There are innovative ministries in cities all over the world. One "avenue [of urban ministry] is to find out what churches in other cities are doing and to network with them" (Greenway & Monsma, 2000, p. 83). This kind of networking is definitely needed. We can learn from the ideas of other churches. A church in Kuala Lumpur, Malaysia has done very well with innovative urban ministry unlike any other church in that city. Their work came as a result of learning from innovative missional churches in Los Angeles (Dream Center) and New York City (Redeemer Presbyterian) and adapting their ideas for the Kuala Lumpur context. We can also aid each other in resourcing, particularly when we are working with multiple languages and cultures.

Established churches in global cities are well-positioned to assist in planting churches in other global cities. Sydney-based Hillsong, for example, has started Hillsong churches in New York, London, and other cities. Most churches do not have the resources to pull this off alone. A small group of Southeast Asian churches is working together to plant churches in cities across the region. Redeemer City to City has developed an extensive network of church planters and pastors with an exclusive focus on the major cities of several continents. Networks like Redeemer City to City build into their model the idea of the newly established churches participating in the ongoing efforts to plant more churches. As this happens, movements that begin in specific cities have the potential to spread into a global movement.

Questions for reflection and discussion:

1. What four elements does the author highlight as essential for perpetuating transformation and how do these uniquely relate to the urban context?
2. What experience have you had with discipleship and leadership development? Do you feel these experiences were effective in preparing you and/or others for ministry in the urban environment?
3. The author lists several factors that create an environment in which a movement can take place. Which of these are present in your church and city? Which of these could your church help to foster?

CANOPY ECOSYSTEM APPROACH
TO URBAN TRANSFORMATION

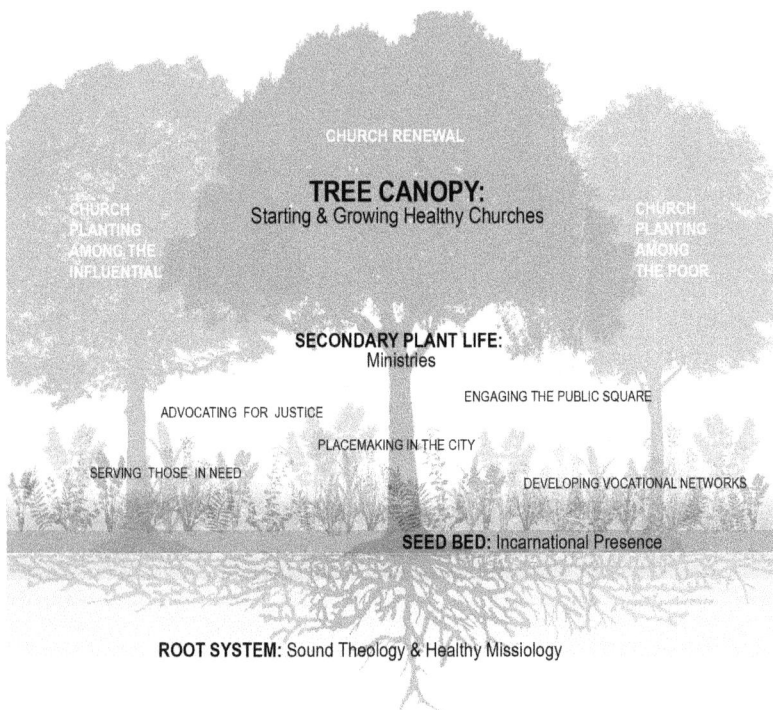

CHURCH RENEWAL

TREE CANOPY:
Starting & Growing Healthy Churches

CHURCH PLANTING AMONG THE INFLUENTIAL

CHURCH PLANTING AMONG THE POOR

SECONDARY PLANT LIFE:
Ministries

ADVOCATING FOR JUSTICE

ENGAGING THE PUBLIC SQUARE

PLACEMAKING IN THE CITY

SERVING THOSE IN NEED

DEVELOPING VOCATIONAL NETWORKS

SEED BED: Incarnational Presence

ROOT SYSTEM: Sound Theology & Healthy Missiology

ROOT SYSTEM ➡ SEED BED ➡ TREE CANOPY ➡ SECONDARY PLANT LIFE ➡ THRIVING CANOPY ECOSYSTEM

Chapter 18
Conclusion

The concept of transformation is far beyond simply doing good works to earn the goodwill of others. In fact, it is at the core of what God has been doing throughout history.

--Sean Benesh (2011, p. 81)

The vision of the New Jerusalem is one which we need to incorporate into our own 'cities' now, our cities of self, household, church, and extended community. We need to be saved, redeemed, holy, peaceful, righteous, joyful, living with the Lord as our Light. God will accomplish the New Jerusalem, but also God can accomplish this vision in and through God's people today.

--Aída Besançon Spencer (2013, Kindle Location 866)

Through the development of a thriving canopy ecosystem, plant diversity thrives. The development of healthy churches and ministries networked together can lead to a self-perpetuating canopy ecosystem that teems with flourishing life. For the ecosystem to be healthy, these networks must remain gospel-centered, united, and clear on their vision for a better city. To grow such an ecosystem, we, as leaders in our churches, need *reflective action*. That is, we need to understand our mission from a biblical framework and be able to exegete our cities. But knowledge and ability are not enough; we must collaborate with others to actively develop a canopy ecosystem in our respective cities. Unreflective action and reflective inaction are both dead ends.

Working Towards a Transforming City

Earlier in the book we looked at the wide range of Christian models of urban transformation. The variety of models can be dizzying, and most of them sound good on their own. Each model offers something valuable to the way we bring change to our cities. Yet many of the models tend to come up short in one of two ways. First, some models are incomplete in the transformation they seek. Some address internal spiritual needs but neglect temporal ones while other models emphasize the need to address external problems like poverty but fail to speak to people's spiritual lives. A healthy model of urban transformation needs to be comprehensive, addressing both internal and external needs. Second, some models are not designed to work from start to finish. Some models presume the presence of healthy churches and a broad base of Christians to work with from the start. Others work well for the immediate moment, but are not designed to continue after one generation. The canopy ecosystem model builds off of the great contributions of these other models while attempting to construct a more comprehensive model to impact the whole city and which incorporates built-in perpetuation. All of this while seeking the good of the city with an idea of what is actually good for the city.

Too often we scramble around trying to do good things in our city with little reflection on what makes a city flourish. In Chapters 4 and 5 we explored the characteristics that make a good city from both the perspectives of urban studies as well as the Bible. These characteristics are not mutually exclusive and cannot be addressed one at a time but rather are interconnected.

Urbanology Perspective	Christian Perspective
Density Vibrancy Diversity Security Economic Opportunity Organic Growth	God-centeredness *Shalom* social vision Kingdom communities

Figure 18.1. Summary of Characteristics of a Good City

The canopy ecosystem model addresses the elements of a good city with which the Church must be engaged. The model begins with a solid, God-centered vision grounded in biblical theology and missiology. The vision is one that prayerfully hopes for *shalom* in the city. A city marked by *shalom* is one that is just, secure, diverse, and provides opportunities for livelihood and growth. The cities best positioned to grow and thrive are those that take advantage of the density, vibrancy and diversity in their context. Christians can only offer change as they fully inhabit the city, living in solidarity with it. Presence is a critical starting point, and this presence is not meant to be solitary in nature. Christians form communities that have been transformed by the gospel of Jesus. These communities called churches point to God's kingdom because they have been drawn into the royal family by the King himself. As churches are started and multiplied in every stratum of society, they can begin to work together to seek the shalom of the whole city (Jer. 29:7). This happens through networks that help ignite ministries and initiatives that intentionally address urban issues while simultaneously training Christians as kingdom citizens. "The church is the only human community through which God works to build the City of God"(Currie, 2013, p. Location 1507). As these citizens look hopefully to the new city of God's making, they inhabit their current city in a new and transformed way, serving, loving, and proclaiming in ways that make the gospel evident.

As networks of churches are formed and as Christians are equipped in the gospel, the work of transformation in the city can begin to take root. Churches and ministries can find ways to serve and aid the poor and marginalized in the city. Christians can become advocates of justice, putting an end to systemic oppression. As the Church works for the welfare of their cities, the importance of civic engagement, cultural production, and vocational excellence becomes apparent. Even the ways we inhabit space have the potential to contribute to the vibrancy of the city. We pray for God to move in our cities while living in a way that allows God to change our cities through us. Potential for God to work among us is created as Christians live out their transformed lives by individually making disciples of others and by collectively seeking the good of the whole city. This creates space for God to spark the kind of renewal that moves from churches to every corner of society.

Choosing a Starting Point

Our entry point for the development of an ecosystem will be unique to each city. Some cities have too few Christians or churches to yet generate a productive ecosystem. In this case we need missional church planters who are actively contextualizing the gospel message for the people of that particular city. Other cities have a large number of churches, but they have been ministering in isolation for decades. Leaders in a city like this must come together to prayerfully develop a vision for their city and begin to collaborate.

No matter what the entry point, cities do not experience change overnight—far from it. Making deep impact in your city will take decades of dedication. In the previous chapter, we noted that Redeemer Presbyterian Church has been working alongside other churches in New York for twenty-five years, and they have seen incremental growth but have yet to reach a tipping point. Rod Garner echoes many urban practitioners when he says, "Staying in the city requires patience and a readiness to take the long view—pleasure when things go well and a refusal to mope when desired outcomes are thwarted"(Garner, 2004, p.

114). David Bosch, the late South African missiologist, describes the incredible sacrifice of wave after wave of missionary monks who sought the welfare of medieval Europe during a dark age. Barbarians raided and destroyed all of the good the monks accomplished leaving behind only corpses. And then another group of monks would arrive and rebuild what had been plundered. This went on for hundreds of years. Bosch (1991) describes these monks as having a "spirituality of the long haul":

> The monks knew that things took time, that instant gratification and a quick-fix mentality were an illusion, and that an effort begun in one generation had to be carried on by generations yet to come, for theirs was a 'spirituality of the long haul' and not of instant success. Coupled with this was their refusal to write off the world as a lost cause or to propose neat, no-loose-ends answers to the problems of life, but rather to rebuild promptly, patiently, and cheerfully, 'as if it were by some law of nature that the restoration came' (p. 233).

Through patience and faithfulness, churches emerge even in some of the most resistant soils.

Effective ministry in the city involves a resolve to commit for the long term. In this age of immediate communication across the world and instantaneous downloads, the pressure for fast results is quickened. There are no short cuts or quick fixes to the ails of a city. Eddie Gibbs tells of Emmanuel Reformed Church in Paramount, California. They remained committed to their community in the midst of ethnic transition and significant economic decline. They then committed to spend 40 years to help restore the neighboring city of Compton (Gibbs, 2009, p. 110). It is reminiscent of Jeremiah's words for the exilic Jews in Babylon in Jer. 29. They are told they will only be there 70 years more, but that they should invest themselves deeply in the city they have been sent to.

We must remember that no two cities are the same; "…it is because urbanism tends to be regarded as international that radical differences between urban sites need to be addressed when considering the nature of any urban reality or process" (Bishop, Philips, & Yeo, 2003, p. 3). I was at a meeting in New York City recently with a church planter from Barcelona, Spain. As the meeting touched on church planting issues, he was acutely aware that the citizens of Barcelona would not respond in the same way as those in American cities. It is critical to know your own city so well that you can adapt to the uniqueness of your context. We need to be particularly aware of the worldview influences that have shaped our cities.[1] In response, we must consider how the gospel addresses the dominant narratives of each city. We cannot keep rolling out church planting stencils and expect that to make a real impact in each city.

The pace at which our cities are growing is unparalleled in history. In addition, the population growth rate of the urban poor is outpacing every other urban population demographic. This swelling of the urban population points us to the greatest priority in global missions today. As more than a million people around the world move to cities each week, is the Church prepared to welcome them with the gospel? Is the church positioned to proclaim the universally great news that Jesus gave his life so that we might experience true transformation?

Every week people are being added to cities that are already pushed to their infrastructural limits. Jobs, shelter, potable water, and clean air are becoming scarcer. Is the urban Church doing its part in building cities conducive to human flourishing? Are Christians truly seeking the welfare of their cities or simply pursuing their own welfare?

---

[1] John Miksic of the Asia Research Institute, Singapore: "It is now acknowledged, however, that the agglomeration of buildings and people was not an evolutionary inevitability. Physical and spatial expressions of social structure, population, political power, economic activity and religion are determined by local factors that vary across space and time…. Different cultures produced cities similar in form, but bearing the stamp of their unique origins. Cities on Java, for example, function differently than cities in Thailand, the Philippines, Myanmar, China and India." (Evans, 2009, p. 43)

As the Church is renewed by the gospel, it has the potential to be a tremendous force for change. The gospel, says Os Guinness (2014), "has a proven record of being the greatest people-changing and world-changing force in history" (p. 21). As billions of people transition into a new urban world, let us, the Church, respond with a biblical vision to reflect the City of God through the transformation of our cities.

Questions for reflection and discussion:

1. What are the elements of the canopy ecosystem model and how do they work together to produce a good environment for urban transformation?
2. In your opinion, what is the current state of the spiritual "ecosystem" in your city? Take into consideration the presence and health of churches as well as their theological and missiological rootedness. Looking at the author's model, where does the Church in your city need to start in fostering a thriving ecosystem?
3. Taking into consideration the necessary starting point for your city, what steps can your church take to help the broader Church in the city develop a thriving ecosystem? Create an action plan. How can theology and missiology needs be addressed? How can the Church live more incarnationally in your city? Are churches many or few, vibrant or wilting? What needs and injustices most urgently need attention? What specific churches and organizations can your church network with?

Sowing Seeds of Change

References

Abrahamson, M. (2004). *Global Cities*. New York: Oxford University Press.

Addison, S. (2011). *Movements That Change the World: Five Keys to Spreading the Gospel* (Revised edition). Downers Grove, IL: IVP Books.

Aghamkar, A. Y. (2000). *Insights Into Openness: Encouraging Urban Mission*. Bangalore: SAIACS Press.

Aikman, D. (2012). *Jesus in Beijing: How Christianity Is Transforming China And Changing the Global Balance of Power*. Washington, D.C.: Regnery Publishing.

Ali, K. A., & Rieker, M. (2008). Introduction: Urban Margins. *Social Text 95, 26*(2), 1–12.

Allen, F. (1986). Toward a Biblical Urban Mission. *Urban Mission, 3*(3), 6–13.

Allen, R. (1997). *The Spontaneous Expansion of the Church: And the Causes That Hinder It*. Wipf & Stock Publishers.

Anderson, L. (2012, December 9). Understanding Immigration Reform. *The New York Times*. Retrieved from http://www.nytimes.com/roomfordebate/2012/12/09/understanding-immigration-reform/comprehensive-immigration-reform-means-no-stop-gap-solutions

Arias, M. (1982). Centripetal Mission or Evangelization by Hospitality. *Missiology: An International Review, 10*(1), 69–81.

Armitage, J., & Roberts, J. (2003). From the Hypermodern City to the Gray Zone of Total Mobilization in the Philippines. In R. Bishop, J. Philips, & W. W. Yeo (Eds.), *Postcolonial Urbanism: Southeast Asian Cities and Global Processes* (pp. 87–104). New York: Routledge.

Asner, G. P., Martin, R. E., Tupayachi, R., Anderson, C. B., Sinca, F., Carranza-Jiménez, L., & Martinez, P. (2014). Amazonian functional diversity from forest canopy chemical assembly. *Proceedings of the National Academy of Sciences*, 201401181. http://doi.org/10.1073/pnas.1401181111

Augustine. (1950). *The City of God* (Modern Library). New York: Random House.

Badger, E. (2013, June 7). The Real Reason Cities Are Centers of Innovation. Retrieved June 10, 2013, from http://

www.theatlanticcities.com/jobs-and-economy/2013/06/secret-why-cities-are-centers-innovation/5819/

Bakke, R. (1997). *A Theology as Big as the City*. Downers Grove, IL: InterVarsity Press.

Bakke, R. (1997). The Challenge of World Evangelization to Mission Strategy. In *Planting and Growing Urban Churches: From Dream to Reality* (pp. 79–93). Grand Rapids: Baker Books.

Bakke, R. (2002). Urbanization and Evangelism: A Global View. In M. Ortiz & S. S. Baker (Eds.), *The Urban Face of Mission* (pp. 29–42). Phillipsburg N.J.: P & R Pub.

Bakke, R., & Sharpe, J. (2006). *Street Signs: A New Direction in Urban Ministry*. Birmingham, AL: New Hope Publishers.

Barker, A. (2012). *Slum Life Rising: How to Enflesh Hope within a New Urban World*. Dandenong, Australia: UNOH Publishing.

Barrett, D. (1986). *World-Class Cities and World Evangelization*. Birmingham Ala.: New Hope.

Barrett, L. Y., Guder, D. L., Hobbs, W. C., Hunsberger, G. R., Stutzman, L. L., Van Kooten, J., & Ziemer, D. A. (2004). *Treasure in Clay Jars: Patterns in Missional Faithfulness*. (L. Y. Barrett, Ed.). Grand Rapids: Wm. B. Eerdmans Publishing Company.

Batty, M. (2007). *Cities and Complexity: Understanding Cities with Cellular Automata, Agent-Based Models, and Fractals*. Cambridge, MA: The MIT Press.

Bauckham, R. (2004). *Bible and Mission: Christian Witness in a Postmodern World*. Grand Rapids: Baker Academic.

Bavinck, H. (1909). Calvin and Common Grace. *The Princeton Theological Review*, 7(3), 437–465.

Beall, J., & Fox, S. (2009). *Cities and Development*. London; New York: Routledge.

Beck, H., & Brown, C. (1986). Peace. C. Brown (Ed.), *The New International Dictionary of New Testament Theology* (Vol. Vol. 2, pp. 776–783). Grand Rapids: Regency Reference Library.

Bellofatto, G. A., & Johnson, T. M. (2013). Key Findings of Christianity in Its Global Context, 1970-2020. *International Bulletin of Missionary Research*, 37(3), 157–164.

Benesh, S. (2011). *View from the Urban Loft: Developing a Theological Framework for Understanding the City* (Kindle Edition). Portland, OR: Resource Publications, an imprint of Wipf and Stock Publishers.

Berkhof, L. (1941). *Systematic Theology*. London: Banner of Truth Trust.

Bertinelli, L., & Strobl, E. (2007). Urbanisation, Urban Concentration and Economic Development. *Urban Studies, 44*(13), 2499–2510. http://doi.org/10.1080/00420980701558442

Bessenecker, S. (Ed.). (2005). *Quest for Hope in the Slum Community: A Global Urban Reader.* Waynesboro, GA: Authentic & World Vision.

Bessenecker, S. A. (2006). *The New Friars: The Emerging Movement Serving the World's Poor.* Downers Grove, IL: IVP Books.

Bess, P. (2006). *Till We Have Built Jerusalem: Architecture, Urbanism, and the Sacred.* Wilmington, DE: Intercollegiate Studies Institute.

Bevans, S. B., & Schroeder, R. P. (2004). *Constants in Context: A Theology of Mission for Today.* Maryknoll N.Y.: Orbis Books.

Bibles, C. (2008). *ESV Study Bible.* Wheaton, IL: Crossway Bibles.

Billings, J. T. (2004). "Incarnational Ministry" and Christology: A Reappropriation of the Way of Lowliness. *Missiology: An International Review, 32*(2), 187–201.

Bishop, R., Philips, J., & Yeo, W. W. (Eds.). (2003). *Postcolonial Urbanism: Southeast Asian Cities and Global Processes.* New York: Routledge.

Blokland, T. (2003). *Urban Bonds: Social Relationships in an Inner City Neighborhood.* (L. K. Mitzman, Trans.). Cambridge, UK: Polity Press.

Bokser, B. M. (1985). Approaching Sacred Space. *The Harvard Theological Review, 78*(3/4), 279–299.

Bonhoeffer, D. (1965). *The Communion of Saints: a Dogmatic Inquiry Into the Sociology of the Church.* San Francisco: Harper & Row.

Bonhoeffer, D. (1995). *The Cost of Discipleship.* Touchstone.

Bosch, D. (1991). *Transforming Mission: Paradigm Shifts in Theology of Mission.* Maryknoll, NY: Orbis Books.

Bragg, W. G. (1987). From Development to Transformation. In V. Samuel & C. Sugden (Eds.), *The Church in Response to Human Need* (pp. 20–51). Grand Rapids: Eerdmans Pub Co.

Branson, M. L. (2003). Forming Church, Forming Mission. *International Review of Mission, XCII*(365), 153–168.

Brock, C. (1994). *Indigenous Church Planting: A Practical Journey.* Neosho, MO: Church Growth International.

Brown, W. P., & Carroll, J. T. (2000). The Garden and the Plaza: Biblical Images of the City. *Interpretation, 54*(1), 3–11.

Brueggemann, W. (1978). *The Prophetic Imagination.* Philadelphia: Fortress Press.

Brueggemann, W. (2002). *The Land: Place as Gift, Promise, Challenge in Biblical Faith* (2nd ed.). Minneapolis: Fortress Press.

Brugmann, J. (2009). *Welcome to the Urban Revolution: How Cities Are Changing the World*. New York: Bloomsbury Press.

Caldeira, T. P. R. (2005). Fortified Enclaves: The New Urban Segregation. In S. M. Low (Ed.), *Theorizing the City: The new Urban Anthropology Reader* (pp. 83–107). New Brunswick, NJ: Rutgers University Press.

Carrasco, J. C. (2007). Transformation. In J. Corrie (Ed.), *Dictionary of Mission Theology: Evangelical Foundations* (pp. 393–395). Nottingham, England; Downers Grove, Ill.: Inter-Varsity Press.

Carson, D. A. (1996). *The Gagging of God: Christianity Confronts Pluralism*. Grand Rapids: Zondervan Publishing Company.

Carter, M., & Patrick, D. (2011). *For the City: Proclaiming and Living Out the Gospel*. Grand Rapids: Zondervan.

Castells, M. (1985). *The City and the Grassroots: A Cross-Cultural Theory of Urban Social Movements*. Berkeley, CA: University of California Press.

Castells, M. (2002). *Castells Reader on Cities and Social Theory*. (I. Susser, Ed.). Oxford: Blackwell Publishing.

Chester, T. (2000). Church Planting: A Theological Perspective. In S. Timmis (Ed.), *Multiplying Churches: Reaching Today's Communities Through Church Planting* (pp. 23–46). Ross Shire: Christian Focus Publications.

Cheyne, J. (1996). *Incarnational Agents: A Guide to Developmental Ministry*. Birmingham, Ala.: New Hope.

Cho, A. (2012, April 19). Interview with author.

Claerbaut, D. (1983). *Urban Ministry*. Grand Rapids: Ministry Resources Library.

Claiborne, S. (2006). The Irresistible Revolution: Living as an Ordinary Radical. Grand Rapids: Zondervan.

Cole, G. (2009). *God the Peacemaker: How Atonement Brings Shalom*. Downers Grove, IL: IVP Academic.

Cole, G. (2013). *The God Who Became Human: A Biblical Theology of Incarnation*. Downers Grove, IL: IVP Academic.

Conn, H. M. (1987). *A Clarified Vision for Urban Mission: Dispelling the Urban Stereotypes*. Grand Rapids: Zondervan.

Conn, H. M. (1992). Genesis as Urban Prologue. In R. S. Greenway (Ed.), *Discipling the City: A Comprehensive Approach to Urban Mission* (pp. 13–34). Grand Rapids: Baker Book House.

Conn, H. M. (1994). *The American City and the Evangelical Church: A Historical Overview*. Grand Rapids: Baker Pub Group.

Conn, H. M. (1997). Introduction to Part 4: Samples: Linking Strategy to Model. In H. M. Conn (Ed.), *Planting and Growing Urban*

Churches: From Dream to Reality (pp. 193–202). Grand Rapids, MI: Baker Books.

Conn, H. M., & Ortiz, M. (2001). *Urban Ministry: The Kingdom, the City, & the People of God*. Downers Grove, IL: InterVarsity Press.

Crouch, A. (2008). *Culture Making: Recovering Our Creative Calling*. Downers Grove, IL: IVP Books.

Crouch, A. (2013). *Playing God: Redeeming the Gift of Power*. Downers Grove, IL: IVP Books.

Currie, D. A. (2013). Ecclesiapolis: Two Millennia of Mutual Transformation between Church and City. In S. H. Park, A. B. Spencer, & W. D. Spencer (Eds.), *Reaching for the New Jerusalem: A Biblical and Theological Framework for the City* (Kindle edition). Eugene, OR: Wipf & Stock Publishers.

Daniels, D. D. (2008). Got a right to the tree of life: religious jurisdiction, religious infrastructures, and urban religious territory. *Cross Currents, 58*(3), 369–383.

Davey, A. (1998). Liberation Theology in Peckham. In M. Northcott (Ed.), *Urban Theology: A Reader* (pp. 8–10). London: Cassell.

Davey, A. (2002). *Urban Christianity and Global Order: Theological Resources for an Urban Future*. Peabody, MA: Hendrickson Publishers.

Dawson, J. (2001). *Taking Our Cities for God: How to Break Spiritual Strongholds* (Rev. Ed.). Lake Mary, FL: Charisma House.

Dayton, E. R. (1987). Social Transformation: The Mission of God. In V. Samuel & C. Sugden (Eds.), *The Church in Response to Human Need* (pp. 52–61). Grand Rapids: Wm. B. Eerdmans Publishing Co.

Dennison, J. (1999). *City Reaching: On The Road To Community Transformation*. Pasadena CA: W. Carey Library.

Desmond, S. A., Kikuchi, G., & Morgan, K. H. (2010). Congregations and Crime: Is the Spatial Distribution of Congregations Associated with Neighborhood Crime Rates? *Journal for the Scientific Study of Religion, 49*(1), 37–55.

Dever, M. (2009). The Pastor and the Community. Presented at the Sovereign Grace Pastors Conference. Retrieved from http://thegospelcoalition.org/blogs/kevindeyoung/2010/06/11/the-pastor-and-the-community-mark-dever/

Dever, M. E. (2007). The Church. In D. Akin (Ed.), *A Theology for the Church* (pp. 766–856). Nashville: B & H Academic.

Dichter, T. W. (2003). *Despite Good Intentions: Why Development Assistance to the Third World Has Failed*. University of Massachusetts Press.

Dodaro, R. (2004). *Christ and the Just Society in the Thought of Augustine.* Cambridge: Cambridge University Press.

DuBose, F. M. (1978). *How Churches Grow in an Urban World.* Nashville: Broadman Press.

Duncan, M. (1996). *Costly Mission: Following Christ into the Slums.* Monrovia, CA: MARC.

Du Toit, L., Cerin, E., Leslie, E., & Owen, N. (2007). Does Walking in the Neighbourhood Enhance Local Sociability? *Urban Studies, 44*(9), 1677–1695. http://doi.org/10.1080/00420980701426665

Edwards, J. (2008). *An Agenda for Change: A Global Call for Spiritual and Social Transformation.* Grand Rapids: Zondervan.

Eitel, K. E. (1996). "To Be or Not to Be": The Indigenous Church Question. *Faith and Mission, 13*(2), 35–57.

Ellison, C. W. (1997). Addressing Felt Needs of Urban Dwellers. In *Planting and Growing Urban Churches: From Dream to Reality* (pp. 94–110). Grand Rapids: Baker Books.

Elliston, E. J. (1989). Contextualized Christian Social Transformation. In D. S. Gilliland (Ed.), *The Word Among Us: Contextualizing Theology for Mission Today* (pp. 199–218). Dallas: Word Publishing.

Enlow, J. (2008). *The Seven Mountain Prophecy: Unveiling the Coming Elijah Revolution.* Lake Mary, FL: Creation House.

Enlow, J. (2009). *The Seven Mountain Mantle: Receiving the Joseph Anointing to Reform Nations.* Lake Mary, FL: Creation House.

Enright, M. J., Scott, E. E., & Petty, R. (2010). *The Greater Pearl River Delta: A report commissioned by Invest Hong Kong, 6th ed.* Hong Kong: Invest Hong Kong.

Evans, S. A. (2009). Media's Role in (Re)Shaping the Values of Today's Urban Buddhist and Its Impact on Gospel Proclamation. In P. H. De Neui (Ed.), *Communicating Christ in Asian Cities: Urban Issues in Buddhist Contexts* (pp. 41–73). Pasadena, CA: W. Carey Library.

Evers, H.-D., & Korff, R. (2000). *Southeast Asian Urbanism: The Meaning and Power of Social Space.* New York: St. Martin's Press.

Field, T. (2003). *Mercy Streets: Seeing Grace on the Streets of New York.* Nashville TN: Broadman & Holman Publishers.

Field, T., & Kadlecek, J. (2001). *A Church Called Graffiti: Finding Grace on the Lower East Side.* Nashville TN: Broadman & Holman Publishers.

Fischer, C. (1984). *The Urban Experience* (2nd ed.). San Diego: Harcourt Brace Jovanovich.

Flew, R. N. (1938). *Jesus and His Church: A Study of the Idea of the Ecclesia in the New Testament.* New York: Abingdon Press.

Flint, A. (2009). *Wrestling with Moses: How Jane Jacobs Took On New York's Master Builder and Transformed the American City*. New York: Random House.

Florida, R. (2008). *Who's Your City?: How the Creative Economy is Making Where to Live the Most Important Decision of Your Life*. New York: Basic Books.

France, R. T. (1984). The Church and the Kingdom of God: Some Hermeneutical Issues. In D. A. Carson (Ed.), *Biblical Interpretation and the Church* (pp. 30–44). Nashville: Thomas Nelson.

Friesen, D. K. (2000). *Artists, Citizens, Philosophers: Seeking the Peace of the City: An Anabaptist Theology of Culture*. Scottdale Pa.: Herald Press.

Fuder, J., & Castellanos, N. (Eds.). (2009). *A Heart for the Community: New Models for Urban and Suburban Ministry*. Chicago, IL: Moody Publishers.

Gallagher, S. D., & Hawthorne, S. C. (2009). Blessing as Transformation. In R. D. Winter & S. C. Hawthorne (Eds.), *Perspectives on the World Christian Movement: A Reader* (4th ed., pp. 34–41). Pasadena, CA: William Carey Library.

Garner, R. (2004). *Facing the City: Urban Mission in the 21st Century*. London: Epworth Press.

Garrison, D. (2004). *Church Planting Movements: How God is Redeeming a lost world*. Midlothian Va.: WIGTake Resources.

Geddert, T. J. (1992). Peace. J. B. Green & S. McKnight (Eds.), *Dictionary of Jesus and the Gospels* (pp. 604–605). Downers Grove, IL: InterVarsity Press.

Georgi, D. (2005). *The City in the Valley: Biblical Interpretation and Urban Theology*. Atlanta: Society of Biblical Literature.

Gibbs, E. (2009). *ChurchMorph: How Megatrends Are Reshaping Christian Communities*. Grand Rapids: Baker Academic.

Glaeser, E. L. (2011). *Triumph of the City: How Our Greatest Invention Makes Us Richer, Smarter, Greener, Healthier, and Happier*. New York: Penguin Press.

Glocalnet: Connecting for Glocal Transformation. (n.d.). Retrieved December 1, 2012, from http://www.glocal.net/

Gmelch, G. (2002). *Urban Life: Readings in the Anthropology of the City* (4th ed.). Prospect Heights Ill.: Waveland Press.

Goldingay, J. (2006). *Old Testament Theology: Volume 2: Israel's Faith*. Downers Grove Ill.: IVP Academic.

Gordon, B. (2006). *The Dream center A2 case study: [community impact]*. Barrington Ill.: Willow Creek.

Gordon, W. L. (1999). A Philosophy of Urban Ministry. In *A Heart for the City: Effective Ministries to the Urban Community* (pp. 73–86). Chicago: Moody Press.

Gornik, M. R. (2002). *To Live in Peace: Biblical Faith and the Changing Inner City*. Grand Rapids: Wm. B. Eerdmans Publishing Company.

Gorringe, T. (2002). *A Theology of the Built Environment: Justice, Empowerment, Redemption*. Cambridge: Cambridge University Press.

Gottdiener, M., & Hutchison, R. (2006). *The New Urban Sociology* (Third Edition). Boulder: Westview Press.

Graham, E., & Lowe, S. (2009). *What Makes a Good City?: Public Theology and the Urban Church*. London: Darton, Longman & Todd Ltd.

Greenway, R. (Ed.). (1976). *Guidelines for Urban Church Planting*. Grand Rapids: Baker Book House.

Greenway, R. (1978). *Apostles to the City: Biblical Strategies for Urban Missions*. Grand Rapids: Baker Book House.

Greenway, R. (1997). Introduction. In H. M. Conn (Ed.), *Planting and Growing Urban Churches: From Dream to Reality* (pp. 17–23). Grand Rapids MI: Baker Books.

Greenway, R., & Monsma, T. (2000). *Cities: Missions' New Frontier* (2nd ed.). Grand Rapids: Baker Academic.

Greenway, R. S. (1992). Confronting Urban Contexts with the Gospel. In R. S. Greenway (Ed.), *Discipling the City: A Comprehensive Approach to Urban Mission* (pp. 35–48). Grand Rapids: Baker Book House.

Grigg, V. (1988). Of Barefoot Dentists...And Rich Young Rulers. *Urban Mission, 5*(5), 43–44.

Grigg, V. (1992). Church of the Poor. In R. S. Greenway (Ed.), *Discipling the City: A Comprehensive Approach to Urban Mission* (pp. 159–170). Grand Rapids: Baker Book House.

Grigg, V. (1993). Intercessors and Cosmic Urban Spiritual Warfare. *International Journal of Frontier Missions, 10*(4), 195–200.

Grigg, V. (1997). Sorry! The Frontier Moved. In H. M. Conn (Ed.), *Planting and Growing Urban Churches: From Dream to Reality* (pp. 150–163). Grand Rapids, MI: Baker Books.

Grigg, V. (2004a). *Companion to the Poor: Christ in the Urban Slums* (2nd ed.). Waynesboro, GA: Authentic and World Vision.

Grigg, V. (2004b). *Cry of the Urban Poor: Reaching the Slums of Today's Megacities*. Waynesboro, GA: Authentic and World Vision.

Grigg, V. (2008). Envisioning a Cultural Revitalization. Retrieved from http://www.visionnetwork.org.nz/attachments/234_envisioning %20a%20cultural%20revitalization%20-%20viv%20grigg.pdf

Grigg, V. (2009). *The Spirit of Christ and the Postmodern City: Transforming Revival Among Auckland's Evangelicals and Pentecostals.* Lexington, KY: Emeth Press.

Grigg, V. (2010). *Conversations on Economic Discipleship: Our Response to Kingdom Economics* (No. #5). Auckland: Urban Leadership Foundation. Retrieved from http://www.visionnetwork.org.nz/ attachments/623_economicdiscipleshipbook.pdf

Grigg, V. (2012). Hovering Spirit, Creative Voice, Empowered Transformation: A Retrospective. *New Urban World, 1*(1), 17–26.

Groll, E. (2012, October). The East is Rising. *Foreign Policy.* Retrieved from http://www.foreignpolicy.com/articles/2012/08/13/ the_east_is_rising

Guder, D. L., Barrett, L., Dietterich, I. T., Roxburgh, A. J., Hunsberger, G. R., & Van Gelder, C. (1998). *Missional Church: A Vision for the Sending of the Church in North America.* Grand Rapids: W.B. Eerdmans Pub.

Guinness, O. (2014). *Renaissance: The Power of the Gospel However Dark the Times.* Downers Grove, IL: IVP Books.

Guthrie, D. (1990). *New Testament Introduction* (Revised edition). Downers Grove, IL: IVP Academic.

Hall, D., Hall, J., Daman, S., & Bass, J. (213AD). Living-System Ministry Ushers in the New Jerusalem. In S. H. Park, A. B. Spencer, & W. D. Spencer (Eds.), *Reaching for the New Jerusalem: A Biblical and Theological Framework for the City* (Kindle edition). Eugene, OR: Wipf & Stock Publishers.

Hall, P. (2006). *Cities in Civilisation.* Orion Publishing.

Hammond, M., & Overstreet, D. (2011). *God's Call to the City: "Should I not be concerned about that Great City?" Jonah 4:11.* Bloomington, IN: CrossBooks.

Hanbury, A. C. (2014, June 26). Southern Seminary alumnus Troy Bush leads Rehoboth Baptist Church toward renewal. Retrieved November 4, 2014, from http://news.sbts.edu/2014/06/26/ southern-seminary-alumnus-troy-bush-leads-rehoboth-baptist-church-toward-renewal/

Harden, M. G. (2013). Redeeming the City in the Margins. In S. H. Park, A. B. Spencer, & W. D. Spencer (Eds.), *Reaching for the New Jerusalem: A Biblical and Theological Framework for the City* (Kindle edition). Eugene, OR: Wipf & Stock Publishers.

Harvey, D. (2009). *Social Justice and the City* (Revised ed.). Athens, GA: University of Georgia Press.

Hays, R. B. (1996). *The Moral Vision of the New Testament: Community, Cross, New Creation, A Contemporary Introduction to New Testament Ethics.* San Francisco: HarperSanFrancisco.

Heldt, J. P. A. (2004). Revisiting the "Whole Gospel": Toward a Biblical Model of Holistic Mission in the 21st Century. *Missiology, 32*(2), 149–172.

Hern, M. (2010). *Common Ground in a Liquid City: Essays in Defense of an Urban Future.* Edinburgh: AK Press.

Heschel, A. (1997). *Between God and Man.* New York: Simon and Schuster.

Hesselgrave, D. (2005). *Paradigms in Conflict: 10 Key Questions in Christian Missions Today.* Grand Rapids: Kregel Publications.

Hesselgrave, D., & Stetzer, E. (2010). *MissionShift: Global Mission Issues in the Third Millennium.* B&H Academic.

Hiebert, P. (2009). *The Gospel in Human Contexts: Anthropological Explorations for Contemporary Missions.* Grand Rapids: Baker Academic.

Hiebert, P. G. (1982). The Flaw of the Excluded Middle. *Missiology: An International Review, 10*(1), 35–47.

Hiebert, P. G. (1987). Critical Contextualization. *International Bulletin of Missionary Research, 11*(3), 104–112.

Hiebert, P., & Meneses, E. (1995). *Incarnational Ministry: Planting Churches in Band, Tribal, Peasant, and Urban Societies.* Grand Rapids: Baker Books.

Hillis, D. (2014). *Cities: Playgrounds or Battlegrounds?: Leadership Foundations' Fifty Year Journey of Social and Spiritual Renewal.* Tacoma, WA: Leadership Foundations Press.

Hillman, O. (2011). *Change Agent: Engaging Your Passion to be the One Who Makes a Difference.* Lake Mary, FL: Charisma House.

Hinson, E. G. (1981). *Evangelization of the Roman Empire.* Macon, GA: Mercer University Press.

Hinton, K. (1985). *Growing Churches Singapore Style Ministry in an Urban Context.* O M F Books.

Hirsch, A. (2006). *The Forgotten Ways: Reactivating the Missional Church.* Grand Rapids: Brazos Press.

Hoefer, H. E. (2001). *Churchless Christianity.* Pasadena CA: William Carey Library Publishers.

Hoehner, H. (2002). *Ephesians: An Exegetical Commentary.* Grand Rapids: Baker Academic.

Hogan, T., & Houston, C. (2002). Corporate Cities- Urban Gateways or Gated Communities Against the City?: The Case of Lippo, Jakarta. In T. Bunnell, L. B. W. Drummond, & K. C. Ho (Eds.), *Critical Reflections on Cities in Southeast Asia* (pp. 243–264). Singapore: Times Academic Press.

House, R. (2005). *School(s) for Conversion: 12 Marks of a New Monasticism*. Eugene OR: Wipf & Stock Publishers.

Hunger Facts. (2014). Retrieved November 20, 2014, from http://www.compassion.com/poverty/hunger.htm

Hunsberger, G. (1996). *The Church Between Gospel and Culture: The Emerging Mission in North America*. Grand Rapids Mich.: W.B. Eerdmans Pub. Co.

Hunsberger, G. (1998). *Bearing the Witness of the Spirit: Lesslie Newbigin's Theology of Cultural Plurality*. Grand Rapids Mich.: W.B. Eerdmans.

Hunter, J. D. (2010). *To Change the World: The Irony, Tragedy, and Possibility of Christianity in the Late Modern World*. Oxford: Oxford University Press.

Illich, I. (1985). *H2O and the Waters of Forgetfulness: Reflections on the Historicity of Stuff*. Dallas: Dallas Inst Humanities & Culture.

Inge, J. (2003). *A Christian Theology of Place (Explorations in Practical, Pastoral, and Empirical Theology)*. Burlington, VT: Ashgate Publishing.

Introducing Viv Grigg, International Director. (n.d.). Retrieved April 21, 2011, from http://www.urbanleaders.org/home/viv-grigg.html

Jacobs, C. (2010). *Power of Persistent Prayer, The: Praying With Greater Purpose and Passion*. Grand Rapids: Bethany House.

Jacobsen, E. O. (2003). *Sidewalks in the Kingdom: New Urbanism and the Christian Faith*. Grand Rapids: Brazos Press.

Jacobsen, E. O. (2012). *The Space Between: A Christian Engagement with the Built Environment*. Grand Rapids: Baker Academic.

Jacobs, J. (1970). *The Economy of Cities*. New York: Vintage.

Jacobs, J. (1985). *Cities and the Wealth of Nations: Principles of Economic Life*. New York: Vintage Books.

Jacobs, J. (1993). *The Death and Life of Great American Cities* (Modern Library ed.). New York: Modern Library.

Jamieson, A. (2002). *A Churchless Faith: Faith Journeys Beyond the Churches*. London: SPCK.

Jardine, M. (2004). *The Making and Unmaking of Technological Society: How Christianity Can Save Modernity from Itself*. Grand Rapids: Brazos Press.

Jeremias, J. (1971). *New Testament Theology: The Proclamation of Jesus*. New York: Macmillan Publishing Company.

Johnson, T. M., & Crossing, P. F. (2013). Status of Global Mission, 2013, in the Context of AD 1800-2025. *International Bulletin of Missionary Research, 37*(1), 33.

Johnstone, P. (2011). *The Future of the Global Church: History, Trends and Possibilities*. Downers Grove, IL: IVP Books.

Karkkainen, V.-M. (2002). *An Introduction to Ecclesiology: Ecumenical, Historical & Global Perspectives*. Downers Grove Ill.: InterVarsity Press.

Kauffman, J. T. (1994). Structures, injustice, and insensitivity: Who is the neighbor anyway? In C. Van Engen & J. Tiersma (Eds.), *God So Loves the City: Seeking a Theology for Urban Mission* (pp. 27–52). Monrovia, Calif.: MARC.

Kehrein, G. (1995). The Local Church and Christian Community Development. In J. M. Perkins (Ed.), *Restoring At-Risk Communities: Doing it Together and Doing it Right* (pp. 163–180). Grand Rapids: Baker Books.

Kelbaugh, D. (2002). The New Urbanism. In S. S. Fainstein & S. Campbell (Eds.), *Readings in Urban Theory* (2nd ed., pp. 354–361). Malden, MA: Blackwell Publishing.

Keller, T. J. (1993). An Evangelical Mission in a Secular City. In L. E. Schaller (Ed.), *Center City Churches: The New Urban Frontier* (pp. 31–42). Nashville, TN: Abingdon Press.

Keller, T. J. (1997). *Ministries of Mercy: The Call of the Jericho Road* (2nd ed.). Phillipsburg, NJ: P & R Publishing.

Keller, T. J. (2005). Our New Global Culture: Ministry in Urban Centers. Presented at the Redeemer Global Network Conference, New York: Redeemer City to City. Retrieved from www.redeemercitytocity.com

Keller, T. J. (2006, May). A New Kind of Urban Christian. *Christianity Today*, 36–39.

Keller, T. J. (2008a). Church Planting. Presented at the London Church Planting Consultation, London.

Keller, T. J. (2008b). The Gospel and the Poor. Redeemer City to City. Retrieved from http://redeemercitytocity.com/content/com.redeemer.digitalContentArchive.LibraryItem/480/The_Gospel_and_the_Poor.pdf

Keller, T. J. (2010a). *Generous Justice: How God's Grace Makes Us Just*. New York: Dutton Adult.

Keller, T. J. (2010b). What is Common Grace? Redeemer City to City. Retrieved from http://redeemercitytocity.com/content/

com.redeemer.digitalContentArchive.LibraryItem/531/
What_Is_Common_Grace.pdf

Keller, T. J. (2012). *Center Church: Doing Balanced, Gospel-Centered Ministry in Your City*. Grand Rapids: Zondervan.

Keller, T. J., & Thompson, J. A. (2002). *Church Planter Manual*. New York: Redeemer Presbyterian Church.

Kim, J.-H. (2008). *The City in Isaiah 24-27: A Theological Interpretation in Terms of Judgment and Salvation* (Th. D. Dissertation). Stellenbosch University, Capetown, South Africa.

Kornbluh, A. T. (2003). Cities of the Future/the Future of Cities. *Journal of Urban History, 29*(4), 483–493.

Köstenberger, A. J. (1998). *The Missions of Jesus and the Disciples According to the Fourth Gospel: With Implications for the Fourth Gospel's Purpose and the Mission of the Conte*. Grand Rapids: Wm. B. Eerdmans Publishing Co.

Kostof, S. (1991). *The City Shaped: Urban Patterns and Meanings Through History*. New York: Bulfinch.

Kotkin, J. (2005). *The City: A Global History*. New York: Modern Library.

Kraemer, H. (1959). *A Theology of the Laity*. The Westminster Press.

Kubiak, T. (2009). Church in the City Center: Diversity and Constant Change. In J. Fuder & N. Castellanos (Eds.), *A Heart for the Community: New Models for Urban and Suburban Ministry* (pp. 273–286). Chicago: Moody Publishers.

Kunstler, J. H. (1994). *The Geography of Nowhere: The Rise and Decline of America's Man-Made Landscape* (Later printing). New York: Free Press.

Ladd, G. E. (1993). *A Theology of the New Testament* (Rev. ed.). Grand Rapids: Wm. B. Eerdmans Publishing Company.

Langmead, R. (2004). *The Word Made Flesh: Towards an Incarnational Missiology*. Lanham, MD: University Press of America.

Larson, C. (2010, October). Chicago on the Yangtze: Welcome to Chongqing, the Biggest City You've Never Heard Of. *Foreign Policy*, 136–148.

Lim, D. S. (1989). The City in the Bible. In B. R. Ro (Ed.), *Urban Ministry in Asia: Cities: The Exploding Mission Field* (pp. 20–41). Taichung, Taiwan: Asia Theological Association.

Lingenfelter, S. G. (1996). *Agents of Transformation: A Guide for Effective Cross-Cultural Ministry*. Grand Rapids: Baker Academic.

Lin, N. (2001). *Social Capital: A Theory of Social Structure and Action*. Cambridge: Cambridge University Press.

Linthicum, R. C. (1987). The Urban World and World Vision. *Urban Mission, 5*(1), 5–12.

Linthicum, R. C. (1991a). *City of God, City of Satan*. Grand Rapids: Zondervan.

Linthicum, R. C. (1991b). *Empowering the Poor: Community Organizing Among the City's Rag, Tag and Bobtail*. Monrovia, CA: MARC.

Linthicum, R. C. (1997). Networking: Hope for the Church in the City. In H. M. Conn (Ed.), *Planting and Growing Urban Churches: From Dream to Reality* (pp. 164–181). Grand Rapids, MI: Baker Books.

Linthicum, R. C. (2003). *Transforming Power: Biblical Strategies for Making a Difference in Your Community*. Downers Grove, IL: IVP Books.

Linthicum, R. C. (2004, May 7). *Relational Power: Bringing Morality Back Into Public Life*. Wheaton Ill. Retrieved from http://www.rclinthicum.org/Paper016b.pdf

Liu, E. (2013). *Why ordinary people need to understand power*. Retrieved from http://www.ted.com/talks/eric_liu_why_ordinary_people_need_to_understand_power?language=en

Low, S. (Ed.). (1999). *Theorizing the City: The New Urban Anthropology Reader*. New Brunswick, NJ: Rutgers University Press.

Luo, M. (2006, February 26). Preaching the Word and Quoting the Voice. *The New York Times*. Retrieved from http://www.nytimes.com/2006/02/26/nyregion/26evangelist.html

Lupton, R. D. (2005). *Renewing The City: Reflections On Community Development And Urban Renewal*. Downers Grove, IL: InterVarsity Press.

Macionis, J. (2004). *Cities and Urban Life* (3rd ed.). Upper Saddle River, NJ: Pearson Education.

Maddock, G., & Maddock, S. (2014). Sowing Seeds of Shalom in the Neighborhood. In D. Cronshaw (Ed.), *Seeking Urban Shalom: Integral Urban Mission in a New Urban World*. Melbourne: ISUM.

Maggay, M. P. (2004). *Transforming Society: Reflections on the Kingdom and Politics* (2nd ed.). Quezon City: Institute for Studies in Asian Church and Culture.

Marti, G. (2009). *A Mosaic of Believers: Diversity and Innovation in a Multiethnic Church*. Bloomington: Indiana University Press.

Martin, R. P. (1993). Center of Paul's Theology. G. F. Hawthorne, R. P. Martin, & D. G. Reid (Eds.), *Dictionary of Paul and His Letters* (pp. 92–95). Downers Grove, IL: IVP Academic.

McClung, F. (1991). *Seeing the City With the Eyes of God.* Tarrytown, NY: Chosen Books Pub Co.

McDonogh, G. (2005). Discourses of the City: Policy and Response in Post-Transitional Barcelona. In S. M. Low (Ed.), *Theorizing the City: The New Urban Anthropology Reader* (pp. 342–376). New Brunswick, NJ: Rutgers University Press.

McGavran, D. A. (1980). *Understanding Church Growth* (2nd ed.). Grand Rapids: W.B. Eerdmans.

McIntire, C. T. (1984). Fundamentalism. W. A. Elwell (Ed.), *Evangelical Dictionary of Theology* (pp. 433–435). Grand Rapids: Baker Book House.

McLaughlin, E. C. (2014, March 2). Dead Mississippi man begins breathing in embalming room, coroner says. Retrieved November 12, 2014, from http://www.cnn.com/2014/02/28/us/dead-man-comes-back-life/index.html

McMahan, A. (2012). The Strategic Nature of Urban Ministry. In G. Fujino, T. R. Sisk, & T. C. Casino (Eds.), *Reaching the City: Reflections on Urban Mission for the Twenty-first Century* (pp. 1–17). Pasadena, CA: William Carey Library.

Meacham, J. (2011, September 26). In God We Trust. *Time*, 31.

Meeks, W. A. (1982). *The First Urban Christians: The Social World of the Apostle Paul.* New Haven: Yale University Press.

Metaxas, E. (2007). *Amazing Grace: William Wilberforce and the Heroic Campaign to End Slavery.* New York, NY: HarperOne.

Mikoleit, A., & Pürckhauer, M. (2011). *Urban Code: 100 Lessons for Understanding the City.* Cambridge, MA: MIT Press.

Mitchell, D. (2003). *The Right to the City: Social Justice and the Fight for Public Space.* New York: The Guilford Press.

Mohler, R. A. (2011). *Culture Shift: The Battle for the Moral Heart of America.* Colorado Springs: Multnomah Books.

Monsma, S. (2008). *Healing for a Broken World: Christian Perspectives on Public Policy.* Wheaton, IL: Crossway Books.

Moreau, A. S., Corwin, G. R., & McGee, G. B. (2004). *Introducing World Missions: A Biblical, Historical, and Practical Survey.* Grand Rapids: Baker Academic.

Mumford, L. (1961). *The City in History: Its Origins, Its Transformations, and Its Prospects.* New York: Harcourt Brace & World.

Murray, S. (1990). *City Vision: A Biblical View.* London: Daybreak.

Murray, S. (2001). *Church Planting: Laying Foundations* (North American ed.). Scottdale, PA: Herald Press.

Neely, A. (2000). Incarnational Mission. In A. S. Moreau (Ed.), *Evangelical Dictionary of World Missions* (pp. 474–475). Grand Rapids: Baker Book House.

Neuwirth, R. (2006). *Shadow Cities: A Billion Squatters, a New Urban World*. New York: Routledge.

Nevius, J. (1973). *The Planting and Development of Missionary Churches* (Reprint of the 4th ed.). Nutley, N.J: P & R Pub.

Newbigin, J. E. L. (1982). Cross-Currents in Ecumenical and Evangelical Understandings of Mission. *International Bulletin of Missionary Research*, 6(4), 146–151.

Newbigin, L. (1954). *The Household of God: Lectures on the Nature of the Church*. New York: Friendship Pr.

Newbigin, L. (1960). *A South India Diary*. London: SCM Press.

Newbigin, L. (1986). *Foolishness to the Greeks: The Gospel and Western Culture*. Grand Rapids: W.B. Eerdmans Pub. Co.

Newbigin, L. (1989). *The Gospel in a Pluralist Society*. Grand Rapids; Geneva: W.B. Eerdmans; WCC Publications.

Newbigin, L. (1994). *A Word in Season: Perspectives on Christian World Missions*. Grand Rapids Mich.: W.B. Eerdmans Pub. Co.

Newbigin, L. (1995). *The Open Secret: An Introduction to the Theology of Mission* (Rev. ed.). Grand Rapids: W.B. Eerdmans.

New Urbanism. (n.d.). Retrieved March 31, 2012, from http://www.newurbanism.org/index.html

Norman, R. S. (2007). Human Sinfulness. In *A Theology for the Church* (pp. 409–478). Nashville: B & H Academic.

North, A. (2014, September 2). How to Talk to Strangers on the Subway. Retrieved October 14, 2014, from http://op-talk.blogs.nytimes.com/2014/09/02/how-to-talk-to-strangers-on-the-subway/

Northcott, M. (Ed.). (1998). *Urban Theology: A Reader*. London: Cassell.

Orsi, R. A. (1999). *Gods of the City: Religion and the American Urban Landscape*. Bloomington: Indiana University Press.

Ortiz, M. (1992). Being Disciples: Incarnational Christians in the City. In R. S. Greenway (Ed.), *Discipling the City: A Comprehensive Approach to Urban Mission* (pp. 85–98). Grand Rapids: Baker Book House.

Orum, A. M., & Chen, X. (2003). *The World of Cities: Places in Comparative and Historical Perspective*. Malden, MA: Wiley-Blackwell.

Owen, N., Frank, L., Leslie, E., duToit, L., Coffee, N., Bauman, A. E., … Sallis, J. F. (2007). Neighborhood Walkability and the Walking

Behavior of Australian Adults. *American Journal of Preventive Medicine, 33*(5), 387–395.

Palen, J. J. (2008). *The Urban World* (8th ed.). Boulder: Paradigm Publishers.

Patrick, D. (2010). *Church Planter: The Man, the Message, the Mission.* Wheaton, IL: Crossway Books.

Perkins, J. M. (1982). *With Justice for All.* Ventura, CA: Regal Books.

Perkins, J. M. (1993). *Beyond Charity: The Call to Christian Community Development.* Grand Rapids: Baker Books.

Perkins, J. M. (1995a). *Resurrecting Hope: Powerful Stories of How God is Moving to Reach our Cities.* Ventura, CA: Gospel Light.

Perkins, J. M. (1995b). What is Christian Community Development? In J. M. Perkins (Ed.), *Restoring At-Risk Communities: Doing it Together and Doing it Right* (pp. 17–26). Grand Rapids: Baker Books.

Peters, R. (2007). *Urban Ministry: An Introduction.* Nashville, TN: Abingdon Press.

Pier, M. (2008). *Spiritual Leadership in the Global City.* Birmingham, AL: New Hope Publishers.

Pier, M. (2012, October 30). Movement Day 2012: Collaborating for the Sake of the City. Retrieved March 5, 2015, from http://nycleadershipblog.com/category/dr-mac-pier/

Pierson, P. E. (2009). *The Dynamics of Christian Mission: History Through a Missiological Perspective* (Kindle Edition). Pasadena, CA: William Carey International University Press.

Piper, J. (n.d.). Urban-Suburban Partnership. Retrieved October 16, 2014, from http://www.desiringgod.org/sermons/urban-suburban-partnership

Plantinga, C. J. (1995). *Not the Way It's Supposed to Be: A Breviary of Sin.* Grand Rapids: Wm. B. Eerdmans Publishing Company.

Polhill, J. B. (1992). *Acts* (Vol. 26). Nashville: Holman Reference.

Portes, A. (1998). Social Capital: Its Origins and Applications in Modern Sociology. *Annual Review of Sociology, 24,* 1–24.

President urges Malaysia to recruit more manpower from Bangladesh. (2012, August 28). Retrieved November 26, 2012, from http://www.thefinancialexpress-bd.com/more.php?news_id=141410&date=2012-08-28

Priest, R. J., Campbell, T., & Mullen, B. A. (1995). Missiological Syncretism: The New Animistic Paradigm. In E. Rommen (Ed.), *Spiritual Power and Missions: Raising the Issues* (pp. 9–87). Pasadena, CA: William Carey Library.

Putnam, R. D. (2000). *Bowling Alone: The Collapse and Revival of American Community*. New York: Simon & Schuster.

Reclaiming the 7 Mountains. (n.d.). Retrieved December 27, 2011, from http://www.reclaim7mountains.com/

Redeemer City to City. (n.d.). Retrieved October 31, 2014, from http://www.redeemercitytocity.com/

Reed, P. (1995). Toward a Theology of Christian Community Development. In J. M. Perkins (Ed.), *Restoring At-Risk Communities: Doing it Together and Doing it Right* (pp. 27–46). Grand Rapids: Baker Books.

Roberts, B., Jr. (2010). *Transformation: Discipleship that Turns Lives, Churches, and the World Upside Down*. Grand Rapids: Zondervan.

Robinson, P. (2010). To Challenge, Relativize and Transcend: Proclamation in the City. In A. Davey (Ed.), *Crossover City: Resources for Urban Mission and Transformation* (pp. 52–63). London: Mowbray.

Robinson, W. I. (2009). Saskia Sassen and the Sociology of Globalization: A Critical Appraisal. *Sociological Analysis, 3*(1), 5–29.

Rogers, E. M. (1995). *Diffusion of Innovations* (4th ed.). New York: Free Press.

Rooy, S. H. (1992). Theological Education for Urban Mission. In R. S. Greenway (Ed.), *Discipling the City: A Comprehensive Approach to Urban Mission* (pp. 223–246). Grand Rapids: Baker Book House.

Russell, M. (2008). Christian Mission is Holistic: Christian Mission Today: Are We on a Slippery Slope? *International Journal of Frontier Missiology, 25*(2), 93–98.

Rutt, D. (2003). Antioch as Paradigmatic of the Urban Center of Mission. *Missio Apostolica, 11*(1), 35–43.

Rybczynski, W. (2010). *Makeshift Metropolis*. New York: Scribner.

Samuel, V. K., & Sugden, C. (Eds.). (1983). Transformation: The Church in Response to Human Need. In *The Consultation on the Church in Response to Human Need*. Wheaton Ill. Retrieved from http://www.lausanne.org/all-documents/transformation-the-church-in-response-to-human-need.html

Samuel, V. K., & Sugden, C. (1987). God's Intention for the World. In V. Samuel & C. Sugden (Eds.), *The Church in Response to Human Need* (pp. 128–160). Grand Rapids: W.B. Eerdmans.

Samuel, V. K., & Sugden, C. (Eds.). (1999). *Mission as Transformation: A Theology of the Whole Gospel*. Eugene, OR: Wipf & Stock Publishers.

Samuel, V., & Sugden, C. (1987). Introduction. In V. Samuel & C. Sugden (Eds.), *The Church in Response to Human Need* (pp. viii–xii). Grand Rapids: W.B. Eerdmans.

Sanneh, L. (1989). *Translating the Message: The Missionary Impact on Culture*. Maryknoll N.Y.: Orbis Books.

Sassen, S. (2001). *The Global City: New York, London, Tokyo.* (2nd ed.). Princeton: Princeton University Press.

Schaller, L. E. (1989). *The Change Agent: The Strategy of Innovative Leadership*. Nashville: Abingdon Press.

Schaller, L. E. (1993). *Center City Churches: The New Urban Frontier*. Nashville: Abingdon Press.

Schlomo, A., Sheppard, S. C., & Civco, D. L. (2005). *The Dynamics of Global Urban Expansion*. Washington D.C.: Transport and Urban Development of the World Bank. Retrieved from http://go.worldbank.org/58A0YZVOV0

Schnabel, E. J. (2004). *Early Christian Mission Paul And The Early Church: Volume 2*. Downers Grove, IL: Inter Varsity.

Seccombe, D. (1998). The New People of God. In I. H. Marshall & D. Peterson (Eds.), (pp. 349–372). Grand Rapids: Wm. B. Eerdmans Publishing Company.

Seitz, C. R. (1997). The Two Cities in Christian Scripture. In C. E. Braaten & R. W. Jenson (Eds.), *The Two Cities of God: The Church's Responsibility for the Earthly City* (pp. 11–27). Grand Rapids: Wm. B. Eerdmans.

Sennett, R. (1994). *Flesh and Stone: The Body and the City in Western Civilization* (1st ed.). New York: W.W. Norton.

Shenk, W. R. (1999). *Changing Frontiers of Mission*. Maryknoll N.Y.: Orbis Books.

Shenk, W. R. (2005). New Wineskins for New Wine: Toward a Post-Christendom Ecclesiology. *International Bulletin of Missionary Research, 29*(2), 73–79.

Sijabat, R. M. (2010, May 15). Indonesia, Malaysia to sign new labor pact next week. Retrieved November 26, 2012, from http://www.thejakartapost.com/news/2010/05/15/indonesia-malaysia-sign-new-labor-pact-next-week.html

Silvoso, E. (2007). *Transformation: Change The Marketplace and You Change the World*. Ventura, CA: Regal.

Sine, T. (1999). *Mustard Seed vs. McWorld: Reinventing Life and Faith for the Future*. Grand Rapids: Baker Books.

Smidt, C. E. (1988). Evangelicals within Contemporary American Politics: Differentiating Between Fundamentalist and Non-

Fundamentalist Evangelicals. *Western Political Quarterly*, *41*(3), 601–620.

Smith, A. G. (2009). Some Historical Views on Asian Urban Extension: Complexities of Urban and Rural Relationships. In P. H. De Neui (Ed.), *Communicating Christ in Asian Cities: Urban Issues in Buddhist Contexts* (pp. 1–40). Pasadena, CA: W. Carey Library.

Smith, B. (2008). *City Signals: Principles and Practices for Ministering in Today's Global Communities*. Birmingham Ala.: New Hope Publishers.

Smith, D. W. (2001). *Seeking a City with Foundations: Theology for an Urban World*. Nottingham, England: Inter-Varsity Press.

Smith, G. (2004). Towards the Transformation of our Cities/Regions. In *Lausanne Occasional Paper No. 37*. Pattaya: Lausanne Committee for World Evangelization. Retrieved from http://www.lausanne.org/all-documents/lop-37-towards-the-transformation-of-our-citiesregions.html

Snyder, H. A. (2013). The Ecology of Urban Mission. *New Urban World*, *2*, 47–60.

Snyder, H., & Runyon, D. V. (2002). *Decoding the Church: Mapping the DNA of Christ's Body*. Grand Rapids MI: Baker Books.

Solecki, W., Seto, K. C., & Marcotullio, P. J. (2013). It's Time for an Urbanization Science. *Environment*, *55*(1), 12–16.

Spencer, A. B. (2013). What City Are We Creating? In S. H. Park, A. B. Spencer, & W. D. Spencer (Eds.), *Reaching for the New Jerusalem: A Biblical and Theological Framework for the City* (Kindle edition). Eugene, OR: Wipf & Stock Publishers.

Stagg, F. (1962). *New Testament Theology*. Nashville: Baptist Sunday School Board.

Starke, J. (2011, May 16). The Incarnation Is About a Person, Not a Mission. Retrieved April 24, 2012, from http://thegospelcoalition.org/blogs/tgc/2011/05/16/the-incarnation-is-about-a-person-not-a-mission/

Stark, R. (1997). *The Rise of Christianity: How the Obscure, Marginal, Jesus Movement Became the Dominant Religious Force ....* HarperOne.

Stark, R. (2006). *Cities of God: The Real Story of How Christianity Became an Urban Movement and Conquered Rome*. San Francisco: HarperSanFrancisco.

Stark, R. (2011). *The Triumph of Christianity: How the Jesus Movement Became the World's Largest Religion*. New York: HarperOne.

Stassen, G., Yeager, D. M., & Yoder, J. H. (1995). *Authentic Transformation: A New Vision of Christ and Culture*. Nashville: Abingdon Press.

Stearns, R. (2009). *The Hole in Our Gospel: What Does God Expect of Us? The Answer That Changed My Life and Might Just Change the World*. Nashville: Thomas Nelson.

Stevens, D. E. (2012). *God's New Humanity: A Biblical Theology of Multiethnicity for the Church*. Eugene, OR: Wipf & Stock Publishers.

Stockwell, C. E. (2002). The Church and Justice in Crisis. In M. Ortiz & S. S. Baker (Eds.), *The Urban Face of Mission* (pp. 159–184). Phillipsburg, NJ: P & R Pub.

Stone, W. P. (2003). Reaching our Cities for Christ. *Malaysia Baptist Theological Seminary Theological Journal, 1*, 81–88.

Stone, W. P. (2004). *The diffusion of Christianity among urban Chinese people in diaspora: The case of metropolitan Kuala Lumpur, Malaysia* (Ph.D. Dissertation). Asbury Theological Seminary.

Strathmann, H. E. (1964). Polis. G. Kittel & G. Friedrich (Eds.), G. W. Bromiley (Trans.), *Theological Dictionary of the New Testament* (Vol. 6, pp. 516–535). Grand Rapids: Eerdmans.

Swanson, E., & Williams, S. (2010). *To Transform a City: Whole Church, Whole Gospel, Whole City*. Grand Rapids: Zondervan.

Sztompka, P. (1993). *The Sociology of Social Change*. Oxford: Wiley-Blackwell.

Talbot, D. (2012). *Season of the Witch: Enchantment, Terror and Deliverance in the City of Love*. New York: Free Press.

Taylor, W. D. (2000). From Iguassu to the reflective practitioners of the global family of Christ. In W. D. Taylor (Ed.), *Global Missiology for the 21st Century: The Iguassu Dialogue* (pp. 3–14). Grand Rapids: Baker Academic.

Tennent, T. (2010). *Invitation to World Missions: A Trinitarian Missiology for the Twenty-first Century*. Grand Rapids: Kregel Academic & Professional.

The 2008 Global Cities Index. (2008, December). *Foreign Policy*, 68–76.

The Atlantic Cities. (n.d.). Retrieved June 5, 2013, from http://www.theatlanticcities.com/

The Global Cities Index: 2010 Rankings. (2010). *Foreign Policy*, 124–128.

The Lausanne Covenant. (1974). Retrieved November 23, 2012, from http://www.lausanne.org/en/documents/lausanne-covenant.html

This Is Our City | ChristianityToday.com. (n.d.). Retrieved June 5, 2013, from http://www.christianitytoday.com/thisisourcity/

Tink, F. L. (1994). *From order to harmony: Toward a new hermeneutic for urban mission* (Ph.D. Dissertation). Fuller Theological Seminary, School of World Mission.

Tizon, A. (2008). *Transformation After Lausanne: Radical Evangelical Mission in Global-Local Perspective*. Eugene, OR: Wipf & Stock Publishers.

Todd, G. (1976). Mission and Justice: The Experience of Urban and Industrial Mission. *International Review of Mission, 65*(259), 251–261.

Traeger, S., & Gilbert, G. (2013). *The Gospel at Work: How Working for King Jesus Gives Purpose and Meaning to Our Jobs*. Grand Rapids: Zondervan.

Twelftree, G. H. (2009). *People of the Spirit: Exploring Luke's View of the Church*. Grand Rapids: Baker Academic.

Uken, C. D. (1992). Discipling White, Blue-Collar Workers and Their Families. In R. S. Greenway (Ed.), *Discipling the City: A Comprehensive Approach to Urban Mission* (pp. 171–182). Grand Rapids: Baker Book House.

United Nations Population Division. (2008). *An Overview of Urbanization, Internal Migration, Population Distribution and Development in the World*. United Nations Expert Group Meeting on Population Distribution, Urbanization, Internal Migration and Development. Retrieved from http://www.un.org/esa/population/meetings/EGM_PopDist/P01_UNPopDiv.pdf

Van Engen, C. (1994). Constructing a theology of mission for the city. In C. Van Engen & J. Tiersma (Eds.), *God So Loves the City: Seeking a Theology for Urban Mission* (pp. 241–269). Monrovia, Calif.: MARC.

Van Engen, C. (2005). Toward a Missiology of Transformation. *Global Missiology*. Retrieved from www.globalmissiology.org

Van Engen, C., & Tiersma, J. (Eds.). (1994). *God So Loves the City: Seeking a Theology for Urban Mission*. Monrovia, Calif.: MARC.

Villafane, E., Hall, D., Agosto, E., & Jackson, B. W. (1995). *Seek the Peace of the City: Reflections on Urban Ministry*. Grand Rapids: Wm. B. Eerdmans Publishing Company.

Volf, M. (1998). *After Our Likeness: The Church as the Image of the Trinity*. Grand Rapids: William B. Eerdmans.

Wagner, C. P. (1972). *Frontiers in Missionary Strategy*. Chicago: Moody Press.

Wagner, C. P. (1996). *Confronting the Powers: How the New Testament Church Experienced the Power of Strategic-Level Spiritual Warfare*. Ventura, CA: Regal Books.

Wagner, C. P. (Ed.). (1993). *Breaking Strongholds in Your City: How to Use Spiritual Mapping To make Your Prayers More Strategic, Effective and Targeted*. Ventura, CA: Regal Books.

Wallnau, L. (2009). *The 7 Mountain Mandate: Impacting Culture Discipling Nations* [DVD]. Morningstar.

Walls, A. F. (2002). *The Cross-Cultural Process in Christian History: Studies in the Transmission and Appropriation of Faith*. Maryknoll N.Y.: Orbis Books.

Ward, P. (2002). *Liquid Church*. Carlisle Cumbria; Peabody, MA: Paternoster Press; Hendrickson Publishers.

Weber, M. (1980). *The Protestant Work Ethic and the Spirit of Capitalism*. (T. Parsons, Trans.). London: Unwin.

White, R. (1996). *Journey to the Center of the City: Making a Difference in an Urban Neighborhood*. Downers Grove Ill.: InterVarsity Press.

White, R. (2006). *Encounter God in the City: Onramps to Personal And Community Transformation*. Downers Grove, IL: InterVarsity Press.

Wilson, B. (2009, August 11). Documents Show Christian World Domination Group Paid For Bipartisan Congressional Hawaii Trip. *The Huffington Post*. Retrieved from http://www.huffingtonpost.com/bruce-wilson/documents-show-christian_b_256825.html

Wilson, E. O. (1986). The Current State of Biological Diversity. In E. O. Wilson & F. M. Peter (Eds.), *Biodiversity (Papers from the 1st National Forum on Biodiversity, September 1986, Washington, D.C.)* (pp. 3–17). Washington D.C.: National Academy of Sciences.

Wilson-Hartgrove, J. (2008). *New Monasticism: What It Has to Say to Today's Church*. Grand Rapids: Brazos Press.

Winter, B. W. (1994). *Seek the Welfare of the City: Christians as Benefactors and Citizens*. Grand Rapids: Wm. B. Eerdmans Publishing Company.

Witherington, B. I. (2011). *Work: A Kingdom Perspective on Labor*. Grand Rapids: Wm. B. Eerdmans Publishing.

Wolterstorff, N. (1983). *Until Justice and Peace Embrace: The Kuyper Lectures for 1981 Delivered at the Free University of Amsterdam*. Grand Rapids: Wm. B. Eerdmans Publishing Company.

Wolterstorff, N. P. (2013). *Journey toward Justice: Personal Encounters in the Global South*. Grand Rapids: Baker Academic.

World Refugee Day: Global forced displacement tops 50 million for first time in post-World War II era. (2014, June 20). Retrieved November 20, 2014, from http://www.unhcr.org/53a155bc6.html

Wright, C. (2006). *The Mission of God: Unlocking the Bible's Grand Narrative*. Downers Grove Ill.: IVP Academic.

Wright, C. J. H. (1990). *God's people in God's land: family, land, and property in the Old Testament*. Grand Rapids, Mich.; Exeter, England: W.B. Eerdmans Pub. Co.; Paternoster Press.

Wright, C. J. H. (2010). *The Mission of God's People: A Biblical Theology of the Church's Mission*. Grand Rapids: Zondervan.

Wright, N. T. (1997). *Jesus and the Victory of God*. Minneapolis: Fortress Press.

Wright, N. T. (2008). *Surprised by Hope: Rethinking Heaven, the Resurrection, and the Mission of the Church*. New York: HarperOne.

Zoughbie, A. E. (1994). *Shalom in the Hebrew Bible: Semantic Study and Theological Implications* (Ph.D. Dissertation). Golden Gate Baptist Theological Seminary, Mill Valley, CA.

Zuidervaart, L. (2005). Good Cities or Cities of the Good?: Radical Augustinians, Societal Structures, and Normative Critique. In J. K. A. Smith & J. H. Olthuis (Eds.), *Radical Orthodoxy and the Reformed Tradition: Creation, Covenant, and Participation* (pp. 135–149). Grand Rapids: Baker Academic.

About the Author

Michael Crane (Ph.D.) has lived most of his life in global cities in Asia and the United States. He is currently teaching urban missions with two seminaries and serves as a co-director for RADIUS Initiatives, an urban transformation think-tank. Michael and his wife have also been involved with urban refugees as well as coaching urban church planters in an Asian global city. Michael has contributed to a number of journals and books and is currently co-writing a book on urban church planting.

About ULP

Urban Loft Publishers focuses on ideas, topics, themes, and conversations about all things urban. Renewing the city is the central theme and focus of what we publish. It is our intention to blend urban ministry, theology, urban planning, architecture, urbanism, stories, and the social sciences, as ways to drive the conversation. While we lean towards scholarly and academic works, we explore the fun and lighter sides of cities as well. We publish a wide variety of urban perspectives, from books by the experts about the city to personal stories and personal accounts of urbanites who live in the city.

www.urbanloftpublishers.com
@the_urban_loft

www.ingramcontent.com/pod-product-compliance
Lightning Source LLC
Chambersburg PA
CBHW071405090426
42737CB00011B/1364